W9-CDH-908

Natural Childbirth the Bradley® Way

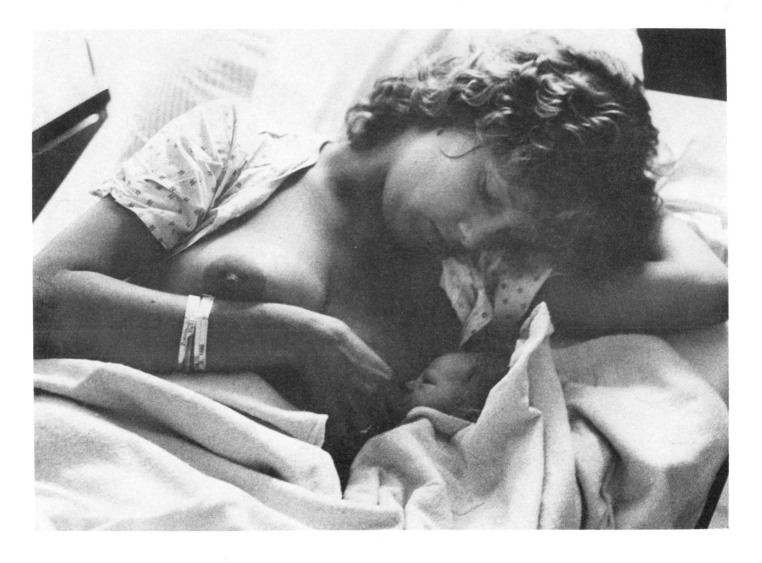

Susan McCutcheon-Rosegg with Peter Rosegg

Natural Childbirth the Bradley® Way

Illustrated by Erick Ingraham and Robin Yoko Burningham

E. P. DUTTON • NEW YORK

Copyright © 1984 by Susan McCutcheon-Rosegg and Peter Rosegg

All rights reserved. Printed in the U.S.A.

No part of this publication may be reproduced or transmitted in any form or by any means, electronic or mechanical, including photocopy, recording, or any information storage and retrieval system now known or to be invented, without permission in writing from the publisher, except by a reviewer who wishes to quote brief passages in connection with a review written for inclusion in a magazine, newspaper, or broadcast.

Published in the United States by
E. P. Dutton, a division of Penguin Books USA Inc., 2 Park Avenue, New York, N.Y. 10016.

Library of Congress Cataloging in Publication Data
McCutcheon-Rosegg, Susan.
    Natural childbirth the Bradley® way.
    Bibliography: p.
    1. Natural childbirth.   I. Rosegg, Peter.   II. Title.
RG661.M38   1984   618.4'5   84-4178
ISBN: 0-525-48113-3

Published simultaneously in Canada by Fitzhenry & Whiteside Limited, Toronto

Designed by Ernie Haim
Unless otherwise noted, photos by Peter Rosegg.

10 9 8

THE BRADLEY METHOD® is the trademark of the American Academy of Husband-Coached Childbirth and is registered in the United States Patent Office. Only those teachers currently affiliated with the Academy may teach The Bradley Method® or use the term Bradley® in connection with childbirth education.

This book is dedicated to my children, Brian, Robin, and Polly.

TO BRIAN, *whose labor taught me patience and the depths of concentration attainable during a hard first labor.*

TO ROBIN, *whose birth taught me the sweetness of an easy labor and the power and rewards of selecting a supportive environment.*

TO POLLY, *whose hard labor taught me not to anticipate what any labor will be like (each is a new experience and takes its own pattern and shape), and whose birth at home made this, although my hardest labor, my best birth.*

IT IS ALSO DEDICATED:

TO DR. WES SOKOLOSKY, *who, bringing along his best smile, kindly attended my home birth of Polly, and who had the uncommon wisdom to do nothing when nothing was called for.*

TO THE HUNDREDS OF COUPLES I HAVE HAD THE PRIVILEGE TO TEACH, *many of whom allowed me to be present during their labors and births and who in turn taught me through the generous sharing of their experiences.*

AND FINALLY TO WOMEN WHO HAVE HAD THE COURAGE TO SPEAK OUT AND PRESS FOR CHANGES IN CHILDBIRTH: Lester Hazell, Doris Haire, Suzanne Arms, Nancy Wainer Cohen, Lois J. Estner, Gail Sforza Brewer, Marjie Hathaway, and, of course, all the Bradley® teachers.

—Susan McCutcheon-Rosegg

Contents

Preface by Robert A. Bradley, M.D.

I highly recommend this book for preparing couples for totally unmedicated births by The Bradley Method® of true natural childbirth. Mrs. Rosegg was a student in our very first Bradley® class many years ago and has given unmedicated births herself. She is well-read and knowledgeable in her subject.

The preparation and focus of *Natural Childbirth the Bradley® Way* follows the natural instinctual behavior of all mammals in bearing their young. I first described and stressed the importance of this human imitation of instinctual behavior in 1947 while in obstetrical training at the Mayo Foundation in Minnesota. At that time, I observed a group of pregnant nurses who volunteered to try my ideas after seeing them work so well with a small number of clinic patients. This first experiment in true natural childbirth without medication or drugs was interrupted by Navy duty in the Korean War, but was reported and illustrated by the *Minneapolis Tribune* in a full-page article, "Better Start for Babies," in 1949.

In 1962 I published an analysis of my first four thousand cases following these principles in private practice, entitled "Fathers' Presence in Delivery Rooms" (*Psychosomatics* 3, no. 6). Over ten thousand copies of this article were requested from all over the world.

These dates and references are brought up because I have not previously compared The Bradley Method®, in writing, with other methods, which I consider "Johnny-come-latelies." The Roseggs, however, have tackled this comparison in their book, and so I would like to set the record straight. The Bradley Method® was preceded only by the late Dr. Grantly Dick-Read's *Childbirth Without Fear* in 1944. I met Dr. Read in Chicago in 1948, and he accepted my invitation to visit with me later in Denver. We had a wonderful visit, but I did have a bit of trouble with some of his theories related to fear and with his assertion that "a little gas or medication wouldn't hurt anything." From the very first, I felt we should use no drugs of any nature in pregnancy, labor or birth unless dire complications warranted them.

Also, from the very first I had included husbands in the birth team as coaches and minimized the role of the physician to resemble that of a lifeguard, who, when watching swimmers, did nothing as long as everything was going along all right. I put the husband where Dr. Read sat, at the head of the bed, to capitalize on the lover relationship and found it worked marvelously.

The Lamaze method came along later, using female "monitrices" as coaches. I tried this and found it most ineffective, as reflected in a low percentage of unmedicated births. With husbands coaching in our method, we have over ninety percent totally unmedicated births. No other approach comes anywhere near that figure.

Inevitable conflicts arose between advocates of The Bradley Method® and the Lamaze method, and as I am an Irishman, I'm guilty of not smoothing but stirring the troubled waters. I was ridiculed for my no-drugs approach, as they continued to claim "a little medication wouldn't hurt anything." Also, I was mocked with the label "Barnyard Bradley" for my insistence on imitating animals and for the term "natural childbirth," which I still prefer to "psychoprophylaxis."

Recent new research on the effects of maternal medication on the fetus and infant verifies the assumptions I first made in 1947: drugs are all bad during pregnancy. Also, the meddlesome interference with nature's instinctual conduct and plans (induction of labor, silly "due dates," routine IVs, monitoring, etc.) are very well covered in this book by these dedicated authors who know whereof they speak.

Mr. and Mrs. Rosegg are not practicing medicine. They are teaching parenthood. Our large American Academy of Husband-Coached Childbirth® located near Hollywood, California, continues to train and affiliate childbirth educators of The Bradley Method®. It is the safest method of having a baby. Regardless of where you have your baby, or whom you choose to have in attendance, do not deviate from nature's great principles.

Foreword by Marjie Hathaway

It is with great excitement that I write a foreword to this outstanding book. We hope it will increase everyone's understanding of The Bradley Method® and will help inform many mothers-to-be that natural childbirth is not dead but is alive and well in their local Bradley® classes.

Our interest in natural childbirth started in 1965. After having three extremely difficult deliveries, I was pregnant with our fourth child, and my husband Jay and I felt there had to be a better way. We learned (the hard way) that medication does not take away the pain. In most cases it just postpones it. Each time I recovered in great pain, while trying to take care of our new baby. We just knew there must be a better way than the "normal" delivery.

Instead, we wanted to have natural childbirth with Jay in the delivery room. After much searching, we could not find any doctors or hospitals in southern California that would allow this radical "new" idea in 1965. Therefore, at last, we flew to Denver, Colorado, where Dr. Robert A. Bradley practices medicine, to give birth to our fourth baby, using the techniques he had perfected and practiced. We were so delighted with our birth that we started teaching and developing The Bradley Method® ourselves for the first time outside of Denver. It took literally years of writing and testing and traveling to confer with Dr. Bradley before we developed the system of childbirth education that now extends throughout the United

States: The American Academy of Husband-Coached Childbirth®.

One of the major tasks the AAHCC® undertook was to train other Bradley Method® teachers. The demand for Bradley® teachers grew so fast, we soon began holding training workshops all over the country. Sue Rosegg was one of the first people to take our training, and over the years she has been a guest speaker at several of our workshops, helping us train many other fine Bradley® teachers. Her application of the principles of The Bradley Method® is an inspiration to anyone looking for a truly natural way to have a baby. Today you can find Bradley® teachers in every state who are trained professionals, ready to teach others and share the wonder of The Bradley Method®.

We have found that it is essential to educate yourself as much as possible during your pregnancy. Read as many books as you can and attend Bradley® classes in your area. This book was not intended as a substitute for classes taught by affiliated Bradley® teachers; attending classes is important preparation, and no book can fill that need.

Bradley® classes are longer than other childbirth classes because we include information on the entire experience of pregnancy, birthing and becoming a family. There are twelve units of instruction and free weekly reviews until birth. Certified Bradley® instructors are also required to keep classes small enough for individual attention. Ask to see your instructor's current Certificate of Affiliation, which will assure you of a trained up-to-date nationally affiliated instructor who is well qualified. You should also ask what percentage of students in her class actually are able to have unmedicated births. Our teachers are ready and willing to give you this information. Our teachers are chosen because of their experience with natural childbirth (most of them are experienced Bradley® mothers themselves), and through AAHCC® they have completed one of the most extensive childbirth training programs in the United States. After you have successfully used The Bradley Method®, you might consider the impact you could have in your community if you took the AAHCC® training and became a Bradley® teacher yourself. Because of the growing enthusiasm and demand for The Bradley Method®, we need many new teachers in all parts of the country.

We are really excited about the impact *Natural Childbirth the Bradley® Way* will have on the general public, and about the possibility of reaching couples interested in The Bradley Method® who were not previously aware of this positive alternative in childbirth. After you have your Bradley® birth, we ask your help in compiling statistics which we hope will help others. Please fill out the feedback form at the back of this book. This information will be entered into our computer to help update and improve ourselves and benefit others. And do have a happy birth-day!

For a free National Directory of Bradley® teachers, or for teacher-training information, call our toll-free PREGNANCY HOTLINE (800) 423-2397, or in California (818) 788-6662, or write the American Academy of Husband-Coached Childbirth®, Box 5224-R, Sherman Oaks, CA 91413.

— MARJIE HATHAWAY
American Academy of Husband-Coached Childbirth®

Acknowledgments

Many people helped in the birth of this book:

Our editor, Jerret Engle, absorbed the message quickly and became an excellent coach. Recognizing a third emotional signpost, she urged and encouraged us on. This book is better for her work.

Heide Lange, our agent, smoothed the way for this book. Her enthusiasm and support kept us going.

Judy Hunt, Susan's sister, gave her creative support in the early days of the manuscript.

Jan Cook, a student and friend, read the first draft when another human being to see it was desperately needed.

Janice Nuckols, a great friend and thoughtful woman, encouraged this project throughout and was the first person to read the caesarean surgery chapter just after it rolled out of the typewriter.

Carol Rosegg, Peter's sister, found us our agent and helped with the pictures for the book.

Sandra Oshiro and Gerry Kato let us use their word processor at a critical time and instead of sending us home in the late hours, fed us and listened to the latest birth stories.

We would like to thank Dr. Rick Renwick for reading and critiquing the manuscript.

Many people helped in the research for this book, either directly or by supplying references to important materials, especially: Lynn Woodward for extensive information on the adverse effects of ingredients in frequently consumed prenatal products; and Rae Grad, editor of the Alliance for Perinatal Research and Services newsletter for information about Bendectin.

A special acknowledgment is due to those people whose writings, lectures, or conversations with Susan had an impact on her teaching and hence on this book: Lester Hazell, Doris Haire, Suzanne Arms, Dr. Grantly Dick-Read, of course, Dr. Robert A. Bradley, Jay and Marjie Hathaway, Dr. Tom Brewer, Gail Sforza Brewer, Dr. Edmund Jacobson, Karen Pryor, Gary McCutcheon, and Helen Wessel.

Finally, we are grateful to the many couples who made their birth and pregnancy pictures available to be used in this book or by our artists, including: Nancy and Steve Stephens, who with Jasmine are on the cover, Suzy and Tim Adkins, Barbara and David Alethea, Christine and Wally Amos, Sarah Bender, Jeannette and Roger Bonvino, Mary and Tony Burris, Lisa and Michael Cain, Josette and Larry Clapp, Beverly Creamer and Jerry Burris, Dr. Jennifer Frank, Teri and Brian Jenkins, Jarri Kagawa, Mifta MacNeil, Dr. Rick Renwick, Elizabeth Reveley and Red Mahan, Pam and Pat Sager, Mickey Selwyn, CNM, and Debby and David Story.

part I

Getting Ready

chapter one

An Introduction

In 1968, I started teaching childbirth to a few friends, and in the next year I completed my first teacher-training course at the American Institute of Family Relations. That course was described as "Lamaze plus." I had really started my career as a childbirth educator, but very soon I felt that there had to be something better. There was. I was fortunate to be in on the first formal teacher-training workshop in the Bradley Method®, taught by Dr. Robert A. Bradley himself in 1970.

Dr. Bradley was a pioneer in getting husbands into the delivery room and has led the movement to return to natural, drug-free techniques in childbirth. Although I was already a certified childbirth teacher, I found in Dr. Bradley's course the real foundation for the next fourteen years as I began teaching what I strongly believe to be the most successful natural childbirth method available today. Since then I have taught over a thousand couples, coached dozens of women in labor, and been present at many more births.

From the time of that first Bradley® teacher-training session, attended by some two dozen people, the Bradley Method® has grown and spread. More than 2,000 teachers have been trained, and at present 1,100 of them are affiliated with the Bradley® organization, the American Academy of Husband-Coached Childbirth®. New teachers are being trained at the rate of three to four hundred a year, and natural childbirth (totally unmedicated and without unnecessary medical intervention) is being sought by thousands of couples.

But since Lamaze or other "prepared" childbirth classes are available in most hospitals, many people mistakenly believe that natural childbirth is already quite common—that "everybody" is doing it. This is just not true. Most births today are still medicated, forceps, or vacuum-extractor deliveries or caesarean surgery—*not* natural, drug-free, normal childbirth. Instead of natural births, most people who take "prepared" childbirth classes are being prepared for deliveries with drugs and mechanical interventions that unfortunately are used routinely in almost all births. When a writer recently asked Dr. Graham G. Hawks, chief of obstetrics at New York Hospital–Cornell Medical Center, how many completely natural births occurred at that hospital, Hawks replied, "I know of only one." At New York Hospital, approximately seventy-five percent of births involved the drug Demerol, thirty-seven percent had forceps deliveries, sixty percent had episiotomies, and an indeterminate number were catheterized. Of those who used Demerol, said Dr. Hawks, "the majority were Lamaze people."[1]

This book is for pregnant couples who are looking for the real thing, birthing normally and naturally without the routine use of drugs or unnecessary interventions—in short, the Bradley Method®.

SUSAN MCCUTCHEON-ROSEGG

TO THE COACH

There is a stereotype about new fathers in this country. You know it well from jokes and cartoons, from television and movies. You recognize the guy out in the waiting room, pacing back and forth, smoking cigarettes by the pack (usually all twenty at once), wearing a path in the linoleum, watching the swinging door. Inside, his wife is alone. And when the door swings wide he hears screams and wonders if they could be hers.

He's a nice guy, of course, so he gets more and more frantic, until someone finally comes out and tells him with a kindly nod that he is a father and, oh yes, the mother is fine. He says something stupid like, "Do I need pink or blue cigars?" And then he goes out and has a drink.

Frankly, that stereotype doesn't fit anyone we know. Today, there are fewer men who think their part in the whole process of birth was finished nine months before and that the nurses and doctors will take care of everything. (And, oh yes, aren't there drugs for all this birth stuff?)

In fact, the nurses have their hands full and most people are amazed to find out that doctors rarely even show up until the last few minutes of birth. And as for drugs, the reality is that truly effective anesthetics can't even be given to a laboring woman until labor is almost over.

Why? Because with the drugs come risks to the mother and the baby. They can affect the mother's heart (causing cardiac arrest) or the muscles she uses to push the baby out, and this can slow down labor, making intervention a necessity. The myth is that the medicated labor is painless. But it is the medicated mother who later talks most about pain (and it is she who is often seen during labor suffering and out of control). She may have thought drugs would see her through labor, so she didn't take the opportunity to get her mind and body ready.

In contrast, the trained, natural-childbirth mother talks primarily of hard work—because she knows what to do in labor. Her body is ready and she knows how to keep herself comfortable and relaxed.

If you have never seen a truly natural-childbirth mother laboring, the first time will come as a surprise to you; it is incredibly different from the woman giving birth with shrieks of agony you may have imagined from novels, television, or the movies.

But the natural-childbirth mother cannot do it alone. Human birth has never been the completely solitary experience that is common among animals. It is an awesome, beautiful moment that should be shared by people who care about each other.

It is hard to imagine a woman laboring and birthing without knowing how to help herself and without a trained coach to support her, though sadly, this happens all the time. First of all, there are physical needs and sensa-tions—like a backache in many cases—that can so easily be alleviated with the help of a caring person. Then, there is a mood to create; a relaxed, warm, loving environment that is only possible with another person whose full attention is on the laboring woman.

Finally, there is a joy to be shared and celebrated, a once-in-a-lifetime moment of happiness, excitement, relief, closeness, and love.

For all these special things, are you going to depend on the doctors or the nurses? Hardly. A busy obstetrician may have one or two *dozen* births a month. He could not spend hours with each laboring woman and still run a practice, even if he wanted to. And what about the nurses? Well, they are essentially trouble-spotters for the doctors. They have little time for a mother with a normal, uncomplicated labor. By now you see the bottle that has been spinning is coming around to stop in front of you.

For some men the question may come down to a simple "Who else?" But for most it is a more positive decision than that. Are you going to leave this responsibility to your partner for someone else and miss this chance for a once-in-a-lifetime experience?

More and more men now actively want to be part of the birth experience of their babies and they want to support their partners in this hard work they have started together. It is one of the most authentic things you may ever do in your life. A lot of people are preoccupied these days with trying to recapture simple values through meaningful human contacts and true-life experiences. This happens at the most fundamental level in birth.

Many men are actively defying the degrading caricatures of the brainless father in the waiting room. They know it is no longer unacceptable to be caring, active husbands and fathers. Our classes are filled with men eager to accept their new responsibilities. They look forward to helping their wives in labor and to sharing the rewards of birth.

In the following chapters, the two of you will learn that labor is really a simple process. Your wife will learn how to work with her body and let it fulfill its task unimpeded by tension, fear, or anesthesia. Don't think you get off without some hard physical work, though. Birth is very much a team effort. Like any other coach, you must get involved right at the start of training. Don't wait until just before the big event. Get started right now.

PETER ROSEGG

NOTE: *When there is no husband to do the coaching:*
Coaches are usually husbands but sometimes there are women who by circumstance or design simply don't have a husband or male partner to coach them. If this is the case, call your nearest Bradley® teacher for help. She often knows women who are experienced and willing to coach or sometimes your Bradley® teacher may offer to coach you herself. If you have a very close friend you can count on to learn everything you are learning, she or he might make an excellent coach for you. Just don't plan on doing it alone. Labor is a lot of hard work and you need and deserve a coach.

Throughout the book we refer to the coach as "he" and often use the phrase "your wife" when addressing the coach. Since this is usually the case we hope that readers other than husbands and wives will understand and accept this arrangement for easier reading. And while at least half of all babies are "she's," we generally refer to babies yet to be born as "he" simply to differentiate them from their mothers. At least *they* are always "she's."

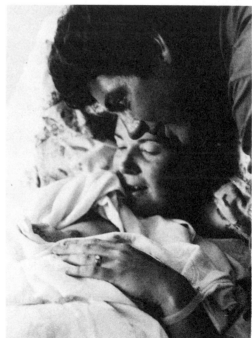

NANCY STEPHENS

6 *Getting Ready*

chapter two

What Is the Difference Between the Bradley Method® and Lamaze?

So you are pregnant (or thinking about becoming pregnant), and you are obviously interested in a natural childbirth since you picked up this book. The first question that probably comes to your mind is: What exactly is the difference between the Bradley Method® and the Lamaze Method? Don't feel alone, that is everyone's first question.

If you have had a Lamaze birth or heard a lot about it, you will want a fairly detailed answer, so hang on a moment. But if you just know the name Lamaze (almost everyone does) and not Bradley® (named after Dr. Robert A. Bradley and often called Husband-Coached Childbirth®), here is the short answer.

Briefly, the Bradley Method® and Lamaze are:

Different in attitude. Bradley® emphasizes being a good consumer and taking responsibility for your birth, shaping it the way you want it, while Lamaze generally prepares a couple for hospital routines and perpetuates the role of the doctor as an all-knowing authority figure.

Different in basic techniques. Bradley® teaches the laboring woman to relax completely and use normal, rhythmic, abdominal breathing during contractions while Lamaze emphasizes three complicated altered-breathing techniques and artificial distractions from the sensations the woman is feeling.

Different in importance of the father (or coach, as we call the mother's caring partner). Lamaze-trained coaches (though as dedicated and caring as the Bradley® ones) are just not given the same depth of information or training.

Different in expectations. Bradley® works determinedly and assertively for an unmedicated, natural childbirth without routine interventions while Lamaze is more accepting of medication and other interference, even when it is not medically necessary.

Different in the rate of successful outcomes. In the Bradley Method®, when we say successful outcome, we mean a totally unmedicated, drug-free natural childbirth without routine medical intervention that enables the woman to exercise all her choices in birthing and give her baby the best possible start in life. And we expect this over ninety percent of the time.

What is a successful outcome in the Lamaze Method? Well, let's take the words of Elisabeth Bing, the country's best-known Lamaze teacher and co-founder of ASPO (American Society for Psychoprophylaxis in Obstetrics), the main training organization for Lamaze teachers. In her book *Six Practical Lessons for an Easier Birth* she says,

> I have often been asked the number of successes and failures among my students. I want you to realize that I do not accept the concept of failure in regard to women I prepare for childbirth. Before we train in our method, we all start off at a point I call minus zero. Everyone of you will achieve zero plus, and this will be *your* point of total success.[1]

We think this is a cop-out. It sounds like a politician responding to a question without answering it. In fact, it is self-serving for a teacher who is training you in a method with a low rate of success to start off with rules that remove yardsticks for measuring effectiveness. *Women do not fail, but methods can fail women*, and it is reasonable for a woman to want to know the rate of success of a method of childbirth training. The latest edition of *Williams Obstetrics* tells us, "It is not unusual for Lamaze prepared women in the United States to receive some narcotic analgesia during labor and nerve block anesthesia for delivery, usually local, pudendal, or epidural."[2] In fact, in a study of 500 consecutive Lamaze-prepared patients compared to 500 hand-picked control patients, only *one percent* (five women) using the Lamaze Method gave birth without drugs.[3]

But with proper Bradley® training and a supportive, noninterfering birth attendant, nine out of ten mothers

birthing vaginally can get all the way through birth without drugs, not because drugs are withheld but because the Bradley® techniques work so well that most women will not feel a need for any.

Actually, Dr. Bradley's own statistics after 14,000 births are even better. Ninety-four percent of the women he attends are unmedicated, three percent require medication for some medical reason, and three percent require caesarean surgery.[4]

That is why we strongly feel that if you want a natural, family-centered birth rather than a doctor-directed delivery, your chances of success are much, much better with the Bradley Method® than with the Lamaze. An unmedicated birth is not an impossible or unrealistic goal. It is within the reach of the overwhelming majority of women.

Most women today know that labor drugs are not good for the baby, but here's something else you should consider about drugs. If you want to have this birth *your* way, you need to get through to the moment of birth unmedicated. Obviously, there are rare complications when medication is required, but most labor drugs are given when there are no medical complications.

Once medication begins, however, the choices slip through your fingers. For example, if you have a drug which might cause your labor to slow down, then you will probably end up needing another drug dripped into you intravenously later to speed your labor up. If you have an anesthetic, your legs must be strapped into the stirrups. If the anesthetic means you cannot push the baby out, the doctor must remove the baby with forceps or a vacuum extractor.

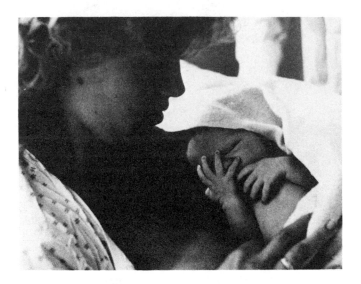

accept medication and its consequences just moments before birth. Teaching an expectant couple how to avoid this pitfall is one of the main things that separate Bradley® from Lamaze. Dr. Silvia Feldman, whose book *Choices in Childbirth* looks at just about every method available, says: "If you're the kind of person who likes to do your own thing and can count (a great deal) on your husband to help you do it, then I recommend the Bradley Method® to you. For those with enough self-confidence, it may be the most rewarding natural childbirth method available in the United States."[5]

Differences in Techniques

If you have had a Lamaze birth, you may still want more specific details on the contrast with Bradley®. You probably know that Lamaze teachers are careful to call what they teach "prepared" rather than "natural" childbirth. Also, you probably realize that there are several kinds of Lamaze training (some quite unlike what Dr. Fernand Lamaze writes about in *Painless Childbirth*). The kind taught in hospitals and some doctors' offices is geared to the practices of particular hospitals or doctors, while Lamaze-training taught privately tends to be more consumer-oriented.

Forceps then make an episiotomy (a surgical cut in the outlet of the vagina) almost certain, and an episiotomy means pain for days after the birth. A drugged mother, and the inevitably drugged baby, find that special moment of togetherness just after birth very difficult or impossible to enjoy. Instead of your being able to take the baby into your arms at once to hold and press to your breast (where he will hear the familiar voice and heartbeat he has known for months in the womb), the baby may need to be taken away immediately for special attention. A wondrous moment that could have been shared by the new family may be lost forever.

Many women have deeply regretted going successfully through hours of hard but rewarding labor, only to

But let's get to some specific differences in techniques. During the early part of labor your uterus (which you can think of as a big bag of muscles holding the baby)

begins to contract for half a minute and rest for five minutes or so. It continues with longer and more frequent contractions for some hours as it really gets to work opening for the baby to emerge. For use during this period, Lamaze teaches three altered-breathing states. But Bradley® stresses the importance of *normal* breathing in labor.

The dangerous thing about altered breathing is that it can lead to hyperventilation. Hyperventilation is a hazard for a mother because it can interfere with the ability of her uterus to contract. But the worst thing about overbreathing is not just what it can do to a mother, but what it does to the baby. Hyperventilation reduces the baby's oxygen supply.[6]

A decade ago the *OB GYN News* reported that "if the mother hyperventilates for a long time before the baby's birth, he will be apnoeic [which means suffer cessations of breathing] at birth." The baby may make no effort to breathe on his own.[7] Dr. Virginia Apgar, who invented the famous Apgar chart used to score the condition of newborns in hospitals across the country, says babies from hyperventilated mothers should be monitored for twenty-four to forty-eight hours after birth to watch for apnea spells.

You have probably heard of breathing into a paper bag (or cupped hands) in labor. That is the Lamaze "cure" for hyperventilation. But a mother's body is ten to twenty times the size of her baby's, so by the time she feels hyperventilation's symptoms, the baby is already affected.

Lamaze, with its complicated breathing, mental exercises, and self-massage, attempts to condition the mother and distract her from the sensations in her uterus by sending competing signals to her brain. Breathing patterns purposely are made more complicated as contractions get stronger. Mothers are told to relax, *but everything they have to do is the opposite of relaxation.*

The Bradley Method®, on the other hand, teaches a systematic relaxation. With eyes closed and her body in the most relaxing position possible, a Bradley® mother uses normal abdominal breathing through the mouth. Her coach tells her in a quiet, soothing voice to just breathe normally, to relax every voluntary muscle in her body, to locate tension and let it go, as the uterus works.

The Bradley® mother and her coach have practiced relaxation techniques for hours, developing just the right mental imagery to keep her on the track, completely relaxing every voluntary muscle group in the body. She is not distracted, hypnotized, or otherwise out of it. She is mentally awake and alert, concentrating on relaxing.

The coach has also practiced the special rub to relieve his wife's backache, and if she needs her abdomen rubbed instead, he knows how to deal with that too. No self-massage here, which uses muscles in the mother's arms and back. We'd rather use the coach's muscles. Many Bradley® coaches come out of labor elated but exhausted compared to their wives who have been concentrating on relaxation for hours. We see this as a sign the couple has done things right.

Here's another important difference in technique. There comes a moment of doubt in many labors when the mother is not so sure she can do this after all. She is extremely suggestible at this time and is literally a mirror of the thoughts and emotions around her. If, at this moment, a well-meaning doctor or nurse says, "Would you like a shot now?" the mother will often say, "Sure, I guess so." How does Lamaze prepare you for this classical shaky moment of doubt? Well, here is Elisabeth Bing again.

> If at any time you should feel the need for medication or sedation, don't hesitate to ask for it. Your doctor will be happy to give you as much relief as he considers medically safe. If he himself suggests medication, he undoubtedly has good reasons for his decision, and I am sure he will explain and discuss them with you.
>   . . . Any medication he may give you will be necessary to insure the health of your baby and your own safety.[8]

And the Bradley Method®? Well, Bradley® couples have been trained for weeks to look for this emotional signpost (self-doubt, uncertainty, suggestibility) and recognize it for what it is: an indication that labor is almost over and the relief of the active, enjoyable, pushing stage is about to begin.

Instead of a shot of medication, the Bradley Method® uses a shot of Praise, Encouragement, and assurance of Progress (we call it PEP). This is a difficult moment for many mothers, but the Bradley® training has devoted a lot of time to helping the couple select a doctor with whom they have an open, communicative relationship rather than an authoritarian one. So this is a time when the coach has been trained to say to the doctor, "Is anything wrong with the mother or the baby? No? Nothing? Well, that's just great. We feel we are doing fine and we would just like to stick with it for a while."

And the coach takes care to acknowledge the laboring woman's work and her upcoming reward: "You're doing just great. Everything is fine and we are almost done. In no time at all you will have a baby in your arms." Support and encouragement are exactly what benefit the woman most at this time.

Most of the Lamaze teachers we know are dedicated and caring people. Some of them are showing up at Bradley Method® workshops, as they drop the altered-breathing techniques shown to be hazardous in labor and look for something safer and more successful.

We also know many second-time mothers who are not happy with their first birth experiences. Sometimes that is hard to admit, even to yourself. Maybe you, like they, are looking for something better. As Dr. Feldman notes in *Choices in Childbirth*, many women start out with a medicated, monitored experience and then "graduate" to a more natural method. Maybe you hope to have the "graduate" experience without going through the undergraduate course.

If so, here is a word about how to use this book. Ideally, we would have you read it all the way through early in your pregnancy and then return to the practice parts as your birth gets closer. But if you are already well along it is not too late to jump in.

The first part of this book deals with important things like exercises, being aware of what you eat, avoiding drugs, learning the mechanics of birth, and choosing your doctor. Selecting a birth attendant (which for most people means a doctor) is the most important single decision you will make in determining how your birth will go, as we will explain a few chapters further on. To choose intelligently, as a good consumer, you really must know what questions to ask. Learning about the full range of normalcy in a natural birth is the only way you can evaluate the answers you get.

It may be tempting to go right from the preliminaries to the controversies at the end of the book and skip the information and techniques for labor and birthing (the middle section of the book). Don't. After the choice of your birth attendant, the next most important thing you need to achieve the kind of birth you desire is for both you and your coach to be physically and psychologically prepared. You cannot be ready without steadily learning the Bradley® techniques nor without lots of practice. Without practice, having a list of childbirth choices and a good birth attendant will not be enough to get you the birth experience you want.

In the next chapter we will explain what to look for in a childbirth educator and how to find a Bradley Method® instructor in your area.

chapter three

How to Choose Your Childbirth Teacher

When should you choose your childbirth educator? Ideally, before you choose your doctor. An independent, natural-childbirth educator will know who is practicing in your area and can suggest those doctors (or other birth attendants) who will meet your desires. (However, don't shy away from a Bradley Method® instructor just because you have already chosen a doctor.) The independent natural-birth educator will also have the scoop on local hospitals and birthing centers.

A natural-childbirth teacher will use the word "natural" with no apology, because the goals of her class will reflect her experience with successful techniques. In fact, she

should be happy to talk statistics with you. Nine out of ten of her students should be experiencing totally unmedicated births.

A teacher who avoids the word natural and uses the word "prepared" childbirth does so because most of her students will have "prepared" but medicated deliveries. The limited effectiveness of the techniques she is using are reflected in her limited goals.

Because they are preparing a woman for what will happen to her in birth rather than teaching what she needs to have the kind of birth she wants, prepared-childbirth teachers often take it upon themselves to withhold information about the risks of drugs or the hazards of procedures that might be used. This is done in "misguided kindness." It stems from the mistaken idea that few women are able to have totally unmedicated labor and birth anyway, so why tell a woman about things that might be avoided if it will just make her feel guilty and unhappy afterward? Advocates of "prepared" childbirth education will often warn expectant couples against natural childbirth, saying, "That will just make you feel guilty if you end up needing medication or forceps, as most women do . . ." But the problem with this approach is that it then becomes a self-fulfilling prophecy: because instructors don't tell students the facts about avoidable procedures, chances are far greater that their students will undergo those very procedures.

The logic of "prepared" childbirth is based on a faulty premise. The average woman *is* able to labor and give birth without drugs or unneeded routine interventions *if* she is trained and supported throughout labor. But when information is withheld future parents are denied the opportunity to make responsible decisions. For example, some prepared-childbirth educators even reassure parents that labor drugs won't do any harm. How many parents have been told that "a little Demerol never hurt anything"? How much better to teach an expectant woman that drugs and interventions have risks; that she can learn to give birth without them if she wishes; that she can find a birth attendant who can be trusted not to use drugs or interfere except in the rare cases in which medical help is indeed necessary.

Once you understand the differences between "prepared" and "natural" birth education, you need to analyze a teacher's ties. Is she an independent teacher, a hospital's teacher, or a doctor's teacher? Let's take a look at each.

The Doctor's Teacher

The doctor's teacher is exactly that: she works for the doctor. If the doctor pays her salary (or sends her all his patients), she can easily be influenced by him and be limited in her point of view and reluctant to explore up-to-date information (which tends to make a doctor who does not keep current uncomfortable).

I tell you this from personal experience since I've worked for half a dozen doctors. Some have been excellent. They have sincerely supported the woman's desire to have a natural childbirth using the Bradley Method®. Others have asked me to omit information on the protective function of the bag of waters, because it was their routine to always break it; or not to explain the value of breast-feeding on the delivery table, since the hospital's head OB nurse was not yet "ready" for this change. I have been asked by doctors to "sell" women on: the fetal monitor; forceps delivery to shorten the pushing stage; lying flat on the back in delivery; being strapped to the table; routine use of IVs; and the three-day hospital stay (with the explanation, to me only, that the hospital needed the beds filled for increased income).

The doctor's teacher may offer a good class, but you will never know how much she didn't get to tell you.

The Hospital's Teacher

Most hospital classes are set up as a defensive response to the "irritation" caused by independent classes. You will usually find that a good deal of time in these classes is spent on justifications for tying women to delivery tables, separating infants and mothers immediately at birth, giving routine episiotomies, staying in the hospital three days, and submitting to IVs and fetal monitoring.

"Part of the instructor's job, as a hospital employee, is to prepare mothers to fit nicely into hospital routines and delivery procedures," says Dr. Silvia Feldman in *Choices in Childbirth*. "A Lamaze educator at one hospital told me proudly, 'Few couples who have been through our classes here in the hospital object to the rules and regulations.' "[1] In general in these classes, the woman is taught passive acceptance of all procedures used in a particular hospital. As might be expected, this reassurance drastically reduces consumer demands for change and updating of services offered. You don't have to think too hard to realize just whom this class serves.

You should, of course, take advantage of all tours offered by a hospital that you plan to use. You will want the chance to see the facilities and the equipment.

The Independent Teacher

You have probably figured out by now that the independent teacher is the one who works for *you*. She has no financial ties to anyone else and therefore cannot be motivated to omit information you should have. She is not motivated to "sell" you on any procedures which current research shows to be harmful. She is able to supply you with any information that may be pertinent to your decisions about birth. The independent teacher is the expectant couple's teacher.

Asking the Right Questions

Choosing a childbirth educator is obviously very important, second only in importance to choosing your birth attendant. Here are some of the questions to ask a prospective teacher.

Are you an independent teacher? Listen to the answers carefully. A teacher who says she's "independent" but teaches in a hospital is not an independent instructor. She bases her claim to independence on the mere fact

that you will be paying her fee and she is not on the hospital's payroll, but she will be under the same pressures to tailor her teaching as the hospital-salaried instructor would be—that is if she wants to continue using the hospital's facilities and drawing her students from among its patients.

Where did you get your teacher training? ASPO (American Society for Psychoprophylaxis in Obstetrics) does Lamaze teacher training and AAHCC (American Academy of Husband-Coached Childbirth®) does Bradley® teacher training. I would ask this even before I asked what method she is teaching. The reason for this will become clear with the next question.

What method are you teaching? Since more and more people are seeking out Bradley® classes, teachers with dwindling classes are prone to say, "Oh, I teach a combination of Lamaze and Bradley®." This sounds like a car salesman: "Whatever you want, I've got it." Beware. It is just not possible, for example, to combine the normal abdominal Bradley® breathing with Lamaze's altered chest breathing. This is why asking a teacher where she got her training is a most important question. Having picked the method you want to use, you will want to be certain you've picked a teacher who knows how to teach it.

Another common response is, "I teach Lamaze, but Bradley® and Lamaze are becoming more alike now. We don't teach so much breathing anymore." At the 1983 ASPO/Lamaze workshops held in five cities across the country, teachers were given an update on breathing. We attended one of these five workshops. At the New York workshop, teachers were given printed material on the breathing. All three were altered breathing

techniques. The first one altered the breathing by having the mother slow down to *half* her normal breathing rate. The second one then has the mother speeding up her breathing to *twice as fast as normal.* The third altered breathing technique is also *twice as fast as normal* breathing *with periodic blowing out.* This is certainly quite unlike the Bradley Method®, which teaches only normal abdominal breathing in labor. Teachers were also instructed to drop the term "chest breathing" and to substitute the term "patterned paced breathing" for the above altered breathing techniques.

The Lamaze leaders also told their teachers to emphasize relaxation more. Now this is indeed like the Bradley Method®, which concentrates on relaxation as the key to a successful labor. But there was tremendous resistance from the teachers at these workshops, who said this new emphasis was turning the Lamaze Method around 180 degrees.

In response to the resistance at the workshop we attended in New York, one leader said, "if [the way you are teaching now] is comfortable for you, and you can rationalize it in your own mind, we certainly cannot take your certification away."

The point is that if a prospective teacher tells you that she teaches Lamaze but it is not like the old Lamaze Method and more like the Bradley®, or that she is teaching the "new Lamaze," you might both be thinking about very different things. If totally natural, coached childbirth is what you're after, why not take a class from a Bradley® teacher who is trained in a proven method and has been teaching it all along? That way you avoid the problem of not really knowing what you are getting.

Have you been to any births recently? Going often to births is important. After fifteen years of teaching I gain some new insights from every single birthing couple I work with, and that benefits my students.

Have you had any children using this method? You would not want a teacher who hasn't had a good birth herself.

How many of your students are experiencing unmedicated natural childbirth? You might ask for the names of some recently birthed couples.

Finally, ask if she is a nurse. Frankly, nurses make poor teachers. Their "real" careers are too often jeopardized if they get into some of the controversial issues of childbearing. For example, if many of her students change from certain doctors with high caesarean surgery rates, she has made a powerful "career" enemy. If she "irritates" the hospital by educating consumers to insist upon little or no separation of mother and infant at birth, she may make a "nuisance" of herself to the nursing supervisor at the hospital where she may already work or desire to work at some time in the future.

The nurse-midwife is no exception. She is not independent of the hospital or the physicians working there and is subjected to a great many pressures. If she is teaching the hospital's classes she must take great care not to antagonize the "traditional physician" or to cast doubt upon the way he practices. That means routine episiotomies, separating mother and infant at birth, and tying mothers down on a delivery table. She may still be a good birth attendant and not do these things to her own clients, but as a teacher she is often walking a tightrope. There will inevitably be issues on which her tongue is tied.

The non-nurse educator's career is birthing. She can expect to do well only if your needs are met completely and safely. Changing current maternity care to safely suit the needs of women and babies rather than perpetuating routines that are more familiar or convenient for the hospital staff is her business.

These are important questions to sort out before you attend a class. Once you've asked them, ask if you can come to the first class and then decide whether or not this teacher is right for you. Remember, your time is limited in pregnancy. You don't want to complete a series of classes and then realize that you feel uncomfortable with your instructor or that you haven't really been taught how to have a baby naturally. You probably won't have enough time left to start over in another class.

To locate the nearest Bradley® teachers in your area, you should write or call: the American Academy of Husband-Coached Childbirth®, P.O. Box 5224, Sherman Oaks, California 91413, (800) 423-2397.

chapter four

How to Choose Your Doctor

Your first parental responsibility begins before the baby is born. It is your choice of a doctor.

It is one of the word games of obstetrics to say that the physician is responsible until your baby is born. Responsibility belongs to those who will ultimately live with the consequences of the decisions made during birthing—the parents. Choosing your doctor is one of the most important decisions you will make in your life, and in the life of your baby.

Once you have chosen a childbirth instructor, get the lowdown from her on the doctors and facilities available to the birthing couple in your area. It is best not to call a teacher, even one you've heard good things about, and announce, "I'm going to Doctor So-and-so." If you make it obvious you are not shopping for a doctor, even if your choice is the worst in town, a teacher may not be inclined to say so—especially over the phone to a stranger.

However, if you discuss doctors with an independent childbirth teacher before you make up your mind, she will be best able to give you the names of two or three doctors, and perhaps some midwives, who are known to be supportive of natural childbirth couples in practice as well as talk. You can always make a more intelligent decision with this kind of candid information.

Do not underestimate the importance of putting time and thought into choosing your doctor. The day you choose your doctor you will have already made many important decisions about your birth experience.

For example: You've already decided whether or not you will get an episiotomy (the cut made in the outlet of your vagina, or perineum, to enlarge the opening). Many doctors do them routinely. If you pick a doctor who does them, you will get one. If you talk him into "trying it out" and only doing an episiotomy "if necessary," you will get one, because he has no experience in helping women give birth without an episiotomy and so he will always think you "need" one.

Some doctors do caesarean surgery for three percent of the birthing women they attend, but there are others who operate on fifteen to thirty percent. There have been books, articles, and congressional health committees investigating and reporting on the current epidemic of unnecessary caesarean surgery. If you picked a doctor with a high surgery rate then you have already decided that you will run a high risk of having unnecessary surgery. If you picked one with a three percent rate then you have already decided that surgery will be reserved for those few complications requiring it. You set the risk.

Some doctors prefer to have every woman on a delivery table with her legs strapped into stirrups. Others are used to helping women give birth in a labor bed. I don't know of any woman who enjoyed being strapped down to a delivery table, but I know quite a few who rave about how relaxed and comfortable it was to give birth in an ordinary bed.

Sometimes people mistakenly think that if they pick a hospital that has an alternative birthing room they will get to have a labor-bed birth. The mere presence of a room doesn't mean a thing. Some of the doctors using that hospital will not use the alternative birthing room; some use it but have the bed broken down into a typical delivery table set up with stirrups.

Some doctors think of forceps or vacuum-extraction deliveries as "controlled" and preferable to natural childbirth. Others are alarmed at the risks to the baby when forceps and vacuum extractors are used instead of the mother's own effort of pushing. If you have picked a birth attendant who sees little natural birth and usually uses forceps or the vacuum extractor, then chances are good that you will not have a natural birth. It will be "taking too long," or you will "need a little help."

Still, many people think that regardless of how their obstetrician "normally" practices, they will be able to just talk to him and tell him how they want things to go for them. We have couples in our training classes who go to physicians who use the common practices of fetal monitoring, routine IVs, pudendal blocks for birth, routine episiotomies, and forceps or vacuum-extractor deliveries. They naively describe the natural birth they would like to have and get the doctor's reluctant agreement. Then, in labor, they are frequently told, "Sorry, it looks like you will need all those things after all." What is the couple going to do? Play doctor? Decide for themselves on the spot that they don't need something even when the doctor says they do? Ignore the critical attitude of the doctor and hospital staff?

That's a pretty tough spot to be in, and what follows is almost always a delivery instead of a birth. The couple is left wondering, "Did we just get the routine, or did we really have to go through all that?"

Doctors who do not keep up with family-centered maternity-care concepts cannot be counted on to provide you, the consumer, with the services you require. Those doctors who will take the trouble to support you in a natural childbirth, including a supportive, nonmechanized environment, and who respond to consumer needs to develop a safer, happier maternity-care system *should* be properly rewarded. The power of the pocketbook is the only effective means we have of changing the birthing picture in this country today. Choose a doctor who supports natural childbirth wholeheartedly and whose actions reflect his words.

Finally, if you pick a doctor whose practice indicates clearly that he or she *rarely* interferes, then you can have total confidence if you are told that everything is not right and that something unusual must be done.

Your choice of a doctor can have long-lasting effects on the life of your child. The risk of minimal brain damage is greatly reduced by choosing a physician who does not interfere with normal labor and birth. The risk of a depressed infant is greatly reduced by choosing a physician who shies away from routine use of anesthetics and analgesics. The risk of toxemia is greatly reduced by choosing a physician who is up to date on maternal health and weight gain during pregnancy.

The risk that you will experience distress and even a resentment of the baby that sometimes follow caesarean surgery (especially when the mother feels she has been victimized by an unnecessary surgical operation) can be greatly reduced by choosing an obstetrician who has a low (three to five percent) rate of surgery.

Consider a Certified Nurse-Midwife

If you are lucky enough to have a nurse-midwife working in your area, she may well be the first person you will want to interview for your birthing. (She can make a good *birth attendant* but not a good teacher. Your teacher should always be independent of your birth attendant and the institution you are birthing in.) A nurse-midwife can provide top-quality maternity care and often has a much broader background and understanding of the variations of *normal* labor than the average disease-oriented physician.

Study after study has shown that the quality of care by the certified nurse-midwife is superior to the average doctor's care. The CNM is a registered nurse (RN) who has continued her education to study nurse-midwifery. When she finishes her training (if it included home births) she has more experience than most obstetricians in normal childbirth. An obstetrician's training focuses on abnormal childbirth which requires intervention. In their training many obstetricians (OBs) never see a woman give birth naturally without an episiotomy or the use of forceps or a vacuum extractor.

A midwife will be most particularly prepared if she has attended a good number of home births. Whether you're looking for a home birth or not, this is your guarantee that she will understand the range of *normality* in birthing. She will be highly skilled in helping women birth without routine episiotomies, and do a much better job of providing the means for relaxed, unstressful, low-tech birthing. She may catch your baby for you in a hospital, but that home-birth background of hers will eliminate the high-tech midwife. If a midwife's training and her experience are all hospital based, then she has been limited to the same high-tech focus on abnormality that most obstetricians have had. The hospital-trained nurse-midwife may turn out to be a junior OB you would rather avoid.

A midwife generally has the time to offer more information on nutrition and give better support to the woman throughout her pregnancy than the average doctor. But she is trained to recognize complications, and when she sees them, she refers the expectant mother to her physician back-up for care.

In fact, during labor a midwife can often spot problems more quickly than the OB. This is simply because the midwife spends hours with the laboring woman, while the average busy OB may manage your labor over the telephone, checking with the labor-and-delivery nurse to see how you are doing. The ordinary RN on duty has less training than the nurse-midwife in spotting problems.

We know that many obstetricians leave standing

orders with the nurses not to call them to attend a birth until the baby's head is showing. Then the woman often has to wait for the doctor to get there before she is allowed to push. This makes for an unnecessarily hard pushing stage for the mother. The nurse-midwife, however, is there all along, waiting to take her cue from the mother. Delaying birth is definitely not in the interest of the infant's health or the mother's.

A first-rate certified nurse-midwife has a better chance to know you as a person than most doctors and is usually much more tuned in to the needs of the natural-childbirth couple.

The Lay Midwife

As it happens, the best birth attendant I know is a lay midwife. She received her basic training in one of the several states that license lay midwives. She has attended many births and is fully competent to do prenatal care, to attend a normal birth, and to spot any complications developing. In many ways her experience with normal birthing is superior to most physicians'. For example, she recently attended a couple from one of our classes birthing at home. Their baby was born with the cord looped three times around its neck—unusual, but not out of the range of normal. The lay midwife calmly slipped the loops one by one over the baby's head in a matter of seconds and the body was born with the next contraction. She had listened to the fetal heart tones frequently and knew the baby had been in no danger. Later, at the hospital birth of another of our couples, the baby's head emerged with the cord looped once around the neck—something quite common. The baby was having no problems, but the physician attending was shouting at the mother (whose control was perfect) not to push. The doctor then pulled out a bit of the loop, clamped it, and cut the cord before the body was born. That meant the baby *had* to breathe immediately since the lifeline supplying it with oxygen had been severed. Fortunately, it did. Neither baby had any problems at birth, but the hospital baby had been put to greater risk.

Today, the lay midwife is a response to a growing home-birth movement. In my own community most physicians have decided to withhold prenatal care from the home-birther. This is judgmental and vindictive. These doctors have decided that home birth is not safe, and by withholding prenatal care they are doing their best to make sure it is unsafe. Often it is lay midwives who step forward to fill the void and help eliminate the unnecessary dangers of home birth. They are essential for screening out women who really should not have a home birth. For considerably less money than a physician charges, they spend many more hours with a pregnant woman before, during, and after the birth. And in most places they courageously face the opposition of the established medical community.

Lay midwives get their training in different ways. Some actually go to schools for formal lay midwifery training, while others apprentice with sympathetic doctors or more experienced midwives. Often lay midwives in a community will be informally organized to share information and support one another.

How to Find Your Birth Attendant

The most important starting point in your search for the right birth attendant is to ask your teacher, "Whom do you recommend?" She will probably respond with her own well-considered list: "Drs. Jones, Smith, or Casey, or nurse-midwife Coleman, or lay midwife Mills." Stick to that list. Remember your teacher sees and talks to women who have birthed with every attendant in town. She knows which ones help women have natural births time after time and which ones *always* seem to have a problem that justifies a forceps delivery or another caesarean surgery. If a doctor's name is *not* on her recommended list there is probably a good reason.

Talk to a few suitable-sounding candidates from her list. Call for an appointment, but make it clear you do *not* want an exam, that you and your husband want to discuss a few things first. Ask if they charge for this kind of visit. Some do, some don't. If they do you will want to know how much so you'll have no surprises later.

If You Already Have a Doctor

If you already have a doctor, ask him questions now and make sure the two of you are not on a collision course. If you don't like his answers, try not to get upset. I get at least two calls a week from women who have reached this collision point (they're usually halfway through my classes and down to their last month or so). It's always possible to change, but the longer you wait, the harder it becomes. Get your teacher's recommended list *now* if the doctor

you've been going to is no longer acceptable to you. Then consider your options carefully.

Don't burn any bridges behind you yet. Start by making appointments to just talk to a couple of the people on your teacher's list. After talking to other physicians who practice in a manner that better suits you, it may suddenly seem far less threatening and traumatic to change doctors and leave the nonsupportive one behind.

If so, *change*. Don't stay with a doctor if you're unhappy. Don't give your birth away. Do not be afraid of hurting his feelings. Believe me, he won't remember the details of your birth even one year later, while you will remember this experience all of your life. If you stay with someone you're worried about, someone you worry will not help you give birth normally, then you will carry fear and tension with you into labor. You will be tensed and ready to argue, and you cannot argue when you are in labor. You cannot possibly use relaxation techniques if you are anxious. Get yourself to a birth attendant you feel will help, not hinder you. Then your energies will be freed to focus on the work of labor.

If you are in a medical plan that does not let you choose your own doctor or you are using a military hospital, I cannot mince words: you are in a poor situation for birthing. You get potluck in labor—whoever is on duty. All your well-laid plans could go awry. You may try to talk to three or four different doctors, describing what you want and getting agreements about your birth, but then in labor you may end up with someone you never have met before, or worse, someone who was hostile to your requests. The doctor on duty is not obligated to honor the agreements you made with another doctor. The tension a woman experiences as she enters the hospital in labor wondering if she will get a doctor who will help or hinder her is not helpful for the work ahead. So I urge you, if you have the option, to switch to a health-care plan that allows you to pick your doctor or other birth attendant.

If you can't switch health plans, I sincerely recommend that you select your own birth attendant even if it means paying out of your own pocket. That may seem expensive, but look at your budget. If you take an annual vacation that costs about as much as having a baby, consider financing the best experience of your life, the birth of your baby, instead of that holiday. The trade-off is worth it. The birth will be far more memorable in your lifetime than two or three weeks spent anywhere.

If both these options are out for you, maximize your chances of having a good birth by following these instructions carefully:

1. Make a detailed list of what you want and don't want in birth, in the order that is important to you.

2. The coach should go along on every prenatal medical visit possible.

3. Try to see a different doctor on each visit. Discuss your requests with each doctor. (Don't bring in your written list; memorize it. Doctors hate to be questioned by someone with a list in hand.) Have the first doctor write what you want on your chart. The doc-

tor is more likely to remember you if he plays an active part in getting your requests down.

4. On later visits ask each doctor to read what the previous ones wrote so you can see if there is anything else to go over. This confirms previous agreements and gets the new doctor actively involved in seeing that your birth turns out the way you want. It also allows you to keep expressing your preferences. (By the way, if you get a hostile reaction from an occasional doctor, be glad you got to see it before labor so you are forewarned.)

5. About three weeks before your birth, you should hand over your written list and see that it is attached to your chart.

6. Have three copies of your list to take with you to the hospital just in case your original was "misplaced" and is not with your chart.

7. Take a supportive person, in addition to your coach, with you to the hospital when the big day comes. This person's function is not so much to intercede on your behalf as to simply be there for moral support as you deal with any situations that might come up. Ask your Bradley® teacher. She may have a "graduate" student whom she can recommend as just the right kind of person.

8. The corollary to informed consent is *dissent.* This is necessary if the concept of informed

consent is to have any meaning at all. So you may need to be ready to decline a procedure that is objectionable to you.

What Are the Questions to Ask?

You can hardly know what to ask and why a particular point is important until you have a good idea of what birthing normally is all about, which you will learn in the pages ahead. Then, in Chapter Twenty-three, when you have more background, we will go over a list of specific questions to ask your doctor. At that point, you will have a complete understanding of why those questions are important and what impact the answers will have on your birth.

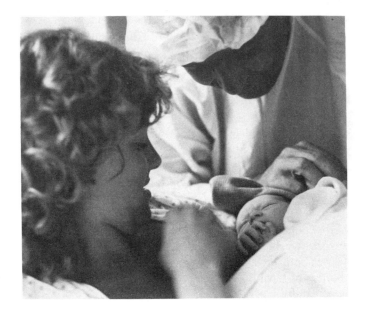

chapter five

Nutrition: How Does Your Garden Grow?

Most of us put more thought and effort into growing a garden than we put into growing a baby. A pregnant woman's diet is often sorely neglected in spite of the fruit she is about to bring forth.

Does It Really Matter What a Pregnant Woman Eats?

Yes, studies have shown that women on poor diets actually have harder labors[1] and that their babies run a higher sta-

tistical incidence of infections in the first year of life.[2] Animal experiments have shown that low-protein diets lead to a reduced number of brain cells in offspring.[3]

Most important, **toxemia**, the most dreaded disease of pregnancy, can often be avoided through proper nutrition.[4] Ironically, one of the reasons doctors were originally afraid of women gaining weight was that women who developed toxemia had sudden weight gains. For a time, it was thought that sudden weight gain was a *cause* of toxemia.

In fact, a woman becomes ill with toxemia as her body cannot throw off toxic substances stored in its cells. She swells up with retained fluids. She has severe headaches, blurry vision, high blood pressure, and protein showing up in her urine. This is all very dangerous for the woman and for her unborn baby. She can go into convulsions and a coma (called eclampsia), but before her condition goes that far the woman usually ends up with caesarean surgery. Dr. Tom Brewer's research has shown that weight gain is not the cause of toxemia at all, but merely a symptom of the problem. Instead, a diet *deficient* in protein and other nutrients can be a primary cause of toxemia. Restricting weight gain is now seen as one of the causes of toxemia, since it restricts the mother's access to the good food she needs.

Still, a woman often comes out of her doctor's office with little or no information about nutrition. Worse, having been scolded by a doctor or a nurse for gaining perhaps five to seven pounds in one month, she may have resolved to diet to avoid gaining "too much weight." She immediately starts cutting calories and skipping lunch, which leaves her irritable and without energy. Some women will actually starve themselves completely the day or two before their visits to the doctor's office just to keep their weight a pound or two lower on the scales.

So the question of what to eat often becomes academic when all the attention is focused on not eating. The woman who gets on the scales and discovers she has gained more than "allowed" never gets to question what she *should* have been eating.

Fortunately, ideas on weight gain have changed and are still changing dramatically. The up-to-date doctor is more likely to encourage you not to worry about weight gain on good, natural foods. This is called positive weight gain. However, if you are going to a doctor still enrolled in the old school of thought, you and your baby may have a real problem.

For example, the human infant has a spurt of brain growth beginning at the last third of pregnancy which continues through the first eighteen months of life. If the child does not get proper nourishment in this critical period, he could have permanent mental disability.[5] And yet, too often in this last important part of pregnancy some doctors advise women to cut calories severely. This usually happens after a scolding by a doctor who has not taken the time to keep up on nutrition developments and is worried about weight gain in the mother. The result is a restriction of calories, including the good ones, right at a crucial time of the pregnancy.

How Much Weight Should You Gain?

Rather than look at weight gain (the outcome of your eating habits), you should concentrate on the habits themselves. It is important for you to know that the American College of Obstetricians and Gynecologists has advised obstetricians to stop the practice of limiting weight gain. Instead, the focus should be on a protein intake for a pregnant woman of about eighty to one hundred grams daily.

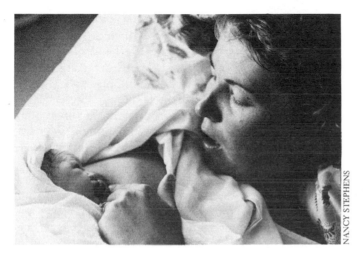
NANCY STEPHENS

So here you are, faced with another responsibility as a parent before your child is even born. It is essential for you and your husband to choose an obstetrician who is up to date on maternal nutrition and weight gain during pregnancy. If you fail to do this, each of your visits to the doctor will start with a scolding on weight gain. This often leaves you with a feeling of personal rejection and ugliness, but most importantly a potential danger to your unborn infant in the form of an inadequate diet.

Sometimes, of course, it is not the doctor who stands in the way of good nutrition but the woman herself. If she is concerned about staying super-skinny throughout pregnancy, she may sell herself on the following fallacy: "It doesn't matter what I eat; the baby will just take what it needs from my body anyway." The idea is that the baby

can cannibalize the mother's tissues for his own needs. That's possibly true to some extent, but that certainly doesn't mean he's getting *all* the nutrients he needs in the amounts needed. The baby must settle for reduced amounts!

Sure, most babies do survive their mother's diets. But one thing is overlooked here. I'm sure you want more than a baby who survives in spite of your diet. You want one who thrives because of it. When your child is born he may be intelligent and healthy enough, but you will never know how much smarter and healthier he could have been if you had eaten properly.

I thought I knew all about good nutrition when I took my first teacher-training course years ago. After all, I knew about the four basic food groups and a balanced diet; but I didn't know enough about protein. Oh, I had heard about it, but I figured if we just ate a balanced diet we would get enough protein.

It was during that training, when I was learning just how important protein really is, that I decided to count my family's protein intake, just to be sure. I discovered we were getting a dismal thirty-five grams of protein a day.

I examined our daily diet habits and discovered that we unthinkingly ate a great many junk foods. Some meals were so low in protein (for example, just cereal, juice, and toast) that it was no wonder at all that I recognized symptoms of low protein intake in myself and my family.

Protein is not a direct source of energy, but it slows down the absorption of carbohydrates and fats so that you get a sort of time-capsule effect. Protein helps allow your blood sugar to rise steadily over a number of hours so that you have a steady prolonged source of energy rather than ups and downs during the day. Protein is the key to *steady* energy. When you're getting plenty of it along with a balanced diet, you feel great! Problems seem so much more manageable, and you find it easy to accomplish a great deal and maintain a sweet disposition.

When your protein intake is low, however, the world doesn't look so good. It seems that little problems are too much to bear. They are so annoying that you think you just can't stand another one. If you switch to eating your highest protein meal (say, forty grams) in the morning you'll be amazed at the energy and enthusiasm you have. Your metabolism gets going great guns and your blood sugar goes up gradually and stays up.

Count your protein intake for one week, aiming at eighty to a hundred grams a day. Most of us fall way below that unless we are intentionally working toward it. To figure how you're doing, use the protein counter in the Appendix. Write down everything you eat daily. To improve you will need to pick high-protein foods that you like or you won't keep at it.

What Is a Good High-Protein Breakfast?

Well, it isn't two pieces of bacon, orange juice, and toast (about eight grams of protein). It certainly isn't the pack-aged cereals that are so anemic they have to have handfuls of vitamins added to them to justify their use at all. Cereals are just about worthless for protein. Those commercials plugging high-protein breakfast cereals are counting the milk you put on the cereal; they could never make those claims counting just the protein in their product.

When I first started working at increasing my protein intake, I mistakenly thought that high-protein food was going to be boring. I thought I would be forever eating cottage cheese to rack up the needed grams for the day. With the threat of monotonous meals looming in the future, I began to think about how to get this protein into my diet and like it. In fact, it only took a little imagination.

One of the most aggravating iatrogenic (that is, doctor-caused) food fads nowadays is skipping eggs for fear of cholesterol. Actually the egg white is loaded with lecithin, a substance that breaks cholesterol cells into teeny particles that can pass easily through the walls of the blood vessels without clogging them. Perhaps cholesterol is a dietary problem, but *not* from the egg, since the lecithin comes already built in for you. (As long as you don't just eat the yolks.) Eggs are cheap compared to other sources of protein. They pack a goodly amount of protein in a yummy package that can be served in many different ways: souffléed, scrambled, fried, in omelettes, boiled for snacks or chopped into sandwiches or salads, and added to lots of foods you happen to be cooking, just for the extra protein. Beyond protein, the egg is similar to milk in that this tiny oval wonder has so many of the other vitamins and elements you need for good health. You would have to munch your way through quite a variety of items to touch as many of the nutrients as come all together in the egg, or in a glass of milk.

Here's a tip. What you bring into the house is what you will consume. Face it, if food is there you will eat it. So at the market put the cookies, frozen dinners, potato chips, rolls, and so on back on the shelves. Bring home protein foods like cheese, meat, chicken, fish, yogurt, cottage cheese, milk, and eggs. Then balance the diet with vegetables, fruits, and whole grains.

Pregnancy is a good time to try whole wheat bread. It will give you some of the B vitamins you need. Beware of breads that are called "wheat" but are not whole wheat. You will be tipped off to such phonies by the list of ingredients, which usually says "caramel dye and wheat flour." They often charge the same price you pay for the real thing.

Yogurt is a fantastic food. If you enjoy it, then indulge yourself, especially during pregnancy. Yogurt lines your intestines with lactic acid and turns them into a B-vitamin factory for you. In the U.S., it is common for women to have "pregnancy mask," a brown freckling across the forehead and the bridge of the nose, extending out toward the cheeks. In fact, this is so common it is considered a normal occurrence of pregnancy. In countries where women usually eat more dark breads and yogurt, however, this is not common and is not considered normal. It is treated as a B-vitamin deficiency.

Liver is a great food. Try it out and see if you can work it into your diet. It is high in protein and B vitamins.

Count your protein intake and make sure you're getting the recommended amount. You should also get some carbohydrate and fat with each meal for a steady and prolonged rise in blood sugar. Most of us reverse this and have large carbohydrate meals with only a little protein. Eating such meals will certainly shoot your blood-sugar level up, but it zooms down fast, too.

Nutrition in pregnancy is important and is really a book in itself. The very best book on the market is *The Brewer Medical Diet for Normal and High-Risk Pregnancy*, by Gail Sforza Brewer with Thomas Brewer, M.D. Dr. Brewer has at all times been twenty years ahead of the American College of Obstetricians and Gynecologists in his nutritional instructions. He promoted eighty to a hundred grams of protein long before anyone else recognized this need of pregnant women. He insisted on a positive weight gain at a time when other doctors were limiting women to eighteen to twenty-five pounds, and was warning women about the hazards of diuretics years before they became suspect for use in pregnancy. In this book it becomes clear that Dr. Brewer is still ahead of his time. If you have had headaches in your pregnancy or if you have had a previous birth with toxemia, then you have no time to waste. A copy of this book will be the best investment in health that you can make.

chapter six

Drugs During Pregnancy

Thinking about taking a drug during your pregnancy? How about just something for that early-pregnancy nausea? It's such a nuisance, isn't it? Or an aspirin for that headache? And there's always that inevitable cold that you're bound to have during the course of nine months, so how about an antihistamine for that troublesome stuffy nose? STOP. LOOK AT THIS NEWS STORY.

ANTI-NAUSEA DRUG, BIRTH DEFECT LINKED.

New Haven, Conn. (AP) Women who took a form of the popular anti-nausea drug Bendectin in early pregnancy may have quadrupled the chances that their infants would suffer a potentially fatal stomach ailment, two Yale epidemiologists report.[1]

Wouldn't you rather put up with a little nausea?

Oh, but that headache. Now there's something you really must have an aspirin for, right? Did you know that the use of aspirin has been shown to prolong pregnancy?[2] Really, nine months is enough, don't you think? You will by the end of your pregnancy. Perhaps you stay pregnant longer because your baby's development has been interfered with and now he needs more time to finish growing. And remember, there are more than a hundred common medications available over the counter that contain aspirin, including Alka-Seltzer, Bufferin, Empirin, Anacin, and Four-Way Cold Tablets.[3]

Wouldn't you rather tune into your body and try to listen to its cues when you have a headache? Your body may be trying to tell you to eat a meal if your blood sugar has dropped to the headache-producing level. Or perhaps you need to slow down for a while. Instead of masking the warnings your body is giving you with medications, be good to yourself and your baby. The two of you deserve it.

Does this mean that you have to put up with a stuffy nose the next time you catch a cold? I'll leave that for you

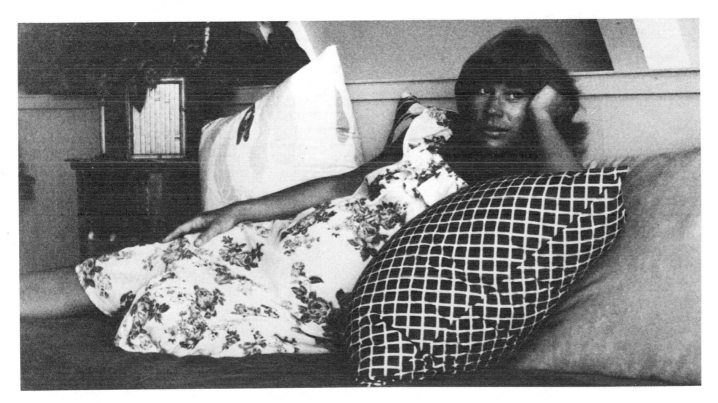

to decide. Nose drops can shrink the placental bed (the site where the placenta is attached to the uterus).[4] The placenta spreads out as far as needed to get access to enough oxygen and nutrients for your baby. (In fact, women who live permanently at high altitudes grow larger placentas to meet the baby's oxygen needs.) Shrinking the placental bed reduces the baby's access to the things he needs. If you take nose drops, the placenta cannot suddenly expand to keep food and oxygen flowing to your baby in optimal amounts during the hours those drops are working. (In addition, some nose drops contain antihistamines, which are also associated with an increased incidence of malformed babies.)[5]

Look at it this way. Most drug dosages are determined by body weight. You would not give your two-year-old an adult aspirin; the dose would be inappropriate to his weight. So what's a safe dose for your child of no years, still in your uterus, yet to be born? *Any drug you take, designed to affect your adult size body, may be approximately twenty times too much for your unborn baby's body.* Alarming, isn't it? How about cutting down the dosage so it won't have an effect on the baby? In that case, it would be a dose too low to have an effect on your body either, so what's the point in taking the drug?

Dr. Bradley is fond of saying, "Don't pollute the bloodstream." But when you find yourself putting up with a stuffy nose during your pregnancy it really wouldn't be fair to blame it all on Dr. Bradley. Warnings about drugs during pregnancy are currently coming from many sources. You should know that the Committee on Drugs of the American Academy of Pediatrics addresses this problem

head on! They have clearly laid it out for pregnant women, stating that "there is no drug, whether over-the-counter remedy or prescription, which when taken by the child-bearing woman has been proven safe for the unborn child."[6]

Would you want to take a drug not proven safe for your baby? No, of course not, not unless your obstetrician prescribed it for you—then it must be safe, right? Look again at the statement by the Committee on Drugs. It does not absolve prescription drugs. They are included in the warning.

Nowadays, most people have already heard that the placenta is not a barrier between your baby and drugs, but few realize that *the prescription pad is also not a barrier!* I'll bet you've read the warning, *Don't take drugs during pregnancy* somewhere else, or perhaps you've heard it on the radio, but the small print that is always tacked on is the last line *unless prescribed by your doctor.* This is the number one loophole through which millions of pregnant women get drugs. It's time for women and their doctors to change this qualifier to something like *Don't take drugs during pregnancy unless necessary to your continued life and health.* A diabetic will need drugs during pregnancy, and so will other women with serious life- and health-threatening problems, but this is not what most drugs are prescribed for in pregnancy.

Does this mean your doctor might write an unnecessary prescription for you that could harm your unborn baby? I'll let you be the judge. Let's take Bendectin, the anti-nausea drug. *The New York Times* reported on June 19, 1983, that "according to manufacturer estimates, in the 27 years during which Bendectin has been sold, more than 33 million pregnant women throughout the world have used it to curb their nausea and vomiting."[7]

In the United States, according to the Yale study I cited earlier, Bendectin was used by about twenty-five percent of pregnant women. That, those doctors added, "suggests a considerable amount of overprescribing."

Overprescribing is an understatement. If twenty-five percent of all pregnant women had this drug *prescribed for them by their doctors,* it was clearly being given for the ordinary harmless nausea that many women experience in early pregnancy and not reserved for the persistent, continuous vomiting that can occasionally require medical help, but certainly does not occur in one out of four pregnancies.

If the obstetricians and pregnant women had been following a line of thinking like *Don't take drugs during pregnancy unless they are absolutely necessary to your continued health and life,* the nausea drug would never have been prescribed for women in those numbers. "If there is a lesson to be learned from the Bendectin story," said Dr. Hugh R. K. Barber, director of obstetrics and gynecology at Lenox Hill Hospital in New York, "it is that no drug or drug-like substance—even vitamins—can be assumed to be completely safe during pregnancy."[8]

You can't expect doctors to step forward to be held accountable for the later-discovered aftereffects of drugs they prescribed for you. That would open wide the door of liability. The drug company will not be quick to even admit there *might* be a problem with a drug they have produced until forced to do so, much less to admit responsibility or accountability.

But let's be fair. Let's not heap all the blame upon doctors. They do not practice in a vacuum. If you call a doctor when you have an ordinary cold and the sniffles, then you must realize this is a statement that you are *not* willing to cope with the symptoms. If you were, you would not be calling about it, because he doesn't have any chicken soup to put on the stove for you; his cupboard contains only drugs.

By calling, you indicate that you want him to *do something* and the only something he can do is *prescribe.* If your intention is to just check out the symptoms, be sure to say clearly that you prefer to avoid drugs during your pregnancy and are willing to put up with the symptoms.

Speaking to a conference on developmental disabilities, Dr. Sanford Cohen of New York University had some good advice. He said that if a pregnant woman's doctor prescribes a medicine, she should ask if it is "absolutely essential" for her health or the baby's. If the answer is no, Cohen said, then she should forget it.[9]

So far, unfortunately, little more than lip service has been given to the idea that pregnant women should not take drugs. I, for one, believe the warnings. And it is time to change the *unless prescribed* rider that effectively cancels the caution to *unless necessary for continued health and life.*

And those nonprescription items you buy at the drugstore, are they really drugs? You know, Maalox for heartburn, Rolaids, Tylenol, and ninety-nine other over-the-counter remedies? Yes, they are real drugs! Even concerned women taking classes for totally unmedicated childbirth often don't realize this. Do you have a blind spot? Are you currently taking an over-the-counter drug?

Occasionally a woman comes up to me after a class and says, "I'm taking such and such, is that okay?" If the American Academy of Pediatrics Committee on Drugs cannot absolve any over-the-counter or prescription drugs, then who am I to absolve a few? False reassurances, however, are often given to women by people who know better (teachers, doctors, nurses) because it is more comfortable for the giver and receiver of the reassurances.

Drugs are not investigated to determine safety during pregnancy for the unborn child. Is this shocking? Not really. Think about it. What is a drug company going to do? Advertise in a local newspaper for a volunteer to test out a new drug—to see if it will deform or otherwise harm her baby? You see the dilemma. But the consequence of this dilemma is even more frightening. Drugs do go on the market without this kind of testing, and that means that *you are the unknowing volunteer* when you take a drug not proven safe for the unborn child.

A drug salesman once told us that when a new drug comes out it's 120 percent safe. By the end of the first year, as side effects are reported back, it's 99 percent safe. Give it a few more years and it falls to 85 percent safe. But by then there will be a replacement drug for it, and this new drug will be 120 percent safe.

This "after the fact" approach has caused and will continue to cause damage to mothers and their babies. For example, at a time when we were feeling rather smug in this country about avoiding the thalidomide disaster (in which babies in Europe were born without arms and legs due to a drug given to pregnant women), the DES (dieth-ylstilbestrol) time bomb was ticking away in the bodies of thousands of children.

It has taken decades for the cancers caused by the use of the drug DES (given originally to avoid miscarriage and premature birth) to reveal themselves. The daughters of the millions of women who were given this drug have a much higher rate of cancer than the rest of the population; male offspring are not free from this either, and the story gets worse as we learn that the mothers themselves are experiencing higher rates.

Years ago I read the story of a woman whose teenage daughter died of the vaginal cancer she developed as a result of her mother taking DES. The mother was asked if she felt guilty. She replied that she did not because her doctor had prescribed it for her and she was doing what she thought was the best thing, following her doctor's advice, with no questions asked. I would not wish guilt on this mother or any mother who took DES, but the fact is that if a lesson is to be learned from DES, it is that *questions should always be asked before taking a drug during pregnancy.* Your consent should at least be *informed consent.* Ask what the known side effects of the drug are, and if it has been tested for long-term side effects. You are the only one who can decide what risks you are willing to accept for which benefits. No one else can decide for you which risks are acceptable to *you,* and which risks are not.

There is no restitution for the physical and emotional agony caused by DES. There is no way to give those affected back healthy, undamaged bodies or to remove the fearful threat of cancer that hangs over them. There is no satisfaction in suing those "responsible"—drug companies, institutions like hospitals, and doctors who used this drug. The sheer numbers of those involved, well into the millions, make the likelihood of meaningful financial settlement a dim prospect.

With the lesson of DES in mind, we realize that it is a word game to say that drug safety during pregnancy is the responsibility of the Food and Drug Administration, drug companies, or the medical establishment. None of these institutions will feel the devastating impact of the tragedy as you will.

Each woman must realize that she is the final guardian of her unborn child. She is the last decision-maker when it comes to putting a drug into her body or undergoing an untested procedure, like a sonogram. It is clear where the buck stops, whether we like it or not. It stops at our own consent. The best thing you can do is simply take no chances. Avoid all drugs during pregnancy except those essential to maintain life and health.

Pregnant or not, it's just good sense to always know the score about any drug you *do* bring into your home for whatever reason. *Always* ask the druggist for the "package insert" whenever you buy a drug. Read it for *known* side effects. (Unfortunately the Food and Drug Administration has lost its mandated patient package-insert program and we must now rely on a *volunteer* effort funded by the Ciba-Geigy drug company).

So an even more important source of information is a *Physicians' Desk Reference* (PDR). It lists all drugs, their known side effects, and when they should not be used. It's a hefty book with a hefty price but it can pay for itself in no time. One of my students had a vaginal infection and her doctor prescribed a drug for her. She looked it up in her PDR and discovered that it should never be used by anyone with a history of kidney infections. She had a history of kidney infections! She let her doctor know this and they dealt with the problem another way. Another student looked up a prescribed drug and decided that she could not accept the risk of the *known* side effects. She felt the problem she was given the prescription for was minor while the risks of this particular drug were major. She discussed this with her doctor and they both agreed that since it was a minor problem that often disappears in later pregnancy, she could do without the drug.

Libraries have PDRs and some bookstores have the PDR on their shelves. If not, you can always order one. You will find it a worthwhile investment, especially as your children grow up. Your doctor has one in his office, so you can ask him to look up a drug he is prescribing and let you read about it or any other on the spot. Every hospital has one, too. It should only take minutes in a hospital for someone to place this information at your fingertips, assuming they want to cooperate with your need for the information. Always ask for it before giving your informed consent.

X-Rays Are Now X-Rated for Pregnancy

And about time. The warnings on x-rays have been out in the medical literature for many years. According to a Food and Drug Administration report, "Data from the Oxford Survey of Childhood Cancers have suggested that radiation exposure in utero increases the cancer risk by 50 percent during the first 15 years of the child's life. A study by MacMahon in the U.S. also showed increased risk of leukemia in children who were exposed in utero to diagnostic x-rays." In short, the so-called harmless diagnostic x-rays that many women have been given in labor are definitely suspect.[10]

Now that we have the sonograms to replace x-rays, you'll finally start hearing more about this. X-rays were often used to determine if the baby's head would fit through a woman's pelvis. This practice is now scoffed at as fairly useless for that purpose. There are too many other factors involved (including head molding and pelvis flexibility).[11] But what you should catch here is the disturbing note of information withheld until a new technique came along. Could ultrasound be like the 120-percent-safe drug? Will we be reading about it as a health hazard in a few years? (It's already suspect and being investigated.) If so we're in real trouble because almost every pregnant woman is sonicated at least once in her pregnancy.

Ultrasound takes a picture of your baby by bouncing high frequency sound waves off him and translating the echo that returns into a picture. We don't know what the long-term side effects of these sound vibrations ("anywhere from 20,000 to millions of vibrations per second") might be. We do know that in the short term cells behave abnormally after just one diagnostic ultrasound exposure. The shape of the cells so radiated changes temporarily and their movement becomes frenetic.

As early as 1962, an article was published in the *Journal of the National Cancer Institute* which linked x-rays with leukemia.[12] Yet when I started teaching in 1968 and until as late as 1976, women were still frequently being x-rayed in labor. That was fourteen years after the study came out. There are studies today casting doubts on ultrasound. But will you only hear about them fourteen years from now after you and your baby have had your ultrasound?

Remember what the FDA doesn't do for us. Remember the statement of the Committee on Drugs of the American Academy of Pediatrics: "There is no drug, whether over-the-counter remedy or prescription drug, which when taken by the child-bearing woman, has been proven safe for the unborn child." And remember, the same applies to diagnostic procedures like x-rays and ultrasound.

chapter seven

Sexuality and Birthing

To begin to understand what happens in birth, you must know how your birth organs work. Of course, they happen to be your sexual organs also, so I don't think you'll be too surprised to discover some similarities between sexual responsiveness and the mechanics of labor and birth.

Take a look at picture 1, a cross-section of a woman's body. The thing shaped a bit like a horseshoe in this picture is the **uterus.** (Dr. Bradley calls it "the baby box." He loves simple terms and clear mental pictures, so we'll interchange his picture words with more technical language and soon you'll have all the right mental images with the correct terminology.) You'll notice the uterus is at somewhat of a right angle to the **vagina** or the birth canal. You will push your baby out of the uterus and down this birth canal when you give birth.

During intercourse, the penis goes into the vagina only. It does not go up into the uterus where the baby is growing, so you do not have to worry about hurting the baby during intercourse. The uterus and the vagina are two separate compartments.

Now, notice the nice neat little funnel toward the front of this picture. This is the bladder from which you

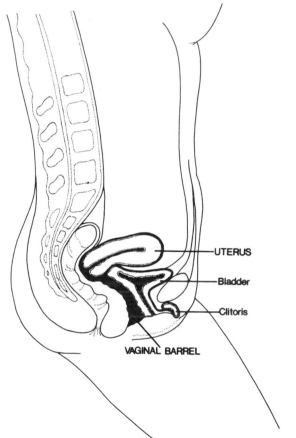

UTERUS

Bladder

Clitoris

VAGINAL BARREL

ROBIN BURNINGHAM

1. The woman in this example is not pregnant.

urinate. In the middle, of course, is the vagina or birth canal and toward the back is the rectum.

If you look for a little thing shaped like a peanut you will find the clitoris. It's loaded with nerve endings capable of receiving lots of stimulation. In fact, it used to be thought that the clitoris is where a woman experiences a climax. Now it is known that it doesn't happen quite that way.

A climax is experienced as a series of muscular contractions or squeezing in the muscles around the vagina and the muscles in the uterus. The muscles squeeze and relax, squeeze and relax, alternately. A climax is just muscles, squeezing and relaxing from about four to twenty times.

By the way, during your second or third pregnancy you may notice your tummy (actually your uterus) hardening and relaxing repeatedly after climaxes during intercourse. Don't worry, you haven't triggered labor. This is very common and normal and it's probably beneficial; those muscles have a chance to rehearse a little.

The clitoris is thought of as a kind of passion trigger, but because it is loaded with nerve endings, direct or prolonged stimulation can often be irritating instead of exciting. In other words, in order for stimulation to be a turn-on instead of a turn-off, a couple needs to communicate. A husband should find out what his wife likes and how much of it.

A woman's nipples are much the same as the clitoris, loaded with nerve endings capable of receiving stimulation. But again, too-prolonged stimulation can have the opposite effect. It can be irritating. Which is why a woman

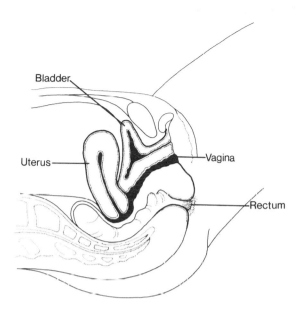

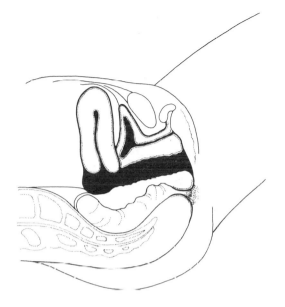

ROBIN BURNINGHAM

2. The vaginal barrel

The vaginal barrel in the excited state

may say, "Oh, I like that," one minute and the very next minute she says, "Don't do that, it doesn't feel good anymore."

Let's take a few minutes here to see what happens inside a woman's body when she's sexually excited. First, her vagina does not merely stretch as the penis enters. If she is sexually excited the vagina barrels outward, expanding to two or three times its nonexcited size. When the vaginal barrel expands outward it bumps the bladder upward and out of the way of the thrusting penis, protecting the bladder from being bruised. The rectal wall is also shoved back for protection.

While the vagina is barreling outward, it elongates by about an inch at each end, and the outer lips of the vaginal barrel stiffen outward somewhat, preventing friction or a dragging sensation as the penis enters.

While this is occurring in the vaginal barrel, the uterus responds too. It balloons forward and upward toward the navel, pulling the bottom part of the uterus out of the birth canal, preventing it from being battered or thumped during intercourse.

How does all this expansion happen? It occurs the same way a man achieves an erection, by engorgement. During an erection more blood goes to the blood vessels

Sexuality and Birthing **43**

than goes out, which has the effect of making the penis stand erect and elongated. The same kind of engorgement occurs in the vagina and uterus when a woman is excited, making the vaginal barrel stand outward and elongate. If you climax during intercourse, the engorgement rapidly disappears, but when you do not climax it can remain quite a while, sometimes causing backache, a pelvic dragging sensation, and general crabbiness.

There is one other time when these same responses occur. Can you guess? Yes, it is when you are pushing your baby out. It is amazing but in a way logical that the same responses that occur when you are sexually excited also occur when you are having your baby. In fact, some women have a birth climax when they have a baby.

The Birth Climax

I happened to be in the hospital taking pictures of one of my couples when the totally untrained mother in the next room gave birth so quickly that no one had a chance to medicate her. She appreciated this since she was able to feel a birth climax.

But this woman didn't know what it was. She said, "Boy, those last few pains sure felt good." When I asked her what kind of a pain feels good, she replied, "Well, you know, it's kind of like during intercourse only a lot stronger." Was it painful at all? "No," she said, "it just

felt good." Yet it was interesting that this mother was so culturally conditioned to equate childbirth with pain that she used that word "pain" in reference to a sensation that she described as positive and exciting.

Most women do not get to experience the birth climax. As long as women continue to have babies in a delivery-room atmosphere, the birth climax will remain an uncommon experience. The labor bed or labor room not only provide a more relaxed and normal atmosphere for having babies, but I think they also enhance the chances of experiencing the birth climax.

Ovulation

In the next picture, you can see just the uterus and the fallopian tubes. The vagina is left out of this picture.

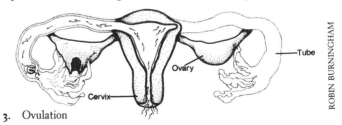

3. Ovulation

The little sacs on each side (called ovaries) are full of eggs. You can see tubes that extend out of the uterus to these egg sacs (the fallopian tubes).

One month an egg will erupt from your right ovary and the next month an egg will erupt from your left ovary. An egg has just erupted in this picture. It will now journey down the tube to the uterus, and if it meets with sperm at the beginning of its journey then you find yourself needing this book. When it doesn't meet the sperm it just falls apart, and you have a regular period at the end of your monthly cycle.

Sometimes more than one egg will shoot off. If both eggs are fertilized (this would take two different sperm), then you really have your hands full at the end of nine months. Your twins would not be look-alikes, however, since they came from two different eggs and two different sperm. Sometimes an egg will split soon after fertilization, and then you would have identical twins.

The actual eruption of the egg from the ovary is called ovulation. It occurs on about the tenth to fourteenth day of each menstrual cycle. (Ten to fourteen days after your last period.) We start off with the ovaries looking smooth like almonds; eventually, after all those monthly eruptions, they look pitted and wrinkled like prunes.

If you know what to look for, you can easily recognize when ovulation occurs. When you have ovulated, your vaginal discharge is somewhat heavier, the consistency of egg white. There is quite a lot of it. Your vagina is well lubricated whether you are excited or not.

This is important to understand. Men often mistakenly think that if the vagina is wet, the woman is ready for intercourse. In fact, if she is ovulating she will be wet even if she is not the least bit excited. She could be thinking of what color to paint the walls and still be wet at this time.

But several days later the man could approach her and think that because she is not as wet, she is not interested in making love. Indeed, she may be very interested. To understand each other and to enhance communication it helps to realize how the body works.

While you are ovulating you may be aware of an aching or burning sensation to the right or left side, depending on where the egg came from, and a slight backache on the same side. It's not all that noticeable until you get into bed. Then you find you are more aware of the sensation and you may be a little restless.

The Uterus

Next in picture 4 you can see the uterus of a woman seven months pregnant. That large round organ in the upper two-thirds of the uterus is called the **placenta** or the afterbirth because it comes out after the baby. The side of the placenta facing the baby is smooth and shiny but the side facing the uterus is rooty- or clumpy-looking where it implants into the uterine wall. You can ask your doctor to show it to you after birth. It looks like a fat piece of liver.

Notice the umbilical cord in this picture. It's usually about twenty to twenty-two inches long, but sometimes longer. The cord is a lovely turquoise blue at birth for a minute or two after the baby is born. The blue is from the three blood vessels inside the cord. One large vein carries

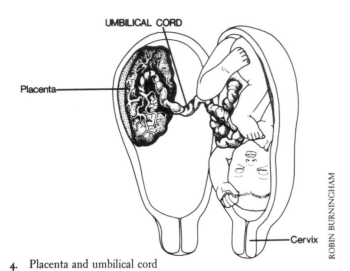

UMBILICAL CORD

Placenta

Cervix

ROBIN BURNINGHAM

4. Placenta and umbilical cord

oxygen and nutrients to the baby and two smaller arteries carry away carbon dioxide and waste products.

If you look closely you can see the blood vessels from the umbilical cord branching out into the placenta. They get smaller and smaller as they branch out deeper into the interior of the placenta. There is no direct hookup between the mother's bloodstream and the baby's. Instead, these small vessels branching out through the placenta run close to the mother's own blood vessels. The nutrients and oxygen the baby needs pass out of the mother's blood vessels and into the tiny capillary veins leading back toward the cord and baby.

The whole thing works in reverse to get rid of waste the baby no longer needs. That waste is passed back into the mother's veins and carried off to her kidneys for her to eliminate with her urine. This is one reason you run to the bathroom more frequently when pregnant. You are handling the baby's disposals as well as your own.

The cord itself is amazing. It is like a fire hose with water running through it forcefully which keeps it from kinking. It might reassure you to know that if you just must have your baby in a taxicab or an elevator, you don't have to worry about doing something with the cord. Most of the blood in the placenta and cord will pump into the baby's body, whether you hold it low or put it to the breast. (This process takes a few minutes or more.) There is no hurry about cutting the cord. The blood will not back up. The vessels inside the cord are surrounded by a jelly-like substance that expands rapidly at birth, pinching the blood vessels in the cord to close them off.

In the past, milking the cord (pinching it between two fingers and running them from one end to the other repeatedly as though milking a cow) was a common practice at birth. The purpose was simply to hurry things up. Recent research, however, is putting this procedure in a bad light. Such milking may be setting up future heart problems for the child by forcing his heart muscle and blood vessels to accept the blood at a faster rate and volume than nature planned. This could put a strain on the heart and blood vessels. Since it only takes a little while to let nature take its course, that seems the wiser thing to do. On the other hand, cutting the cord *before* allowing the cord blood to go to the baby deprives him of as much as one-quarter of his blood volume and is suspected of causing anemia during the first year of life.[1] Perhaps even more important, the cord contains a good deal of oxygenated blood and can prevent anoxia (lack of oxygen) in the newborn infant.

In picture 5 you see the baby in the uterus, nine months along.

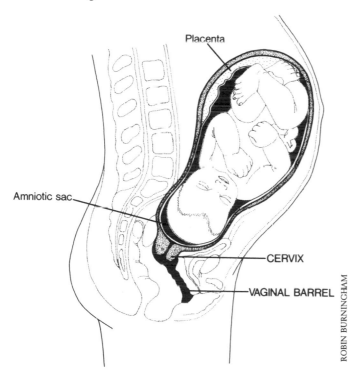

5. Baby in the uterus at nine months; notice the cervix.

ROBIN BURNINGHAM

Did you know your baby is floating in a bag of water? In this illustration you can see the thin line indicating the bag called the amniotic sac. This tough little bag holds approximately one quart of liquid. Your body actually changes this water eight times every twenty-four hours. No wonder pregnant women naturally retain water. You may have noticed your wedding ring feels a little tighter as a result. Your blood volume also increases by almost a third. A certain amount of water retention is not only normal but probably quite beneficial.

It is always surprising to hear of an occasional doctor who gives out diuretics almost routinely to his pregnant patients. Fortunately, most doctors wouldn't consider this, because diuretics can be dangerous. They actually decrease your blood volume at this critical time. They can also reduce the volume of blood circulating in the fetus, making it more difficult to get oxygen to the baby's brain.[2]

The bag of water or amniotic sac is a marvelous thing. If you were punched in the tummy you might feel pain, but your baby would not experience the punch as a direct blow to his body. Instead, the force would be spread throughout the water so the baby felt a much gentler, equalized sensation all over. In fact, this is how your baby will feel labor as long as the bag of water is intact: as a gentle, equalized pressure. It's somewhat like a hug and a squeeze each time the uterus works during labor.

Your baby swims around in this sac while he's small enough, and he urinates in it a little. He may swallow a bit of the water, but he won't choke because there is no air in his lungs, just water. He even practices breathing by inhaling some of this fluid in and then moving it out of his lungs. He receives his oxygen via the cord. The sac is a comfortable, secure home for your baby until he is ready to be born.

Now here's something you will want to remember. If you put your hands on your hips you can feel your pelvis like a girdle of bones within you. Until about the eighth month most babies are floating around just above the pelvis. That's why you can feel him kicking you in the ribs.

As you enter your ninth month things begin to get extra crowded in there, so the baby will settle down lower into the pelvis. You will then have a little more room to breathe but you will find yourself running to the bathroom more frequently, if that is possible. This is because of the increased pressure on the bladder.

This settling-in is called engaging. Your mother-in-law may call it "dropping." Sometime in your ninth month it is quite possible the doctor will tell you the baby is engaged. By the way, what do you think this tells you about when your labor is going to start? *Engagement tells you nothing at all about when labor will begin.*

My first baby couldn't be bothered to engage until I was pushing him out! Yet another of my babies was well engaged two months before birth. It is important for your peace of mind to remember that there is no way to accurately predict the week, or the day, or the hour your baby will be born.

chapter eight

The Mechanics of Labor and Birthing

At last, we come to what will actually happen when you are having a baby. This chapter will help you understand the birth process so later you can learn to work with it effectively.

The first thing most couples want to know is: How long does labor take? Well, the textbook says one thing, but that is not always what happens. The book says your *first* baby will take about twelve to fourteen hours of labor. Second and later babies come a little faster, after eight to ten hours of labor.

But after years of teaching, we have decided that a lot of mothers just aren't reading textbooks. We see every-thing from the *speedster*, to the *textbook* laborer to the *putterer*.

The speedster gives birth after a fast five or seven hours of hard work. That's really fast particularly for a first baby. The textbook laborer has the ten to fourteen hour labor and then there is the putterer. The putterer has extremely easy, light labor for several hours or more. Her uterus works perhaps for thirty seconds, maybe every seven to ten minutes. She is not working hard. In fact, she is usually at home continuing her daily activities.

Finally, after a number of hours, her uterus stops playing around and gets down to work. In the long run her

The Mechanics of Labor and Birthing **49**

labor may last twenty hours or more, but that isn't bad at all when you realize that she really isn't working hard all those hours.

So you have already learned a most important thing about having a baby. Every woman will produce a baby at her own speed, and in a normal labor, her own speed is the best speed.

The First Stage of Labor

We will divide labor into three stages. It is just a convenient way to describe things. Your doctor will talk of labor in these same stages, so it is good to know their names.

This is important. Look back at picture 5 and take particular note of the *cervix*, the bottom part of the uterus that hangs down a little into the birth canal.

The cervix looks like the neck of a turtleneck sweater. Here it doesn't look like that because this picture is cut in half making the cervix look like two ends hanging down. But use your imagination and in your mind put the two halves of the uterus and cervix together.

Dr. Bradley calls the cervix the "door" to the uterus, simply because this has to open before you can push your baby down and out the canal. If you think of the cervix as the door to the uterus, you will always know its function during labor.

Let's suppose a woman is having a textbook labor of fourteen hours with her first baby. The only thing that is happening for about twelve of those hours is that the cervix is opening. Once it is open she has just one canal, instead of her two separate compartments of the uterus and the vagina, so she can push her baby out. *So the real work of labor, the long work that takes most of those hours, is just getting this door open. The opening of the cervix is called first stage.*

The cervix is pulled open and pulled back over the baby's head, like pulling a turtleneck sweater over your own head. It doesn't just flap aside as the baby moves down the canal. The cervix is pulled back closely over his head. It seems to disappear.

Where does the cervix go? It is drawn into the upper body of the uterus. This upper part of the uterus actually gets a little thicker which is great because once the cervix is open the thicker, upper uterus acts like a piston to boot the baby out.

So what will pull the cervix back and over the baby's head? *Contractions.* You have probably heard them called "pains." In this book we'll use the accurate term and call them what they really are, contractions.

But what exactly is a contraction? Well, flex the bicep in your arm. That's a contraction. A muscle flexing or shortening is all a contraction is. And that is all labor is— muscles working.

Look at picture 6. It simply shows the uterus, not cut in half, but the way it really is. It is just a big bag of muscles. In fact, this muscular bag is made up of three layers of muscle tissue. A contraction is just this bag of muscles flexing for you.

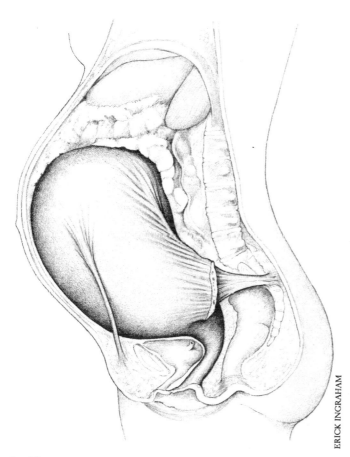

6. The uterus is a muscular bag.

ERICK INGRAHAM

A woman's muscles may flex for thirty seconds at a time when she begins labor. She may rest for five to seven or possibly even ten minutes at first. After a while this muscular bag will begin flexing for forty-five seconds at a time and she may rest for five minutes or less. After more time goes by, her uterine muscles will contract for sixty to seventy seconds and her rest periods will be about three minutes or less. Her uterus has long muscles that go from the top down toward the cervix. A contraction starts at the top as these long muscles begin to flex. They contract and shorten and continue to contract, gathering strength, and keep on flexing until she gets a good stretching and pulling sensation at the cervix to open the door a bit. Then they relax. The muscles gradually stop their efforts for several minutes. They not only contract but they also retract, or stay somewhat shortened, after each flex. This is what draws the cervix up and over the baby's head.

After a rest the muscles will flex again. Starting at the top, the muscles build up to their work. They keep shortening, sweeping her along to the peak of their strength as they contract all the way down toward the cervix to give her a good, strong, stretching and pulling sensation which opens the door a bit more. Then the sensation gradually diminishes. Her muscles get to rest and so does she.

Finally, at the end of first stage the uterus may be flexing for ninety seconds and her rest periods may be one and a half to two minutes long. But nature is very kind. This is a lot of work, but she always gets a rest between contractions all the way through labor. Now, look at the cervix in picture 7.

You can see that the two-inch neck of the cervix has

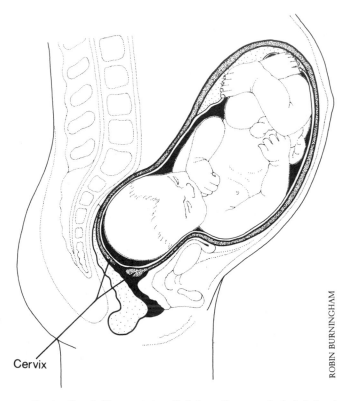

Cervix

7. Cervix effaced: The cervix is pulled down flat onto the baby's head.

ROBIN BURNINGHAM

This flattening of the cervix is called **effacement**. If, most likely in your ninth month, your doctor mentions that your cervix is beginning to efface, you will know what he is talking about. By the way, what do you think this tells you about when your labor is going to start? You are probably on to us by now.

Effacement tells you nothing at all about when labor will begin. You cannot predict the hour or the day. A wise doctor never burdens an expectant mother with unreliable predictions which only build up her expectations and then let her down. To predict "this weekend, for sure," or "next week, definitely," starts the woman on an emotional roller coaster.

With one of my pregnancies I was examined early in the day and told not to expect anything to happen soon since I was not the least bit effaced. I gave birth later that evening. With another pregnancy I was completely effaced (and the cervix was even slightly open) two months before I went into labor. So, while effacement tells you nothing about the day and hour of your birth, it is nice to know what the doctor means if he says, "Hmm you're effacing."

Now let's look at the cervix in picture 8.

You will see that the door is really beginning to open.

The mother reaches the end of the first stage when her cervix is completely open. It is as if that turtleneck sweater has been pulled down onto the head and the neck of the sweater is stretched open. In picture 9 the cervix is completely open. This is called ten centimeters (or, sometimes, "five fingers") dilated. Through the first stage her cervix opens, or dilates, gradually until she is "complete," meaning completely dilated.

been pulled flat. It is not open; it has just flattened out along the baby's head, much as if you had just started to put on that sweater, pulling the neck down flat onto your head but not actually pulling it open and over your head yet.

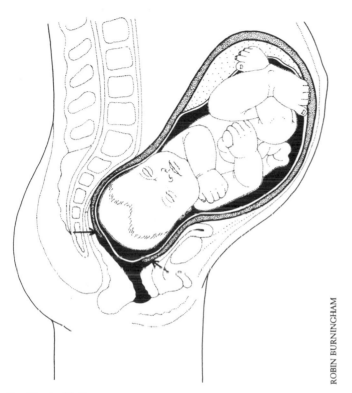

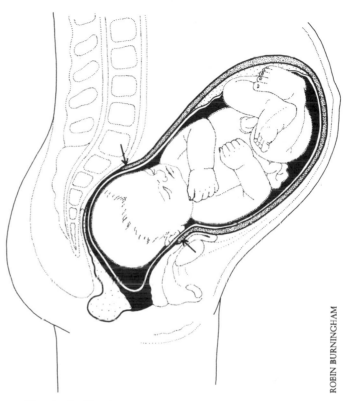

8. Cervix dilating

9. Completely dilated

ROBIN BURNINGHAM

Remember, the part that is opening is up inside, so its progress cannot be seen just by looking at the vaginal opening. It can be checked only by inserting two fingers into the vaginal opening far enough to feel the cervix and to estimate the amount of dilation (which takes some

training and experience). Even at this point the number of centimeters tells you very little about precisely when the baby will be born. Some women may dilate at a fairly even pace, perhaps about a centimeter an hour. Others may be measured at four centimeters one hour and jump to ten

The Mechanics of Labor and Birthing **53**

the next. Yet another woman may seem "stuck" (she really isn't) at three or four centimeters for some hours before opening wider. *So knowing how far dilated you are really tells you nothing about how many more hours or minutes it will be before you give birth.* Vaginal exams can set up the same kind of emotional roller coaster that the news about effacement or engagement did earlier. And they increase the risk of infection and other problems, as we will discuss later.

The Second Stage

Once the cervix is open, the next thing the mother will do is push the baby out. The second stage begins with her first push. Pushing can be exhilarating after a woman has learned how to work *with* her body. It is the icing on the cake.

In second stage she will still have contractions and rest periods, but now they are pushing contractions. Her uterus now works like a piston to push her baby out. The uterine muscle will apply about thirty-five to forty pounds of force, but that is not enough. She will have to apply additional force to push the baby down and out the birth canal.

When a pushing contraction starts, her uterus begins working to move her baby out. She will push and push and push with it and move her baby down the birth canal.

Then her uterus rests and she rests too. As she rests, the baby slides back a bit. It is not exactly two steps down, one step back—but that is the general idea.

After resting a few minutes, her uterus begins to contract again, and she repeats the performance for a minute or two and then rests again. This is hard and sweaty, but exciting, work. It may take half an hour to two hours or more to push her baby out. Picture 9 shows where she will be at the end of that pushing time. This is still second stage until the baby is all the way out. This is called "crowning" because the vaginal lips look like a crown around the baby's head.

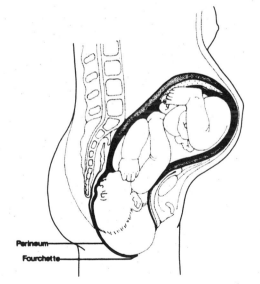

10. Crowning

ROBIN BURNINGHAM

Look at picture 10. This is just moments before the head emerges. Notice the perineum. It is stretched flat as a pancake, extending all the way up to the fourchette (see the arrow on the diagram). For comparison, look back to picture 7 where the perineum is a rather thick muscle. It is remarkable the way this muscle stretches so beautifully.

Some doctors will perform a routine episiotomy at this time. That is a surgical incision with a pair of scissors cutting into the perineum. The mother would not feel the cut, because pressure from the baby's head cuts off the circulation to her perineum and makes it numb. This procedure is called a "pressure episiotomy" and no Novocain is necessary since nature's anesthetic works quite nicely. An anesthetic would be injected after the baby is born, while the cut is being sutured.

But a growing number of women do not believe an episiotomy is necessary or desirable. And we know several doctors who agree and rarely perform episiotomies. These births turn out very well. (In Chapter Twenty we will discuss episiotomies in detail.)

In picture 11 the baby's head is emerging and the perineum is already shrinking back. Contrary to popular belief, this is not the "most agonizing moment." Nature provides its own anesthetic, the same one that makes possible the pressure episiotomy. The baby's head pushing against the perineum cuts off the circulation there. The feeling is similar to when you sit on your leg too long, also cutting off the circulation. When you get up your leg feels numb and tingly, and this is exactly how your outlet will feel when the baby's head emerges.

Picture 12 shows the baby's head out, but the baby's body is still inside the mother. The work is almost done. The perineum is all the way back to normal and looks like a nice, thick muscle again. In a natural birth the doctor or birth attendant never needs to pull on the head. The unmedicated mother is quite capable of pushing her baby out.

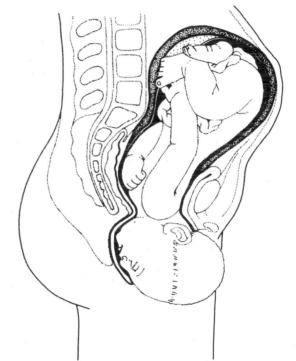

11. Baby's head emerging

ROBIN BURNINGHAM

The Mechanics of Labor and Birthing **55**

wards. Once the baby's entire body is out, the second stage is over.

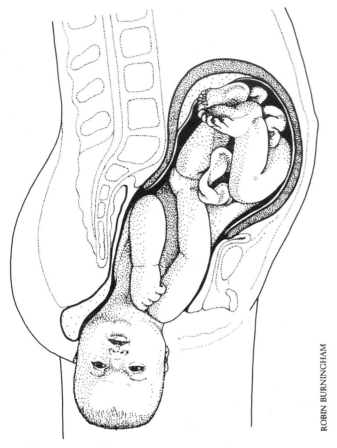

12. Birth

After a pause, she will give another push and the baby's body will come out quickly, all slippery and wiggly-feeling. This is delightful, and you feel so empty after-

The Third Stage/(and a Summary)

The third stage is easy enough. The mother will simply push out the placenta or afterbirth. We certainly hope that she gets to nurse her baby right away, even on the delivery table. Nursing immediately at birth makes the uterus contract strongly and prevents bleeding. It stimulates the production of a natural hormone called oxytocin which contracts the uterus and speeds the birth of the placenta.

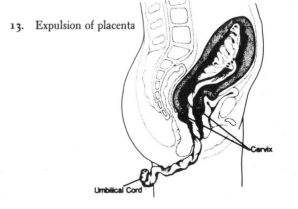

13. Expulsion of placenta

Once the baby is out, these final contractions cause the uterus to shrink. The placenta does not shrink with it, so as the uterus contracts underneath, the placenta breaks loose. This can be seen in picture 13. At this point it will be easy to push the placenta out. Often just a push or two does the trick. Letting the placenta break off naturally and pushing it out makes for an efficient, safe third stage for the mother.

To summarize briefly:

First stage is getting the cervix (the door to the uterus) open. This is all that happens during most of the hours of labor.

Second stage is pushing the baby out after the door is open. This can take half an hour to two or three hours.

Third stage is expelling the placenta.

It is an incredibly simple process. The door opens, you push your baby out, and then the placenta is pushed out.

The Baby's Role

Now that you have a clear idea of what happens in the woman's body during labor, let's consider what her baby will be up to. Take a look at picture 14. Most babies are in this position when the mother is ready to begin pushing. They are not quite facing toward the spine, not quite to the side, but somewhere in between to the right or the left. As she is having her baby his face will turn to her back. This is much like a key fitting into a lock. (See picture 15.)

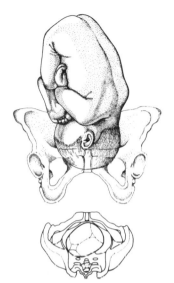

ROBIN BURNINGHAM

14.   Position of the baby in relation to the pelvis (common position)

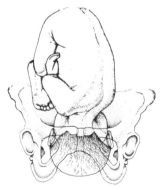

ROBIN BURNINGHAM

15.   Like a key fitting into a lock

The Mechanics of Labor and Birthing   **57**

The baby will then move down the spine and through the pelvis, which Dr. Bradley calls "the baby sliding board." As the baby emerges, his head turns to its original position so it is once again in line with the shoulders. Here there is usually a short pause while the baby's head is outside the mother's body but his body is still inside as in picture 16.

16. Head is completely out; body still inside the mother.

This is a wondrous moment. Quite often (in an unmedicated birth) the baby's eyes are already open. Imagine. There is your child with his body still within you and his head out with eyes open wide. Hardly believing what is happening, you give another push. This part goes quite rapidly. You can feel your child's little body as you push the rest of him out.

At this moment, with your baby's head out and the body just about to emerge from your own, you can look over your tummy to reach out for your baby. We have seen this spontaneous emotional reaction often and it is beautiful to watch. Very often the baby is the only one in the room with dry eyes. Why should the baby cry when he goes right from the womb to mother's arms with no delay? From the first moment of birth the baby will continue to hear the same familiar heartbeat and feel the same warmth from the mother's body. No, the baby does not cry, but everyone else in the room does from the sheer, wonderful joy of it.

It is fortunate when parents are able to find a doctor who is tuned in to the new family as a unit. The importance of allowing the parents *immediate touch contact* with the baby cannot be overestimated. Getting to hold or touch the baby five minutes later is not quite the same thing. The intensity of this particular emotional response is diminished with each passing minute.

The baby may actually help himself to get down and out of the birth canal. If you take an unmedicated newborn and press on his feet or hug him snugly, he will push back with his feet. This is recognized as a normal reflex. When the uterine muscles flex, the top of the uterus comes down on the baby's bottom and feet. What do you suppose he does? He pushes back, helping his journey down the canal.

When a mother has not received any drugs during labor and birth, she will find her own pushing efforts to be vigorous and effective. She and her baby will be working together toward the moment of birth.

There is another way the baby is helping to be born. If you put an unmedicated newborn face down on a blanket, he will pick up his head and turn it to one side. The mechanics of lifting and turning the head are exactly what occurs as he emerges over the perineum.

I'll never forget the doctor's reaction at the birth of one of my children. At this moment, when the head was right at the outlet and turning, the doctor exclaimed with amazement, "Look at that baby spin around!" He was accustomed to the medicated mother and infant and his experience had been limited to manipulating and extracting the infant himself.

When you are in labor yourself, you will want to picture the harmony of the work involved: the baby with built-in reflexes to help in birth, the uterus working in its designed way, and you, the skilled mother, relaxing at the right times and working at the right times with a supportive partner caring for you and coaching you through labor.

Now you have a good idea of what your body and your baby will be doing in labor. So let's go on to some important exercises to get you ready for birth.

chapter nine

Exercises:
Getting Your Body Ready for Birthing

Exercises are a bore. But to give birth comfortably your body does need some special tuning up. You will find that in preparation for giving birth we are not so interested in building muscles as we are in stretching and limbering them up.

WARNING: Just being in great physical shape is no help to a person who has not learned how to swim and finds herself in the middle of a lake. So, although we will start with exercises, by themselves they will not give you a happy labor and birth. You still need to learn how to labor and to practice the labor and birth techniques you will learn. Also, please note that this book deals with normality, so those who have a medical problem or condition that

may be affected by the exercises taught here will want to check with their doctor before undertaking them. It might help to show the doctor this book.

Tailor Sitting

Here is your first exercise. It is called *tailor sitting* after the way old-time tailors used to work. Actually, it is a posture rather than a conventional exercise, and it is not all that easy. You do have to work at getting your knees as close to

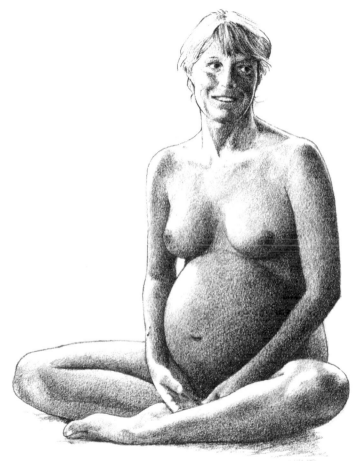

ERICK INGRAHAM

17. Tailor sitting

the floor as you can. Try touching your knees to the floor in this simple tailor-sitting position while you read the rest of this chapter.

If at first your knees are nowhere near the floor, don't force them. You will have to gradually work up to it at a pace that is suitable for you.

Why are you doing this? When you push your baby out your legs will be comfortably apart. This is at the end of your labor and may take half an hour to two hours or more. If you have prepared yourself for birth, with lots of tailor sitting, then the muscles on the upper insides of your legs will be stretched and lengthened so you will be comfortable in the pushing position.

The untrained mother frequently gets sore legs and even cramps. Can you imagine trying to enjoy the momentous experience of birth with a cramp in your leg? Nothing joyful about that.

TO THE COACH

Keep your wife out of all the soft, cushy chairs at your house. When she sits in a soft chair, her bottom sinks down and her knees come up. Start coaching now, by helping her to remember to do her exercises and use these postures. They're easy, and it is not a matter of taking extra time to do them, since they go easily with watching television, reading, or many other activities. If you take the coaching job seriously, your wife's favorite chair will gather dust from now until the birth of your baby.

(If you catch her complaining to friends about how you make her do her exercises, perhaps she's actually bragging about how much she is cared for and about your active part in getting ready for birth.)

Squatting

Here's your next exercise, or really just another posture: *squatting*. Simply stand with your feet about a foot or so apart, heels flat on the floor, lean slightly forward and drop gently down into a squatting position. Leaning forward helps you to keep your balance. Now you can push your knees farther apart with your elbows. Check the illustration.

This usually takes two to do at first or you may find yourself falling over backwards. Don't despair if you have trouble keeping your heels flat on the floor. With practice, the tendons at the backs of your ankles will lengthen and you will soon be able to squat without help and with your heels flat on the floor. Remember to keep your knees wide apart.

And come up *bottom first* as you unbend your knees. This helps you to deflect the baby forward, out of the pelvic ring. You avoid tamping the baby down into the bony pelvis and impeding circulation to your legs. You can put your hands on your thighs and push to help raise yourself the rest of the way.

Why are you squatting? Well, squatting does an even better job than tailor sitting of preparing your leg muscles for a comfortable legs-apart position at birth. But more importantly, it helps to stretch the perineum, making it more flexible, something you'll really appreciate when your baby's head emerges.

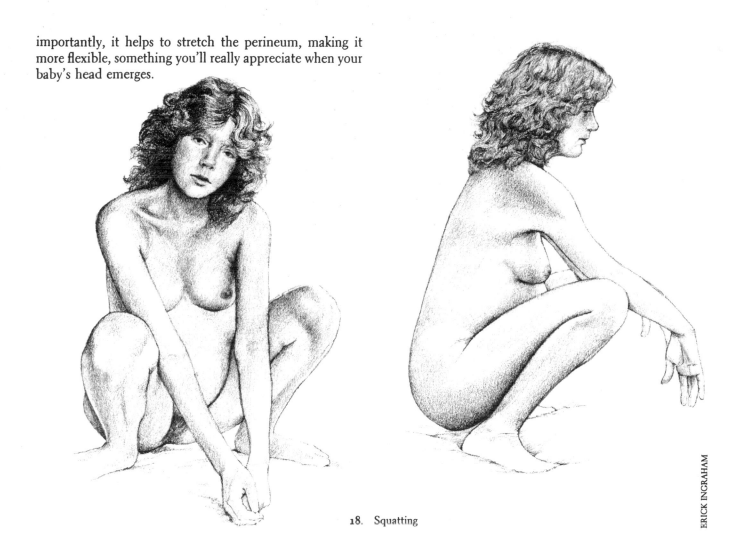

ERICK INGRAHAM

18. Squatting

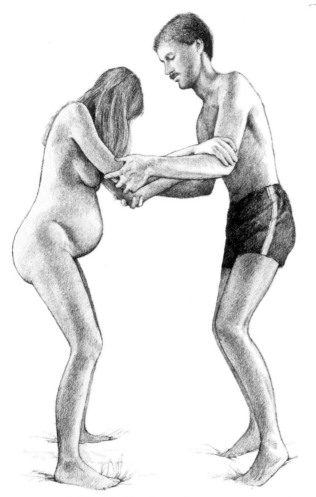

The **perineum** is the skin and muscle tissue between the vaginal outlet and the anus. It does the most stretching at birth.

Squatting is one of your most important exercises.

TO THE COACH

To help the mother get started in the squat you should hold her forearms strongly. Be ready to support her weight with a slight pull as she goes down. Try it with her now before going on.

19. A little help from the coach as you start to practice squatting

ERICK INGRAHAM

Keep her working on the squat until she can do it easily by herself. Don't let her feel discouraged. It takes most women who are not used to squatting a week or two before they are able to do it alone. How much squatting should she do? Lots!

Pelvic Rocking

This next exercise is great for the common complaint of backache during pregnancy. It is called *pelvic rocking*, and it is primarily for your comfort.

Simply get down on your hands and knees, with your hands directly under your shoulders and your knees either directly under your hips or a little farther back. (In other words, make a box.) Now start off with a sag of your tummy and a sigh. You'll notice your bottom sticks out more when you do this. The next step is to tuck your bottom under, then relax once again.

The only movement is in your pelvis. Don't get your shoulders going up and down. This should be done at a slow, steady pace. There is nothing particularly beneficial about speed. As you tuck your pelvis under, tighten your abdominal muscles at the same time, and when you return to normal do not sag exceedingly. (There's no need to bounce your tummy off the floor.)

In addition to easing backache, pelvic rocking often helps prevent varicose veins. When you get down on all

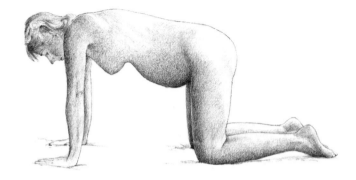

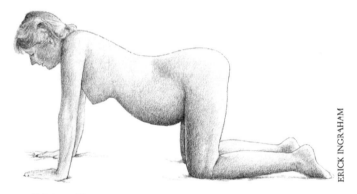

ERICK INGRAHAM

20. Pelvic rocking

fours the weight of the baby drops forward, out of the pelvis and off the large blood vessels running along the back of the uterus. This takes pressure off some of the main blood vessels leading down to your legs. So if you have a tendency toward varicose veins, you'll want to use pelvic rocking at brief but frequent intervals throughout the day.

Legs Apart Exercise

Here is an active exercise to get you ready for the "legs-apart" position for birth. So far the tailor-sitting and squatting postures you have learned are passive stretching exercises, but the legs-apart exercise will *actively* strengthen the abductor muscles which you use to open your legs. And this exercise takes teamwork. The pregnant woman sits on the floor, propped up with pillows. Your knees are bent and your feet are pulled back toward your bottom. The coach places his hands on the outside of the pregnant woman's legs at the knee or a little lower on the calf and applies mild pressure as if to hold the knees together while the woman uses her thigh muscles to push them apart. The resistance the coach applies puts the abductor muscles to work. Look at the illustration to see this exercise, which you should do three times a day. Remember, Coach, don't overdo it. This is not a contest of strength. You should allow her to slowly get her knees apart. You are not trying to keep them together, just to see that it takes a little more effort.

Practicing Your Exercises

Don't save a certain time of day for your tailor sitting and squatting. Anytime you're sitting down around the house, working, watching television, or reading, tailor sit or squat.

ERICK INGRAHAM

21. Legs-apart exercise

When you bend over to pick up something light, squat. Don't bend with your back. You have hinges in your knees, as Dr. Bradley is fond of saying, not in your back.

Pelvic rocking is a good thing to do in the afternoon, say, at two different times, twenty repetitions each. (Dr. Bradley feels pelvic rocking before bed helps restore and improve circulation to the legs after you have been up and around all day.)

There are other physical exercises you could do, and some women may want to get into a program of prenatal exercise or yoga. But these four movements are easy, simple, and quite specifically geared to getting your body ready to give birth. Whether you do a lot of other exercises, or nothing else at all, you should be sure to do the tailor sitting, squatting, pelvic rocking, and legs-apart exercises regularly.

There is one more exercise to learn, one that you will find beneficial for birth and throughout the rest of your life.

The PC Muscle and Your Most Important Exercise

Now, you're ready for the best exercise you'll ever learn. Its benefits go beyond birthing. You may have heard of the muscle this exercise strengthens—the pubococcygeal muscle. (There's a mouthful for you.) It's sometimes called the Kegel muscle, after the doctor who invented these exercises. We'll call it the **PC muscle** for short. The PC mus-

cle is a sling or hammock of muscle attached to your pubic bone in front and the tip of the spine in back. It's actually wrapped around the vagina, urethra, and rectum as thick muscular bands.

This sling will hold the inner organs up high *if it is strong enough to do so.* The picture on the left shows a woman with a nice strong muscle. You can tell by looking at her uterus. It's up high and headed toward the navel. Her vagina is long and narrow, and the rectum is well supported. Her bladder is funnel-shaped.

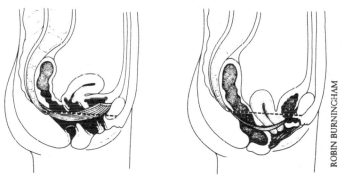

22. The PC muscle: A strong sling of muscle. A weak sling of muscle.

Now take a look at the picture on the right, showing a weak PC muscle.

Just look at what happens when this important muscle is weak and saggy. The bladder is not a nice neat funnel; it's collapsed! Every time this woman sneezes or coughs she probably leaks urine, to her embarrassment. Her uterus not only isn't high and toward the navel, it's actually falling down into the vagina. This condition can be so serious that the uterus starts to protrude from the vagina. This is called uterine prolapse, and it can result in a hysterectomy (removal of the uterus).

Intercourse may become quite uncomfortable. When the uterus sags into the vagina like this, a woman is likely to complain of a shallow feeling, as if the penis were thumping into something. It certainly is, it's hitting the cervix; and the vaginal barrel is not the long narrow canal it should be, it's squashed, short, and loose. The vaginal walls are too far apart. They can't possibly come into good contact with the penis, depriving both man and woman of a strong sensation during intercourse.

In fact, look closely at the vaginal barrel in picture 23. Here you do not see the PC muscle, which is wrapped around the vagina. What you do see is the *effect* the muscle has on the vaginal barrel.

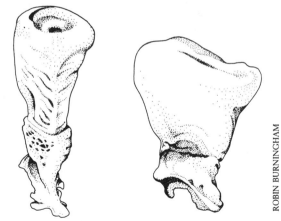

23. The vaginal barrel: Well-supported   Weak support

ROBIN BURNINGHAM

The vaginal barrel on the left is well supported by a strong muscle and looks like a squeezed toothpaste tube. The walls are narrow (so they will make good contact with the penis). The vaginal barrel on the right, however, shows the result of little support from a weak muscle. The vagina is too short and wide. The vaginal walls are too far apart to come into good contact with the penis and the vagina is shallow, which will cause the "thumping" sensation during intercourse. Did you know that women have hardly any tactile nerve endings in the vagina? What feels good during intercourse is the PC muscle. In particular there are two one-centimeter spots in the muscle itself that are loaded with nerve endings.

If the muscle is strong and tight around the vagina, the woman is capable of feeling a great deal of pleasure during intercourse from the deep-touch stimulation of the nerve endings in the PC muscles. If the muscle is weak, all those great nerve endings are wasted. They're too far away to receive sufficient stimulation from the thrusting penis. So, with a good, strong PC muscle you can get more enjoyment from sex.

Dr. Arnold Kegel taught PC exercises to every woman he saw in his gynecological practice. He was concerned with teaching women to flex this muscle to keep the uterus up high and to prevent it from dropping downward with a saggy muscle. Over the years he heard again and again, "Dr. Kegel, since you taught me those exercises I've started climaxing during intercourse. Do you think the exercises had anything to do with it?"

It turned out that Dr. Kegel had accidentally stumbled across the biggest find of the century in female sexual response, and he hadn't even been looking for it! Here was a basic key to female climaxing: having a PC muscle in good tone.

The PC Muscle and Birth

But this is a book about childbirth, so how does this muscle fit into the birth picture?

Simple. The baby is pushed out through the birth canal, of course, and the birth canal is surrounded by the PC muscle. You might think by looking at the pictures that the mother with the short canal would just drop her baby out, while the mother with the long narrow canal would have things harder. *Not so.*

The woman with the wide, loose vaginal barrel will find herself in trouble when she's actually pushing her baby down her saggy birth canal. As her baby passes through her vaginal barrel, the soft unsupported tissue is likely to be pulled forward and dragged downward with the baby's progress. This can result in pinched, torn tissues. This mother is likely to suffer damage to her vagina.

Such damage rarely happens to a trained mother who has learned and practiced the exercise for the PC muscle. She has a strong hammock of muscle surrounding and supporting her vaginal barrel. The tissues are firmly held in place and well supported as the baby passes through.

You now have some great reasons to want to make sure you have a strong, well-exercised muscle: to make love happily; to stay healthy; and to enjoy giving birth to your baby.

How to Identify the Kegel Muscle

The next time you are urinating, with your legs apart, stop the flow without putting your knees together. This does not mean you have a strong muscle, but it helps you to be sure you know exactly what muscle we're talking about.

The exercise itself is simple. It is the same squeezing motion you performed to stop the flow of urine, only you can squeeze much stronger and tighter when you are not urinating. We have three ways for you to exercise this muscle.

How to Practice the Kegel Exercise

The Beginning PC Exercise

Flex the PC muscle tightly. Make it a deep flex. If you are pinching your buttocks together then you are using the wrong set of muscles. A feeling of strain in the lower abdomen would mean the same thing.

If you observe a proper flex closely, what you should feel is the PC muscle tightening first at the back near the rectum and then as you continue to tighten harder you feel it moving foward and toward the clitoris. After a little practice you should be able to flex tightly and deeply just the PC muscle, with abdominal muscles and buttocks uninvolved.

Now, how often should you flex this muscle? Well, let me ask you this. If I asked you for five minutes of actual exercise a day, wouldn't you think that extraordinarily reasonable? Just five minutes? Right. And how many flexes does that make at a quick second or so a flex? 300 flexes! But come on now, it's only five minutes of actual exercise, and if you pause to rest for a second or so between contractions, it's still only a ten-minute-a-day exercise program. It was Dr. Kegel himself who recommended contracting the muscle 300 times a day.

Do not stop at just flexing the outer lips of the vaginal opening. This is just a very slight flex. *Concentrate on flexing deeply inside the vagina and way up high.*

TO THE COACH

If you are a husband coaching your wife, remember—she can be a great athlete and still have a saggy PC muscle. Or she could be totally out of shape otherwise and have a strong one. It doesn't relate to her general strength. A husband is the best person to know what condition her muscle is in. Can she squeeze and hold your penis during intercourse? Don't criticize her, but encourage her to exercise regularly.

It is important that you do this beginning PC exercise program each day until you get a good tight flex. It should

feel as distinct as clenching your hand. As soon as you get to this point (days for some, a week or two for others), then you will want to move right on to the intermediate PC exercises which will get you to a very elastic (stretchy) strong muscle. (The kind that supports the vaginal barrel and prevents damage.) Then go on to the advanced PC exercises, which will give you the ability to consciously release (like opening the hand) to give birth to your baby.

The Intermediate PC Exercise

When you have achieved the definite flex of the PC and are able to repeat it numerous times, you are ready for this intermediate exercise. Discontinue the 300 flexes.

Here we'll ask you to flex your muscle thirty-six times a day, but when you do, hold it to the count of ten before releasing. Try it now. Flex, two, three, four, five, six, seven, eight, nine, ten, and release. Again, flex, two, three, four, five—*don't let it slip, keep holding it tightly and deeply*—eight, nine, ten, and release. The trick is to hold that flex as strongly on your tenth count as you do on your first.

With this new exercise you are well on your way to achieving a strong, supportive hammock of muscles. We suggest you do this twelve times in the morning, before you get out of bed, twelve times in the afternoon, and twelve times at night before going to sleep.

Advanced PC Exercise

When you have the ability to hold that flex as in the intermediate exercise you can discontinue the thirty-six flexes a day, and you are ready for the advanced conscious-release exercises. You will use this releasing ability deliberately when you are pushing your baby out.

Flex just the outer third of the vaginal barrel, now the middle part of the vaginal barrel, and now think of flexing way up high.

Now release up high, release the middle third, and release the lower third of the vaginal barrel.

You can think of it like an elevator going up three floors, stopping momentarily at each floor, and then going down three floors as you let go of this contraction.

At this point you can do about a dozen regular flexes a day to retain the tone you have gained and then do about six one-two-three, release-two-three exercises.

Just a couple of times before the birth of your baby you should try placing your hand on your perineum, and as you are doing a release-two-three exercise try going beyond that and actively bulge your perineum outward as you release even more. It helps to feel that slight bulging down and out as you release the muscle and direct a small amount of downward pressure toward the vaginal outlet. Don't practice the bulging regularly, just try it out a couple of times before birth so you will be aware of what you are aiming for when you are really pushing your baby out.

A Lifetime Exercise Plan for After the Birth of the Baby

You can begin PC contractions again right after birth. In fact if you've had an episiotomy it restores circulation and helps to promote healing, and since the exercise has such impact on your health, you will undoubtedly want to continue PC exercising to prevent uterine prolapse. Although the Kegel exercises are the well-known prophylactic measure to prevent and even correct uterine prolapse, many women are never informed about them. You will want to develop a lifelong exercise habit for these muscles that becomes effortless for you. I do my PC exercises at red lights. Since I manage to hit every one in town, I easily get at least a hundred PC contractions in each day with hardly a thought to it. Find something that you do every day that you can connect your exercises to and make them a lifelong habit for health.

part II

The First Stage of Birth

chapter ten

Getting Ready for Labor

As you begin to think about your own labor and birth, you are probably already asking yourself: When is this going to happen? Will I know? What are the normal signs? You already know that the flattening of your cervix, known as effacement, is a step toward giving birth, but that it doesn't tell you when birth will happen. And you already know that engagement, or the baby "dropping" lower into your pelvis, is also usually a part of the process, but that doesn't tell you when labor will begin either.

In fact, early in your pregnancy your doctor probably gave you a "due date," but frankly, that doesn't tell you much about when birth will happen either.

First of all, unless you are absolutely sure when conception took place, there is no firm date from which to begin counting the gestation period. Counting from the last menstrual period already allows a week or two of leeway on either side of what might be your real due date. But most importantly, no two women are alike and neither are any two babies. So it is quite impossible, even if you know the date of conception, to say exactly when a baby will be born.

The best that can be hoped for is to have a good estimate, and that is all that a realistic due date can be. Your doctor would be doing you a real favor if he would tell you to expect your baby "toward the end of August or early September" rather than "August 25" or even "the fourth week in August," when you ask (as you certainly will), "When am I due?" And you would be doing your family and friends a real favor if you would give them that kind of loose estimate about when the baby is due.

There are several reasons for this. First of all, you are going to reach a point when you will be ready to strangle the next person who says to you, "Still pregnant?" It puts a lot of stress on you to know that everyone is watching the calendar as closely as you will be if you have set a specific date in your mind.

Remember, no one has been pregnant forever and the baby knows when it is time to be born. It will happen when the baby and your body are ready.

Furthermore, while you will often hear women say, "My labor began at 3 P.M. on Wednesday," in many cases there is nothing that precise about when labor begins. At that point a series of things will be happening in your body over a period of time that could be as long as a week or more. The uterus may try out a contraction or two and then decide to wait for another day. Or you might have contractions over several hours and get quite excited (naturally), only to have the uterus stop and wait to start again later in the week.

This is often called "false labor," but there is really nothing false about it. It is part of a process that will begin and stop on its own until it is ready to begin in earnest. Who is to say that those early contractions are not really an important part of the whole process of giving birth?

If you count your labor from the first of those tentative contractions of the uterine muscles, you will be able to

amaze (and probably frighten) your friends by telling them how long your labor was. But if you wait until labor is definitely underway with good, strong, working contractions that require your complete attention, you may well have a much shorter labor to tell about.

How you count your labor is important to you psychologically. It could make the difference between a birth you will later describe as hard work, to be sure, but a manageable, joyful experience, and a birth you will describe as difficult and exhausting. But it is not just your attitude that is at stake, especially if you are giving birth in a hospital.

The latest trend in obstetrical medicine is to set time limits on birth and to intervene in the process if those limits are not met. For example, in *Active Management of Labour*, by Drs. Kieran O'Driscoll and Declan Meagher (London: W. B. Saunders Co., 1980), obstetricians are urged to put a twelve-hour limit on birth from the start of labor. If within a few hours the woman is not on schedule, labor will be "speeded up" with drugs. Though it seems incredible to put a single, hard-and-fast time limit on all women who give birth (even though it should be obvious that women of different sizes, ages, physical conditions, and temperaments will have different birth patterns), it frequently happens.

There are often other time limits imposed on labor, as we will examine later; but for now, it is important for you to realize that birth is a natural process that will occur when your body is ready, with no reference to some imprecise due date, and that once labor begins it will also move forward at its own rate and not on some schedule imposed by others.

Your body knows what to do. It will naturally lead

you through the three stages of birth: opening the cervix, pushing out the baby, and expelling the placenta. From the preceding several chapters you have gotten a pretty good idea of what happens within the body during labor. Now it is time to begin to learn the labor techniques. These are the skills that will help you tune into your body and work with your labor.

Relaxation is simple but not easy—at least not until you learn to do it thoroughly and well. That will take more than just learning the theories of relaxation. You must practice until it does become natural for you.

So be forewarned. You can flip through this book devouring all the information on controversies in childbirth and making lists of choices for yourself. But if you skip or just skim through this and following chapters on labor skills, you may as well put your list aside. You will only get to use it by going into labor fully prepared with a lot of practice behind you.

Relaxation

Your primary concern in labor, above all else, is to relax. You have to learn to relax as if your life depended upon it. This section will lay the groundwork for the skill of relaxation. If you cannot find a Bradley® class in your area you will want to come back to this section again and again. Master it thoroughly. It is your foundation, and everything else builds upon it.

The purpose of this extreme relaxation is just to stay out of the way with a limp body and allow the uterus to do its work unimpeded by other bodily tensions. This may sound easy. It is simple, but not easy. It takes all of your concentration to keep your whole body really limp and sagging, letting go everywhere as the uterine contraction builds and builds to a peak of strength.

The uterus is just a bag of muscles, but it is the largest collection of muscles you have and when it flexes you can really feel it as a powerful sensation. You will not eliminate this sensation with what we will teach you, but you will learn to do the right things while that muscular bag is flexing, so that you are working for you and your baby, not against yourself.

Take a look at picture 24. As you recall, you have long muscles that go from the top of the uterus down to the cervix, the muscles which contract or flex to pull the cervix back. Each time they flex or contract during labor, they get a little shorter and stay retracted. They just continue to shorten all through first-stage labor until the cervix is drawn completely back and open. But you can also see the opposite muscle group here, the circular muscles which are most heavily concentrated at the bottom of the uterus near the cervix. These muscles keep the door of the cervix closed while you are pregnant; but in labor, while the long muscles flex and shorten, the circular muscles must lengthen and relax to allow the cervix to be drawn back. These are involuntary muscles. They will work for you in labor no matter what you do, yet you can have an effect on them. Let's see how.

Remember how a contraction starts at the top of the uterus. The long muscles reaching down toward the cervix

 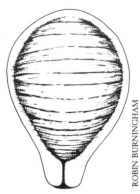

24.

ROBIN BURNINGHAM

Long muscles of the uterus contract or shorten to pull the cervix back for you.

Circular muscles of the uterus relax and lengthen to allow the long muscles to pull the cervix back.

begin to flex. They work a little bit more and continue to shorten. They keep on flexing and shortening until you get a good, strong, stretching and pulling sensation at the cervix. Now, what do you think the untrained mother does when she feels a contraction start slowly and work more and even a bit more? You are right, of course, she tenses her body and clenches her teeth to get ready for another one of those contractions. We call this fighting labor.

The woman who fights labor makes contractions last longer. She makes her work much harder by tensing against it. When you are tensed, the uterus has to work harder to get the same amount done with each contraction. It is not accomplishing twice as much, just working twice as hard. So, you must acquire the know-how and concentration to relax. This is a skill that must be acquired

through practice, and the untrained mother is not very good at it.

Often when a woman is fighting labor, a well-meaning nurse will say, "Try to relax, honey." The mother bravely tries for a couple of contractions. But does she genuinely relax her body and go limp? No, instead she imitates relaxation by holding herself still. She cannot consciously and deliberately let everything go loose and slack. Muscle groups throughout her body are tensed and contracted. She gets no comfort from an imitation of relaxation.

The Best Position for Labor

Relaxation begins with a comfortable position that makes it easy; it is quite difficult in a position that causes stress or strain. If you could walk through a labor ward in most hospitals, you would find almost all of the untrained mothers lying flat on their backs throughout most of labor. Yet all the current research shows this position to be dangerous to the laboring woman and to her unborn child. Why? The largest blood vessel runs in back of the uterus. If you think of your baby's weight as a bowling ball, you can easily imagine what happens to this large blood vessel when you lie on your back. It is pinched between the pelvic bones and the weight of the baby. And when this circulation is interfered with, your baby's oxygen and nutrient supply is impeded.

A coach should remind the pregnant woman not to lie on her back from about the seventh month of pregnancy through the end of labor. Sounds easy, doesn't it? You think to yourself, "I know it and she knows it, so she won't lie on her back." Yet, when a woman is in labor she is so wrapped up in what is happening inside her body that there is a tendency to remain in whatever position she happens to be in. So if in the hospital, for example, she is examined (for which she must be on her back briefly), she will likely just remain on her back out of inertia. If the coach simply says, "Okay, it is time to get off your back. Let's turn over now," she will readily comply. She just needs some encouragement and help getting started.

Since the pregnant woman cannot lie on her back and she probably won't care to lie on her tummy, that leaves the side as the best lying-down position for labor. (There is an alternate sitting-up position we will go into later.) Picture 25 will show you a comfortable and safe position for labor. It is important, so please study the details carefully. This is a balanced position, worked out by a physical therapist. Each part of the body is equally supported and no part is resting on any other part. There is no lopsided stress or strain on any part.

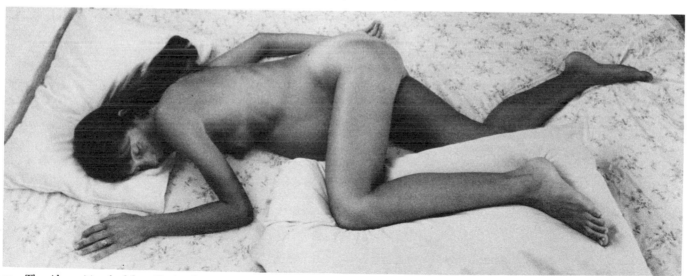

25.   The side position for labor: Notice the arm behind, off the pillow.

- Notice the slight curve to the spine and to the whole body.

- The chin should be slightly toward the chest but not on it. Avoid tilting the head back, causing strain on the muscles.

- Elbows and knees should be bent. Keeping them straight creates strain and tension, which you want to avoid completely during labor.

- Use a *flat* pillow under the head. This will keep it level with the neck and in line with the body. Avoid fluffy pillows that prop the head up at an unnatural angle, causing ten-sion. The pillow can be pulled forward and tucked into your chest if this is comfortable.

- The top leg should be extended outward, bent at the knee, and then supported with at least two pillows, one on top of the other. Long pillows that support the entire leg and the foot are best. Having the top leg almost level with the top hip will avoid tension and an aching sensation there.

- Place the bottom shoulder and arm on the bed behind you. Do not rest the shoulder on the pillow. If it is placed on the pillow, the shoulder will feel strained.

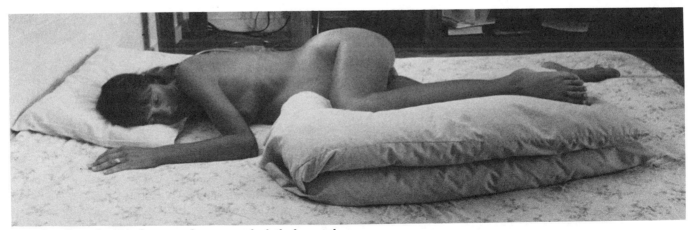

26. The pillows should be long enough to support both the knee and toe and high enough to have the knee somewhat level with the hip.

Remember, this is a balanced position. It is designed to avoid strain and tension. You will find this most comfortable on a firm mattress (like those on hospital beds) or on a carpeted floor at home. If your bed is too soft it will not be comfortable when you practice, because your body is not given the support it needs. Try this position and have your coach check you out, comparing your position with the illustration and checking all the points.

TO THE COACH

Is your wife grumbling about the arm and shoulder behind her? They are often not very comfortable at first, because she may be stretching muscles and ligaments that haven't been used this way before. Practice is what makes her ready for labor.

What about pulling her arm under herself, as she may do in sleep? This is a poor substitute for the preferred position because of the pressure on the lower arm. The circulation is cut off quickly in the arm, and discomfort soon sets in. She can get away with sleeping like that for a while, but labor takes intense concentration, and the discomfort from a less-than-perfect position can distract her terribly. This position you have just learned was designed to maximize comfort.

Now ask her to turn over and help her get up in the position on her other side. Be careful to arrange the pillows to support the entire upper leg and foot and to keep that leg even with the hip. In labor you will want to turn her over from her favorite side to her other side every hour or hour and a half to ensure even circulation. She need only stay on her less favorite side for about ten minutes before turning back, if she prefers.

Two Keys to Relaxation

Once you have mastered this position for labor, there are two keys to skilled relaxation. The first is observation. Here is an exercise in observation, *not in relaxation*, for you both to try. Take turns with one of you lying in the side position while the other reads the exercise aloud.

- Tighten up all of your facial muscles hard. That is extreme tension. It is easy to spot. Now relax.

- Now tighten your shoulders very hard. Just hunch them up. You are very aware of that tension, aren't you. Since you are so aware of it, it is easy to release it now.

- But extreme tension is not what you stumble over in labor. The tension you will need to watch for is much more subtle than that. Here are some samples of what you need to look for in labor and to deliberately, consciously release.

- Tighten just a few muscles in your face. Just a slight frown and a few tight facial muscles.

You would probably not notice this tension while working around the house or while preoccupied at work. Now, relax your face.

- Could you spot that kind of tension in labor? You must be aware of it to release it. *Observation is the first key to relaxation.*

- Now, tighten your shoulders just slightly, hardly enough for anyone else to see. You must be able to recognize the sensation of slight tension in order to concentrate on releasing it. Now relax. You cannot relax to any great depth unless you are skillful at observation.

- *The ability to relax during contractions directly relates to your degree of comfort during labor.*

- Tighten your leg extremely. That is easy to spot. Now release. Tighten just a few muscles in your leg ever so slightly. Imagine that a nurse comes in to check you in the hospital, and when she leaves you are not quite as deeply relaxed as before. Would you notice it? You must be aware of tension, the flexed or shortened muscles in your body, before you can deliberately release them.

- You cannot be skillful at relaxation until you are good at deliberately and continuously observing your body. Look for tension, notice it, and let it go.

Now the woman should read this exercise in observation (remember it is not a *relaxation* exercise) to her coach. A coach should be just as familiar with the subtlety of sensations in tension. Try making the same comparisons before going on.

The second key to skillful relaxation is *consciously releasing tension.* (Some birth classes confuse observation exercises with relaxation and never take you on to the next step.) Once you are familiar with the feeling of tension and are able to recognize it, you will be able to *concentrate on deliberately letting it go.*

This is not at all like relaxing to go to sleep. Most of us climb into bed and wait for our bodies to relax. Few of us know how to deliberately release tension from our bodies.

You cannot hold yourself still in labor and wait for your body to relax and sag just because you are in a sleep position. Relaxation will never come. You must practice observing your muscles over and over and then *deliberately releasing tension.* Never be satisfied. You can always let go a little more. Be prepared to spend fifteen to twenty minutes a day in the last months of your pregnancy consciously practicing relaxing your whole body.

Relaxing Through a Contraction

Now it is time to put the relaxation skills you are learning together with the special position and to practice what you will do in a real working contraction of labor. Coach, have your wife lie on her side and check to be sure her body is arranged properly and well supported by pillows (no parts resting on other parts and no dangling hands or feet). Be sure her eyes are closed so she can concentrate. Read the following demonstration aloud at least twice and then put the book down and try it twice on your own. Your goal is to help the laboring woman be totally relaxed for the first stage of labor, which takes practice and skill.

Speaking quietly into her ear with conviction and loving attention, talk her through a contraction as follows, urging her to relax her whole body from head to toe. Pause for a moment between naming each muscle group to let her consciously eliminate the tension before moving on to the next one. This practice contraction should last about one minute:

Practice Exercise A: Relaxing Through a Contraction

- Relax your whole body. Let it sink into the mattress.

- Drop your head down into the pillow, don't hold it up with your neck muscles.

- Relax all the muscles in your face. Really think about them and release.

- Smooth your forehead. Let go with all the tiny muscles around your eyes. Have a relaxed open throat and let your jaw hang open. Don't try to swallow. (It's even OK to drool on the pillow—that is how relaxed you are, just like you are when you are in deep sleep.)

- Let go of all the tension in your neck. Let it go out of your shoulders. Locate any tightness there and let it flow away. You can always release a little bit more.

- Don't just hold yourself still. Really release and let the tension go. Look for any tightness and deliberately release. Relax as if your life depended upon it.

- Let go with your arms and let any tension go out through your hands and your fingertips. Have loose, limp fingers.

- Relax your chest and your abdomen. Think of your tummy sagging and floating out and away from you as it sinks down into the mattress. The stronger the contraction becomes, the more you release and let go with your tummy, sagging extremely. You can always release a little bit more.

- Let go of any tension in your hips and thighs. Let your legs sink down into the mattress and the pillows. Locate any tension in your legs and let it flow out through your feet. Your whole body should be loose and limp.

- Let that big bag of muscles flex for you and just concentrate on that powerful sensation of the biggest muscles in your body working and working to open the door to the uterus.

- Let your whole body sag and go limp and get out of the way so that big bag of muscles can do its job. Concentrate on relaxation and release extremely. You can always let go a little bit more.

- Think your way up and over this contraction, locating any tension that is left in your body and letting it go, letting it ease out through your hands and feet.

The practice contraction is over. Do not go on until you have read this twice aloud and done it twice without the book using your own words. You simply start at the head and say what you see: facial muscles, jaw, neck, shoulders, and so on. You don't have to memorize this series exactly as it is written here. But you do have to practice saying it your own way, again and again. Anything you desire to do skillfully requires practice. Repetition is the best way to get it down pat.

TO THE COACH

During labor you have an important part to play in helping the pregnant woman to relax. Indeed, coaching contractions is one of the most important things you are going to be doing during that time. And for this, practice is essential, so that when the day comes the basic coaching skills are second-nature to you.

Don't think for a minute that it is all right to know these things in theory but that you probably will not actually need them. You will need them. These techniques really work and will be much easier to do after a long familiarity through practice.

Though even your wife may think that a lot of practice is unnecessary now, after the birth you both will be happy you took the time to get ready properly. One thing couples in our classes always tell others when they return after their births is, "We are glad we practiced a lot. It

really paid off and we think that is the most important advice we can pass on to you."

The first few times you actually coach a contraction can be awkward. It is play-acting, after all, something that most people are not too comfortable with, even in the privacy of home. No one laughs when we coach in class, but there will probably be a lot of giggling the first few times both of you try to coach through a pretend contraction. Laugh together, let the laughing go, and keep at it.

As you practice, don't coach in a monotone or a dull, droning voice. After all, you are not trying to hypnotize her or put her to sleep. The pregnant woman in labor must *think* her way through a contraction. She must use her brain, actively observing her body and concentrating on deliberately releasing tension in her muscles no matter how slight the tension seems, so you want to help her keep mentally alert and thinking. You will need to talk with inflection, thinking yourself about what you are saying, helping her continue with her concentration. Just saying, "Relax your arms, relax your legs, relax your thighs," won't do it. Use different words with an earnest, urgent, actively inflected voice.

You will find the coaching role in labor similar to the role of a swimming coach. When the swimmer puts it all together, the coach stands by saying, "Stroke, kick, breathe, reach out farther, keep kicking, etc." The swimming coach is the objective observer and is able to give direction as needed. When the new swimmer is in the middle of the pool and feeling tired or discouraged, the coach offers encouragement and praise. The labor coach is also an objective observer. He (or she) can see how close the laboring woman is to her goal while the woman may be thinking she will never get there. But like the swimmer, the laboring woman must know her skills and practice them. Then and only then can coaches be of great help.

chapter eleven

More on Relaxation: Backaches to Breathing

There is another important skill for the coach to learn, and that is how to deal with the backache that the laboring woman frequently experiences. Most women, but not all, have a backache while experiencing strong contractions. The ache begins as a contraction begins, gets stronger as the contraction gets stronger, and goes away as the contraction ends.

Why? The uterus is kept in place by ligaments. If you look back at picture 6 on page 51, you will see one of the two round ligaments in the front, mooring the uterus to the pelvic floor. You may feel these ligaments during pregnancy if you bend over and then stand up too fast. The muscles can sort of buckle under, giving you a sharp pain

that quickly disappears. (Remember, there are no sudden, stabbing pains in labor.) Nothing is wrong with you or your baby, and you are not starting labor. What you felt is just a kink from standing up too fast.

You have two ligaments in the back, too, called the uterosacral ligaments. Take another look at picture 6 and you will see them. They look like two thick rubber bands stretching from the uterus to either side of the spine. With each contraction in labor, the uterus pulls forward and puts traction on its anchor point through the uterosacral ligaments, causing the backache that occurs in many labors.

TO THE COACH: THE BACKACHE

Coach, your wife cannot concentrate a hundred percent on her task if she is bothered by this uncomfortable backache. So it is your job to clear this obstacle to her concentration. You must take care of the ache. You do this by applying counterpressure in the form of a back rub. It sounds easy, but don't forget, in a "textbook" labor you may be rubbing while contractions occur for fourteen hours. One coach recalled it this way:

"With our first baby I rubbed Sandy's back for twelve hours. My arms were killing me for days after the baby was born. But I couldn't stop and I couldn't feel sorry for myself. She surely did need that back rub and I was the only one around who cared enough to give it to her constantly. She labored beautifully, quietly concentrating completely. She says the back rub she received freed her to put all her attention on her relaxation and breathing."

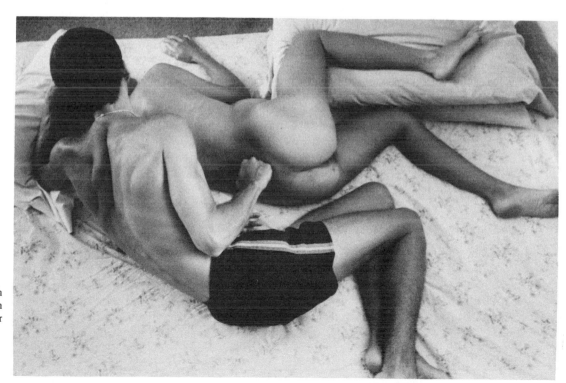

27. Backrub: Do with great attention to detail, in precisely the right spot for her.

As coach, you need to get this back-rub technique down pat if you expect the laboring woman to do well with labor:

- Be sure to rub exactly where it aches. Obviously, she will be able to tell you just where that is. The spot is not in the small of the back nor all the way down at the tailbone, but usually somewhere in between. You should rub this spot in a small, tight circle. She will tell you just where to rub, and she is the one to please.

- The heel of your hand or the front of your fist usually works best for this back rub. You may find it helpful to wrap your hand in a soft cloth, like an old T-shirt.

- Have your hand in place before the contraction starts. Don't wait for her to tell you the contraction is under way and then try to put your hand on her back. That's sloppy. It is exactly what the untrained husband does when trying to help his wife, and it's exactly why she tells him to leave her alone.

- Rub with a slow, steady rhythm in one direction. If you break the rhythm it distracts her attention immediately and she may snap at you.

- Press your hand firmly into the back and then rotate it in a circular motion. Do not slide your hand over her skin. That is irritating and will soon leave a raw feeling. Press inward—it will require *a lot* of pressure—and let the skin move with your hand in that circular motion. This is a deep massage.

Be forewarned—the most common error is to rub too fast. It must be a slow, steady, deep rub. And don't make the mistake of changing the direction of the rub in the middle of a contraction, even though your arm may feel tired. You will get an instant cranky reaction. The laboring woman is acutely aware of the minutest details (even though she may not seem to be), and a sudden shift in direction is sure to distract her attention from relaxation. Be sure your rubbing motion is steady and rhythmic, with no jerky, uneven movements.

A sloppy back rub may be even more disturbing to the laboring woman than the backache. She senses the coach is tired and not doing a thorough and careful job. She may also feel annoyed because he seems to lack empathy for the intensity of the sensations she is feeling. So to get the back rub right, it will be necessary to practice. It is a little like an isometric exercise, and you may be surprised at how hard she will want you to push. One coach said we should have told him to practice by rubbing a brick wall.

To practice, get the pregnant woman into the side position again and check her out to make sure she has no part resting on any other part and no limbs dangling. The coach needs to find a comfortable position too, to get good leverage, since a lot of pressure will probably be required. Locate the place where the backache will probably be felt, between the small of the back and the tailbone. Now begin the back rub as you coach some more practice contractions, coaching and rubbing for sixty to ninety seconds and resting for a few minutes in between. Look back at Chapter Ten if you need a reminder about coaching the muscle groups from head to toe to help her relax.

Even before labor begins, the back rub is quite soothing and you will have little trouble getting her to let you practice it. And once you have learned the back rub, it will serve you well long after the baby comes. The same technique offers great relief for the backache that often accompanies the beginning of a menstrual period. If you can help your wife with that you will earn her eternal gratitude.

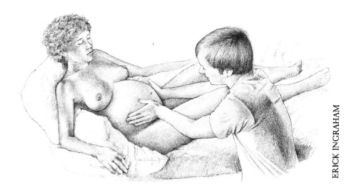

ERICK INGRAHAM

28. For round ligament ache: Rub in two places, using a circular or back-and-forth motion.

Round Ligament Ache

Though less common than the backache, occasionally a woman will have an ache in front in the round ligaments which attach the uterus to the pelvic floor. Like the backache, this ache starts at the beginning of a contraction, gets stronger, and diminishes as the contraction goes away. It is handled much like a backache, except the laboring woman will definitely not want as hard a massage on her tummy as she would on her back. You must talk to her to learn the exact degree of pressure that she desires (it may be very little) and exactly where to rub.

As with the back rub, have your hands in place before the contraction begins, massage with a steady, even rhythm, and never switch directions in the middle of a contraction. Use a circular or back-and-forth motion, but now it will be in two places on the front instead of one on the back. And like the back rub, this massage must be done with concentration and concern because the pregnant woman is very sensitive to sloppy or half-hearted effort.

Do not confuse the round ligament ache with a

More on Relaxation: Backaches to Breathing **89**

crampy sensation low in the abdomen. That crampiness can be taken care of by relaxing the tummy extremely. How do you distinguish between the two? Easy. A crampy sensation would be experienced all across the lower part of the abdomen. Round ligament ache would be limited to two areas, perhaps spreading down the legs.

29. Contour-chair position

An Alternate Position for First Stage

The massage for round ligament ache is hard to do while the laboring woman is on her side in the position we have taught you for labor, but there is an alternate, called the contour-chair position, which some women find helpful for first stage. I have personally never used this position for first stage because I truly believe that deeper relaxation is possible in the side position. (Although sitting and standing may shorten labor somewhat, I do not consider mere speed a benefit, especially if it is paid for at the price of lessened comfort.)

However, some women are just not comfortable on their sides during labor. If you find that you are one, then this contour-chair position is a good second choice. It will still get you up high enough to avoid some of the problems that come from lying flat on the back. Look at picture 29 to see the position. Hospital beds are good for this position because their backs can be rolled up to a forty-five-degree angle (anything less puts too much weight on the vessels bringing blood to the uterus and oxygen and nutrients to the baby), and the bottom can often be cranked up to support the knees. At home a lot of pillows will be needed, or perhaps a large bean-bag chair. Even in the hospital, you will need one or two pillows to support each arm, another for the head, and more still for under the knees if the bed does not crank up. If you cannot get enough pillows, don't bother with this position at all. Arms that just dangle rather than being supported cause strain on muscles and increase tension. Of course, elbows and knees are slightly bent in this position as in the side position to avoid strain and tension. Try this position out now, so that if you need to use it you will be familiar with it.

Breathing in Labor

What about breathing during the contractions? As mentioned earlier, you will learn no altered-breathing states in the Bradley Method.® You have been breathing all your life, and by now you are quite good at it. It is important for both the laboring woman and her baby that her breathing be calm, steady, and normal. All you need to learn is how to observe your breathing, so that if it becomes too fast or irregular you can deliberately return it to a calm, steady rhythm. Remember, normal breathing is a reflection of good relaxation, and relaxation is the real key to a successful labor.

Let's return to that poor, untrained mother for a moment. Does she breathe normally during labor? No. Instead she may breathe in three common patterns: sometimes she panics and breathes in a rapid *pant* (this is actually quite dangerous since it can cause hyperventilation); or she may breathe in irregular gasps; or she may simply stop breathing during a contraction and hold her breath.

All these ways of mishandling breathing spell panic, tension, and discomfort for the mother. The laboring woman needs to keep her breathing simple and normal since her primary aim is complete, skillful relaxation. To insure that relaxation, the laboring woman should use abdominal breathing, which simply means putting calm, steady breaths deep and low into the abdomen. Therapists in various fields use calm, abdominal breathing to relax excited patients, from asthmatics to the emotionally upset.

The key to abdominal breathing is just to *listen* to the quiet, regular rhythm of your breathing. Think of putting your breath low in the abdomen with an extremely relaxed abdominal wall. The abdomen will naturally expand outward with low abdominal breathing, so you do not need to push the abdomen out or try to hold it there. If you are listening within your body to the calm, quiet, steady rhythm of your breathing, it is impossible to breathe too quickly. If you are concentrating on putting the breath low in the abdomen, it is easy to avoid the chest breathing that can quickly lead to hyperventilation.

Here is the way to check this simple, natural breathing. The coach should sit on the floor with his back to the wall, forming a contour chair for the pregnant woman, who sits between his legs. A thin pillow between the two of you should make this position more comfortable. Reaching around her body, the coach should put his hands on the woman's abdomen, just about at the top of the pubic hair line. Now, the pregnant woman should try abdominal breathing. There will be some movement in the chest, of course, but the real action in this kind of breathing will be felt down low in the abdomen. Do not tense the abdominal wall or try to push it out; simply put the breath way down low, and the abdomen will expand out and away naturally, and the coach will feel the abdomen rise gently beneath his hand.

There are four main points to coaching the breathing during a contraction. Read them aloud twice and then close the book to make sure you have the four points and can express them in your own words.

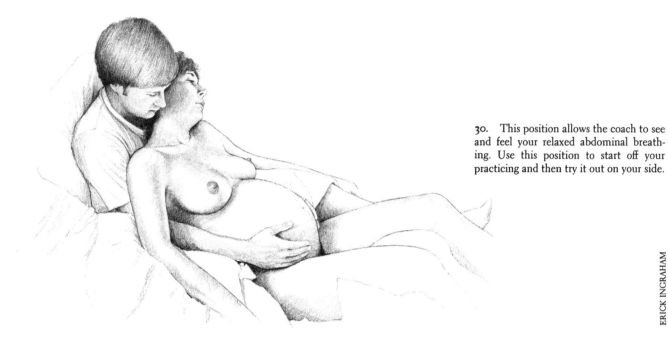

30. This position allows the coach to see and feel your relaxed abdominal breathing. Use this position to start off your practicing and then try it out on your side.

ERICK INGRAHAM

Practice Exercise B: Relaxed Breathing

- Listen to the sound of your breathing.

- Hear the quiet, even, steady rhythm.

- Think of putting the air way down low in the abdomen.

- Relax the tummy extremely and let it just expand outward naturally as you breathe in.

Try coaching just the breathing for a while, until both of you are satisfied that it is going well. Now we can put the coaching of the breathing together with coaching head-to-toe relaxation for one more practice contraction so you will see how the whole thing works.

Putting It Together

Now that you have learned to coach relaxation and breathing separately, practice putting the two together. They go hand in hand. The trick is to coach a little breathing and a lot of concentration on relaxation in each contraction. That is, start out with the four points of the breathing and move right on to head-to-toe relaxation, returning to the breathing very little during the contraction unless the laboring woman seems to need it.

Remember, relaxation for labor is not like relaxing to go to sleep. As long as you keep in mind the purpose of coaching—to help her achieve skillful, deliberate relaxation of muscle groups and breathing in a calm, rhythmic manner low in the abdomen—then you cannot miss. So read the following exercise aloud twice, then close the book, and with the mother in the side position, practice several complete contractions. Don't forget the back rub. Just in the practice sessions, you should also say the things in parentheses.

31. Putting it all together: Coach and rub the back at the same time.

MASTER EXERCISE I

First-Stage Contractions: Breathing and Relaxation

(A contraction begins. You feel it starting to work. Your uterus flexes for you, a little more, and just a little bit more, until you get a good, strong, pulling, stretching sensation around the cervix to open that door.)

- Breathe with a steady, even rhythm. Not in the middle of your tummy, but way down low. Listen to the quiet ease of your abdominal breathing.

- Concentrate on relaxing your tummy extremely. Think of it just floating outward and away from you as you breathe in.

- Drop your head into the pillow. Think about it. Don't hold your head up with your neck muscles. Just let it drop down into the pillow.

- Smooth your eyelids, and concentrate on all those facial muscles being loose and slack. Smooth your brow. Let your eyes rest. Let all the tension go from your face. Loosen your jaw and let it sag open. Have a relaxed, open throat. Don't try to swallow.

- Drop your shoulders. Have no tension in them at all. Relax your back and let your tummy relax completely, floating out and away from you. You can always relax your tummy a little bit more. There is always some leftover tension to ease away.

- Each time you exhale, you let go a little more. Let your whole body sag and relax and get out of the way so that big bag of muscles can open the door for the baby.

- Locate any tension that is left in your shoulders and your arms and let go of it so it eases out through your hands. Let your hands be limp and let your fingers be loose and limp. Everything just sinks down into the pillows and the mattress.

- When you feel that muscle flexing you think your way through the contraction. The whole body is relaxing to let the uterus do its work.

- Let go of any strain or tension in your chest. Drop your whole body into that bed. Let go. Release everywhere. Relax your tummy extremely. Concentrate on letting go and letting it float out and away from you. Keep your breathing very calm and quiet and steady and way down low in the bottom of your belly.

- Think, drop into the bed, and really let go. Don't just hold yourself still. Keep loose and limp, and let your PC muscle relax completely. Let your vaginal barrel be open.

- Let go as if your life depended on it. Breathe at a nice, normal pace. Observe your body. Look for any tension and skillfully let it go so it just eases out of your body. You can always let go just a little more. Think, observe, release.

- Let your hips be slack and sink down into the bed. Let go of any tension in your thighs. Let it all go out through your legs and feet. Your legs are loose and easy now. Your feet are loose and limp as well.

- That's it. You are doing great. Don't stop thinking about relaxing now. You think your way up and over a contraction. That's what you are practicing right now. Concentration. Don't let your mind stray to other things. Keep thinking about relaxation. Look for any tension and deliberately release it away. Sag, go loose and limp.

- Think of your uterus as that big bag of muscles that is opening the door for your baby. It is just a bag of muscles flexing. The more it flexes the more you relax with it. Stay out of the way with your body. Don't get in the way. The more you relax the better those muscles work. Think of your baby's head pressing on the cervix as you let go and open, AND OPEN. Let the vaginal barrel be relaxed and open.

- Breathe with a nice, quiet, steady rhythm. Listen to the sound of it, way down low in the bottom of your belly. You can always relax a little more and a bit more. Never be satisfied. Keep thinking. Breathe and sag. Picture what is happening inside you. The bag of muscles flexes to open the door for the baby.

- Think your way up and over a contraction. (And the contraction peaks and ebbs away to the end.)

Practice this Master Exercise every night until it becomes automatic.

32. During an occasional contraction, put two fingers lightly on the abdomen to check the breathing. You should feel the abdomen move outward as she breathes in.

ERICK INGRAHAM

How to Time Contractions

A contraction is timed from its beginning to the peak of its strength. The laboring woman will let you know when a contraction begins by saying, "There's one," or with a raised finger or a simple grunt. She needs to signal you in the same way when a contraction has reached its peak and begins to subside. This will tell you how long the contraction is.

Why not time the contraction from the beginning to the end? Because it is only really working for her until the peak. Then the uterus is just relaxing and the sensation is fading, so it is hard to know exactly when it does end. So time contractions from the beginning to the peak.

To determine how far apart contractions are, time from the *beginning of one contraction to the beginning of the next.* You do not time from the end of one contraction to the beginning of the next because it is so hard to say when a contraction ends.

But wait, this is important. When we say, "The contractions are seventy seconds long and three minutes apart," that is not the result of timing just one contraction. The human body is not a machine and it does not work like a clock. Often a good, strong contraction will be followed by a short one, or several long ones and several short ones will alternate. Sometimes a contraction will just fizzle after a few seconds. This is all normal and no cause for alarm. So, in timing contractions it is important to time and record several—say five or six—and then take a *conservative* average to determine the length and interval of the contractions.

For example, if you timed five contractions and three were forty-five seconds long and two were fifty-five seconds long, what would you say? You would say the contractions were about forty-five seconds long. That is, you would go by three contractions out of the five. Acting on one or two contractions instead of the low average of about half a dozen could give you, the laboring woman, and everyone else a false idea of where you are in labor.

You have learned a lot in the last two chapters. You now know the best position for labor (and an alternate), how to relax, how to coach relaxation, how to deal with the backache many women have (and the round ligament ache a few have), and how to listen to the breathing to keep it quiet, steady, and normal. In class you would review these things many times, and you should return often to these chapters. There are a few more basic labor skills to learn, but first we will look at another common question: pain.

chapter twelve

About Pain—and More Relaxation Tools

What about pain? It is something that every pregnant woman certainly wonders about. Is a painless labor possible? Yes, painless labor is indeed possible, *but it is certainly not a promise.* I have experienced painless childbirth, so I am very much aware of the possibility. But what about the women in our classes? We find that about two out of five describe their labors as painless. That is not even half the people we teach.

I can promise you control in labor. All you have to do is want it. If you are motivated to really want an unmedicated childbirth with a labor that is dignified and manageable, you can have it simply by listening to your breathing to ensure it continues in a calm, quiet, relaxed rhythm. The woman who is breathing excitedly or holding her breath is the one who is panicky and out of control.

Personally, I do not consider control enough. So I know you will want to really get into relaxation because it is the key to comfort in labor. How well you skillfully release tension will to a large extent determine your degree of comfort.

How does relaxation affect pain? Does it diminish our response to pain or does it reduce and eliminate the sensation itself? Well, relaxation can do both. If you have pain, then relaxation influences your response to it in a way that eases labor. As you know, tightening up makes labor harder.

But relaxation does more than that. Women who have had painless labors often say that they think it is a matter of doing things right in the first place: not tightening up but going with the strong sensations and looking upon them as "just muscles working." What makes labor painless for them is total relaxation and not fighting to control pain. A deeper, more complex explanation can be found in Dr. Edmund Jacobson's book *How to Relax and Have Your Baby.* His specialty is not babies but relaxation. He has applied what he believes about relaxation to labor quite successfully, though, as he explains, ". . . relaxation proceeds to relieve pain mechanically . . .

> It requires action of the whole nerve-muscle-brain-nerve-muscle circuit to experience pain. The muscular part of this circuit is under your control and can be relaxed. By relaxing all efforts to perceive the pain and to do something about it, like withdrawing, you can put out of commission the uterine pain circuit."

There are undeniably strong sensations in labor which are felt by every woman, but whether these are described as pain is a subjective matter which depends a lot on expectations and experiences. For example, the childbirth teacher who has experienced hard pain in labor often teaches that this is the only way it can be and almost always has students who have hard pain. The woman who is certainly *not* going to have a painless childbirth is the one who is absolutely convinced that birth must be an agony. She is less apt to *analyze* the physical sensations she feels.

Instead, as her powerful uterine muscles flex, she *reacts* automatically with her built-up expectations. Labor will be manageable for her, with good control possible just by listening to the sound of her breathing, but comfort is something lost to her.

Those women who have experienced hard pain sometimes find it difficult to believe that anyone could experience painless childbirth. Occasionally, over the years of teaching, I have observed a few women who seem to have a real psychological need to deny that painless childbirth is possible. Perhaps this stems from a feeling that if someone else didn't have pain, that somehow invalidates the painful experience of a woman who does have pain.

On the other hand, women who have no pain in labor certainly did feel the uterus contracting very powerfully and they certainly had moments when they felt the emotional booby trap of "I don't think I can do this anymore." Such women understand that labor can be painful with anything less than perfect relaxation, so they have no need to invalidate or deny the pain of those who experienced it. *The reality is that there is such a thing as painless childbirth and such a thing as painful childbirth. It is not necessary to invalidate either experience.*

The pain discussion is a critical part of the class, and I never fail to mention the entire range of experiences possible. I like to have each class hear the story of one couple who had a painless birth; another couple who describe their labor as having no pain or mild cramping at the beginning, going on to moderate pain, and ending up with hard pain for a short time; and finally one couple who had hard pain for most of labor. This covers the real range of experience, and it is very important for women to hear the whole range. (All these women, by the way, will describe their labors as quite manageable, even those who experienced hard pain most of the way.) Most women in class do listen and hear this range, not "selecting out" any experience, and they come back after birth eager to share how it was for them, because they understand it is acceptable to have had either experience.

Women give many clues about how labor is going to be for them. As we mentioned, the woman who has already decided before labor that it definitely will be painful is almost certain to find it so. Like water taking the shape of its container, experiences often take the shape of expectations. And the woman in class who is eager to be reassured that childbirth is painless seems to have a strong chance of having hard pain. What she *wishes* for is a painless birth but it is not what she *expects*, as shown by her anxiety as she tries to get reassurance.

Most women who do experience hard pain tend to do so at the end of the first stage. But remember, there are no sudden, sharp, stabbing pains in labor. Rather, there is a strong building up of sensation with each contraction. In between contractions there is a chance to rest. (The speedster, by the way, rarely experiences painless childbirth. Her contractions are too close. There is not enough time for her to get accustomed to the sensations and to get deeply into relaxation, though she keeps good control with the breathing. The putterer is more likely to have a painless birth since she has lots of time to get used to the sensations and get deeply relaxed.)

The woman in my class who I predict (to myself only)

will have a painless birth is the one who is quite comfortable with her body and with physical strain and sweat. She will really get into the relaxation techniques, rather than only going for the physical exercises. This woman listens to all the various birth stories and is prepared in a matter-of-fact way for the backache, for powerful sensations, and for hard, sweaty work. She is not looking for any authority figure to reassure her or guarantee her a painless birth. She simply has faith and confidence in the process of labor and birth. I am not talking about religious faith, but about a belief that birth is normal and an expectation that her body will function normally as millions of others have done before. She truly has the idea that labor is nothing more than muscles flexing.

This is the woman I expect will have a painless or near-painless birth. I am often, but not always, right. This woman usually comes back to the class after birth and tells of her physical sensations in terms of stretching, pulling, straining, low in the abdomen. She uses words that typically would apply to *working muscles*. Those who report that labor is painless almost always say their favorite technique was *picturing what was really happening in their body while they deeply relaxed and let go with it.* (This technique, called "mental imagery," will be explained more thoroughly in a moment.) The woman who said her favorite technique was breathing seldom experienced a painless childbirth.

But let me make it quite clear that women who have experienced both a medicated birth and a trained, natural childbirth are quick to tell you that *medication does not make childbirth painless.* They invariably say their natural childbirth was, by far, the most comfortable of the two. And most women who have had a medicated childbirth, and no other kind, talk about little else but the pain and discomfort.

So let me repeat. I do not promise any woman a painless childbirth. It is a possibility, not a promise. And you do not need a painless childbirth to have a good, natural, unmedicated birth experience, one that you will enjoy remembering.

Mental Imagery

This is nothing more than vividly picturing what is happening inside your body each and every time you feel a contraction. A contraction is a powerful sensation. Your uterus is the biggest set of muscles in your body, and when it flexes you have a strong physical sensation. You feel as if it could pick you right up off the bed. Do not underestimate labor, for it is the hardest work you will ever do. So you must be prepared for strong sensations. You certainly do not want to tense and tighten up against this contraction sensation. You want to mentally hook up what you are feeling to an accurate image of what is causing it.

You will have to concentrate on going limp, sagging, letting go, and visualizing the long muscles flexing and contracting while the circular muscles lengthen and relax outward in an ever-widening circle, opening the door to the uterus, your cervix. That is why you feel that stretching, pulling, straining sensation low in your abdomen.

In this wonderful series of pictures you see the uterus not cut in half but as it really is. You can clearly see that the cervix is not just two ends hanging down into the canal but in fact goes around in a circle just like the neck of a turtleneck sweater.

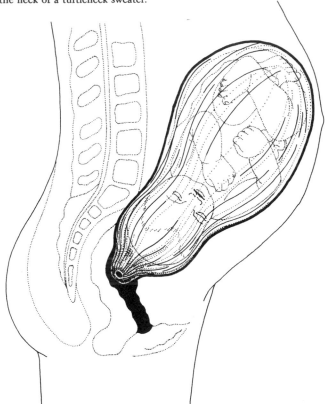

33a. In the first picture labor has not started. No effacement has occurred either. The opening you see in the cervix is just the cervical canal.

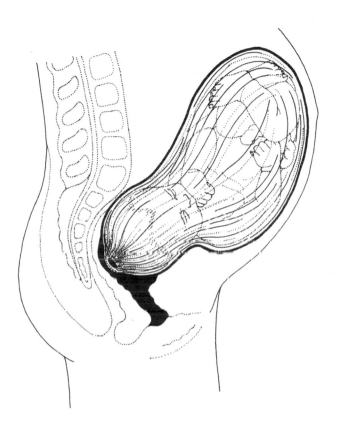

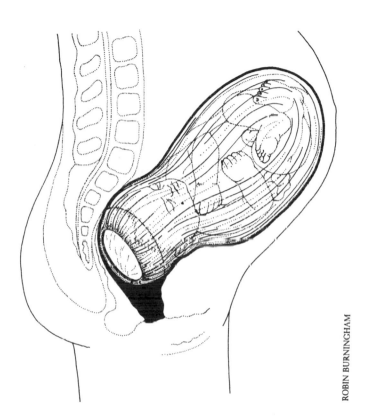

ROBIN BURNINGHAM

33b. The cervix is effaced, pulled back flat onto the baby's head, but not dilated yet.

33c. Here you can see the cervix opening into ever-widening circles as it dilates. The dotted line shows you how the cervix will continue to pull back over the baby's head. Do not confuse this with crowning. This is not at the outlet but up inside where you do not see it opening.

About Pain—and More Relaxation Tools **101**

It is not enough to just know this is happening in an abstract way. You have to apply mental imagery, that is, picturing what is happening vividly and deliberately during a contraction. You have something concrete to work with in labor when you visualize just what is happening. If you do, you will find yourself analyzing what you feel and where you feel it rather than simply reacting emotionally with fear and tension to a strong sensation. A contraction is not your enemy; as it pulls stronger it is also working better for you. Keep this in mind during a contraction.

And remember, nature is very kind. As your uterine muscles flex and relax, you always get a rest between contractions. Your body works in an intricate and harmonious fashion. There is no onslaught of forces against you, no sharp sudden pains or piercing agony, but there is a definite sensation of a powerful set of muscles working. Visualizing this is as important as the relaxation or breathing during a contraction. If we could give you just one gift with this book it would be the faith in the proper working of your own body and the ability to visualize just what is happening during labor.

Coaching mental imagery is not difficult. Start by taking another look at the picture of the uterus and hold that picture in your mind as you read this exercise. You were already introduced to some of the words and phrases in Master Exercise I. Just remind the mother what is happening inside her body.

Practice Exercise C: Mental Imagery

- Stay out of the way with your whole body and let that big bag of muscles do all the work for you, opening the door to the cervix.

- Visualize what is happening inside you. Picture those long muscles flexing and pulling the cervix open. Picture the circular muscles relaxing and lengthening in an ever widening circle to open the door for the baby.

- The more it works for you, the more you relax with it. The more you relax, the better the uterus works for you as you open and open.

- Concentrate on what is happening inside you. Go loose, limp, sagging while your uterus works for you, and hook up what you are feeling to the picture of that big bag of muscles working.

You certainly have the idea by now. Read over Master Exercise I, read these samples of coaching mental imagery, then put the book aside and coach several practice contractions, using your own words for all the techniques you have learned—breathing, head-to-toe relaxation, and mental imagery.

Floating Technique

There is just one more technique for the first stage of labor that you may find very helpful toward the end. During the last sprint of the uterine muscles, as the cervix goes from seven to ten centimeters of dilation, contractions will be quite strong soon after they get started. This usually corresponds to the "self-doubt" emotional signpost, which you will learn more about later. You have already learned muscle-grouping, consciously relaxing from head to toe. But when you reach the last part of first stage you will probably find it more helpful to think about relaxing the whole body at once. The contractions seem to be coming in waves now, so it is valuable to think of relaxing the whole body and letting it float up to the peak of a contraction's strength so you can just slip over the top.

TO THE COACH

The floating technique is simply more relaxation. The only difference is that you are talking about the whole body being loose and limp at once. This will be useful as the laboring woman moves into her hardest and fastest work. When coaching her to float up and over a contraction, do not get off the track with talk about floating on clouds or cotton candy or other such images. The symbolism of the wave is very specific. Contractions seem just like waves, building and building and reaching a peak of strength, just as a wave rolls up to a peak and then goes over. The laboring woman can relate very well to this idea of staying limp, floating up to the peak of the contraction, and then slipping over the top to the other side.

You coach this technique much as you have done up to now. Start with the breathing, go to full-body relaxation, urge her to think about locating tension and letting go, use mental imagery, and add phrases like these:

Practice Exercise D: Floating

- Let your whole body sag into the bed and float up and over this contraction. Just keep floating loose and limp.

- Just a little farther now, keep floating, the peak of the contraction is just ahead. Let go and you will slip right up and over the peak and down the other side.

Read this over twice and then do several practice contractions with the book closed, using your own words for all the coaching techniques you have learned. And don't forget the back rub.

chapter thirteen

The Six Needs of a Laboring Woman

It should be clear by now that during the first stage of labor, the pregnant woman's attention is centered on what is happening inside her body. So the labor environment, or what is happening outside the woman's body, is really the responsibility of the coach. Dr. Bradley has identified six needs of the laboring mother. Meeting those needs is really at the heart of the coach's role in the Bradley Method.® As you read through them here you will realize that you already have learned about many of these needs and how to meet them. But remember, every laboring woman needs someone who has taken the trouble to learn as much as she has learned, someone who can remind her of the goal as

she tires and someone to help her help herself. This is why a loving, supportive coach is the very essence of the Bradley Method.®

ONE: **Darkness** and **Solitude**. The laboring woman needs a dark or dimly lit room. Bright lights disturb concentration and she needs one hundred percent concentration on relaxation to work properly with labor. Solitude while the two of you are working together is also important. This means no mothers or mothers-in-law. If children are to be present at birth, this is not the time to have them in the room, except for short visits so they can see that

Mommy is doing fine. Solitude also means no pregnant neighbor from across the street, despite the temptation to show off a bit.

It is very distracting for most women to have observers in the first stage of labor. The laboring woman finds herself wondering what everyone thinks about how she is doing. The coach in turn spends less time thinking about the laboring woman and more time on what the observers think of his coaching. A laboring woman is not performing. She should simply work for herself and her baby. Keeping the room (even a hospital room) dark and keeping observers to a minimum is the coach's responsibility. Whether they are in-laws or hospital personnel this requires tact, but it should not be left to the laboring woman to deal with. As her work gets serious she will have other things to think about.

TWO: **Quiet.** It should be obvious to anyone who has ever concentrated on anything, even reading this book, that noise distracts concentration. At home it is usually not difficult to keep noise under control. Hospitals are understandably noisy places, but fortunately, labor rooms do have doors.

THREE: **Physical Comfort.** Be extremely fussy about the laboring woman's comfort. Make sure she has all the pillows she needs, especially a flat one for under her head so her head and neck are properly aligned with her shoulders. Do not allow as much as a toe to go unsupported; if needed, get another pillow for it. Help her to find the perfect position.

Physical comfort also means the laboring woman should not have a dry mouth. In between contractions she can have sips of water or she can suck on a wet washrag. These are things that must be thought of and made available before her labor really gets going. If she says that she is hot but not to worry about it, do worry about it. Get a window open or whatever is required. If she is cold, get her blankets. She is too busy to fuss a lot, so it is up to you to be a perfectionist.

Also, the coach should remind her to turn over every hour or hour and a half. If she has a favorite side that is okay, but she does need to get off it occasionally to restore circulation. Remind her to go to the bathroom. She will tend to put it off because she is afraid of having a contraction on the way. Usually though, just because she is worrying about it, if she does have a contraction on the way to the bathroom it will be a light one.

Don't leave physical comfort behind at home. Once you are in the hospital or birth center start all over to get everything perfect.

FOUR: **Physical Relaxation.** You already know a lot about physical relaxation. It is different from physical comfort, but relaxation depends upon comfort. Remember, it is the subtle, minor degrees of tension that are the hardest to let go of. Help the laboring woman avoid just holding herself still, that is, lying there looking as if she is relaxed but with all her muscles slightly tensed. Don't bark out orders, but in a sincere concerned voice direct her concentration toward releasing all those slightly flexed muscles everywhere.

The Six Needs of a Laboring Woman **105**

FIVE: **Controlled Breathing.** You already know that panting is a symptom of panic. It is so serious that one anesthesiologist considers it a good reason to medicate women in labor, to prevent rapid breathing and avoid the hyperventilation that tends to follow. His concern is specifically aimed at the untrained mother who is panicky and at the Lamaze-trained mother who has been taught faster-than-normal breathing. This doctor's concern is legitimate, even if his solution is excessive. You know that what is needed is to have the laboring woman *listen* to her breathing to assure the continuation of quiet, rhythmic, abdominal breathing. If the coach is listening to the breathing he will know if she is breathing too fast or holding her breath. The real key is perfect relaxation, because normal breathing is a reflection of good relaxation.

SIX: **Appearance of Sleep and Closed Eyes.** Closed eyes are a guarantee that there will be no visual distractions. The woman who keeps her eyes open is trying to escape from the contraction rather than go with it. The appearance of sleep is your ultimate goal. Of course, the laboring woman is not sleeping. She is thinking and concentrating on what is happening inside her body. She is mentally alert, and this is reflected in a body that is genuinely limp and relaxed, not just still. But to those who do not know what is happening, the woman laboring with the Bradley Method® appears to be sleeping. Nurses often comment upon it. The appearance of sleep is the ultimate goal, one that can be met when all the other needs of the laboring woman have been attended to.

106 *The First Stage of Birth*

TO THE COACH

Coach, you know what the laboring woman does during a contraction, and you know that between contractions she rests mentally. You know what you will be doing during contractions—coaching and rubbing her back if needed—but what do you do between contractions? Unfortunately, you do not fall into a chair and rest. Instead, this time is your opportunity to deal with the six needs or any other problem that comes up.

- Rub her shoulders, if she likes.
- Take care of her dry mouth with a wet washrag, sips of water, or ice chips. Remember, she will be breathing through her mouth during the contraction, so she will feel dry.
- Wipe off her face and forehead with a damp cloth. This is sweaty work for her, and the dampness can be uncomfortable.
- Also, use this time for some of the fun things in labor, like taking pictures.

A Practice Plan

At this point you have a number of very important things to practice, so we have prepared this weekly practice plan.

The Mother's Weekly Practice Plan

- For fifteen minutes every day practice skillful relaxation by yourself. This does not mean taking a nap; that isn't practicing anything. Lie down with the idea that for fifteen minutes you are going to push your brain. Remain mentally alert and think. Of what? Dinner? The color of the crib? No, that is drifting, the opposite of concentration.

  You should think of *observing* your muscles over and over from head to toe. Be aware of your body. Seek out slightly contracted muscles. Look for subtle tension. *Then concentrate on deliberately, consciously releasing it.* And remember to listen to your breathing. Normal, abdominal breathing is conducive to deeper relaxation. For fifteen minutes you will observe and release, constantly concentrating on a deliberately and skillfully limp, loose body.

- If you have been doing your PC contractions faithfully, you should now be ready to go on to the Intermediate PC exercise practice plan. Simply change to flexing to the count of ten. When you reach seven or eight, think about tightening even more. Contract your muscle in this manner at least thirty-six times a day—twelve in the morning, twelve in the afternoon, and twelve at night. Remember to flex deeply.

- Continue to squat, tailor sit, and pelvic rock, do the legs apart exercise and continue to count your protein intake to make sure you are getting eighty to a hundred grams a day.

The Coach's Weekly Practice Plan

- Practice coaching your wife in relaxation and breathing, doing about five practice contractions a night before going to sleep. Check her labor position, listen to the breathing, and rub her back. In between practice contractions think about meeting her other needs—rubbing her shoulders, wiping her brow, and so on. Turn back to Chapter Eleven if you need a refresher in coaching, but soon you should be adding your own words and developing your own style. Talk it over with her to find out what words and images work best.

For coaches who are not husbands:

- Be sure to set up times when you can practice together. You may need to think more about developing familiarity and rapport so you will be comfortable as a team with the laboring woman. Touch is important in coaching. If this is a barrier while you are practicing, work toward both of you feeling at ease as you rub her back and shoulders.

Review Questions
for Both Mother and Coach

Put yourselves through this little test, talking over the answers to the questions and looking back to the right sections if you are not satisfied with your own answers. When the birth gets close you will feel a lot more comfortable if you know what is happening and what needs to be done without having to take time to look it up.

1. What are the three stages of labor?

2. Why is it harmful to lie flat on your back during late pregnancy and labor?

3. What is effacement? What is engagement?

4. What does effacement or engagement tell you about when your labor will start?

5. What are the two keys to learning relaxation as a skill?

6. What is the best lying-down position for labor? What is an alternate position?

7. Have you decided where you will labor? Have you set up the pillows to actually see what it will be like?

8. How do you breathe in labor?

9. What are the four points to coaching the breathing?

10. When coaching a contraction, do you emphasize relaxation or breathing?

11. What happens to the untrained mother's contractions when she has not learned skillful contractions and fights labor?

12. What are the six needs of the laboring woman, as defined by Dr. Bradley?

chapter fourteen

The Emotional Map of Labor

You now know about the physical side of labor, and how to begin coaching it, but you should also realize that your journey to birth is marked by emotional signposts as well. You should realize from the outset that a natural birth experience is more easily attainable if you learn the emotional signposts that go with labor. That's what this chapter is all about. Before we get to the map of emotions, however, remember that no two labors are alike. And as discussed before, one of the crucial differences is time. Just as several people may start a journey with the same map, if one walks, one bicycles, and another drives, they will have vastly different experiences. The person in the car may go

speeding by some sights so quickly he will barely notice them. The walker may pass these sights so slowly that he doesn't see them as distinct milestones. Meanwhile the cyclist moves by all the signposts at a speed that allows him to observe each distinctly.

While we will be giving you a very reliable emotional map of the experience of labor that most people have from beginning to end, you will NOT get to choose the speed at which that experience will occur.

The map we will use as our point of reference is of the so-called *textbook* labor—twelve to fourteen hours. The emotional signposts we will discuss are pretty standard, but the time it takes to progress from one to another is *extremely variable*, and the time is not nearly as important as the signposts themselves are. Beware of paying more attention to the time than you do to the signposts along the way.

By the end of this chapter your goal should be to understand the loose pattern into which the details of your own unique labor experience will fall, so you will be able to tell what is happening along the way.

The First Emotional Signpost: Excitement

If you are going by the textbook, your contractions will start off short and easy, with rest periods of five or possibly more minutes. You could have an hour of this or several hours.

The beginning emotional signpost is elation, excitement, a bit of nervousness, feeling, "Oh, my gosh, today's really the day."

Contractions at this point feel like a hardening or tightening sensation, if you start off slowly and easily like our textbook labor. Your uterus pulls forward and hardens somewhat. You probably do not have any backache during these early contractions. During this time your cervix might dilate to about two centimeters or so.

You feel quite happy and excited; you have been waiting for this day for nine months and maybe longer. This is it at last, you feel with some elation. Of course, you may feel a tiny bit of stage fright too. You feel both eager and anxious.

Self-Help

You really don't have to do much now except keep a relaxed tummy throughout each contraction. Be sure you keep that abdomen hanging loose at all times. This is easiest to do with proper breathing and closed eyes during the contraction, but for heaven's sake, don't climb right into bed if you start off slow and easy. It can get pretty boring at the other end of twelve or fourteen hours!

When you have a labor that starts slow and easy, enjoy it. This is the fun part. Later on you'll be working hard. Just close your eyes, sag your tummy, and breathe with a rhythm during a contraction. Then go on reading, watching TV, or whatever you were doing before.

TO THE COACH: COACHING THE BEGINNING EMOTIONAL SIGNPOST

In the beginning emotional signpost, the woman is happy, excited, elated, nervous. There's often a smile, and when you see that you know she has a long way to go! The more nervous type does not walk around smiling, but it's obvious that she's not in hard labor.

ERICK IN·GRAHAM

34. First emotional signpost: Excitement; today's the day.

What's your coaching job? Well, she's not working hard yet and neither are you. When a contraction starts, she just stops whatever she's doing, sags her tummy, and breathes with a rhythm way down low in the bottom of her abdomen. (Very few women need a back rub when displaying the beginning emotional signpost.)

The coach sets the atmosphere. Encourage her to relax and enjoy this part. A number of couples find they have plenty of time to go out to a favorite restaurant. He has a hearty dinner while she has something light. (Some doctors think light nourishment can be essential to a normal labor and approve of this; others do not.) Go back home and enjoy yourselves. Savor the excitement and help set up an approach, an attitude to this part of labor that you can draw upon later. This is a time to enjoy. Later it will be hard, monotonous work for both of you. This is a time for those silly things. Take a couple of pictures of yourselves. At the time, picture-taking seems so unimportant, but later these may be pictures you'll treasure.

The coach's major job is keeping his wife at home. Don't let her talk you into rushing off to the hospital at this beginning signpost. Most women are convinced that the sooner they get to the hospital the sooner they'll have the baby. This is not true. At this point it can even work the other way around. When she arrives too early, labor has a tendency to disappear on her.

If her labor starts off slow and easy and you dash off to the hospital right away, she may just wind up being hungry, thirsty, poked-at, and interrupted while she labors ten, twelve, or more hours in the hospital. The surest way *not* to have a natural birth is for her to be psychologically beaten down and frustrated by a long stay in a hospital with all its routines and interruptions.

Remember, babies are rarely produced with anything less than hard work. Even speedsters usually work *hard* for at least two or three hours.

Labor is what the word implies: hard work. So please don't go to the hospital when she displays the beginning emotional signpost. Before you ever think about the hospital, she should be so wrapped up in her work that she can no longer be bothered flashing a grin at the camera! If she is talking glibly during contractions or in between them, you're not far along.

The Second Emotional Signpost: Seriousness

A few hours pass by. Now your uterus gets down to serious work, and so do you. And that is exactly what the next emotional signpost is. You are serious. Excitement gives way to concentration. Now when you have contractions you definitely feel a *need* to sit down, or even lie down, and get comfortable. You need to concentrate on some real relaxation and to listen to your breathing.

You do this not merely because you are eager to try things out, but because you must work with the contractions. And if you have a backache, you are serious about getting a back rub.

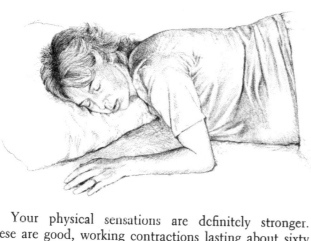

Your physical sensations are definitely stronger. These are good, working contractions lasting about sixty seconds. (Anything less than forty-five seconds just isn't doing much work at getting the cervix open.)

Self-Help

Now, when you feel a contraction, you fully understand the need for total concentration on a limp, sagging, let-go body. You work diligently because you do not want these contractions to get ahead of you. You can feel the long muscle pulling to open the cervix. Now you are working hard, and you will be for the next several hours or more, if you continue to stick to the textbook.

The serious emotional signpost is total absorption in the work and the need to be undistracted. It is a do-not-disturb and get-to-work attitude.

ERICK INGRAHAM

35. Second emotional signpost: The uterus gets serious and so does she.

TO THE COACH:
SERIOUS EMOTIONAL SIGNPOST

She is in total concentration, dedicated to her work. She snaps at you if you distract her or don't rub her back exactly right.

She won't exactly *jump* from the beginning emotional signpost to the next one. She drifts into it. First, she wants the back rub if she has any backache. Then you notice she definitely needs coaching now. She is serious about working with contractions.

Coach, you should become serious too. Clear the way for a smooth, steady course. A few hours go by, her uterus gets *more* serious, and she gets *even* more serious. It is different now. She is totally absorbed. There is determination you may have never seen in her before as she focuses inward and prepares to greet the next contraction with a totally yielding body. It is this intensity, which often takes hours to establish, that I look for in a woman to know she is now *really* into the serious signpost. She no longer jokes and laughs—she's busy. She wants to be ready for each contraction.

She will be doing this for hours (in the textbook labor), so get a good number of these hours of work behind you at home before going to the hospital. Don't make the mistake of dashing off to the hospital the minute you see the serious signpost.

One wise coach of ours spent three or four hours at home with his wife in the beginning emotional signpost. Contractions were five to seven minutes apart. She didn't need coaching at this point.

When they got down to work, her contractions were mostly five minutes apart and were lasting about fifty-five seconds. She seemed to be showing the serious signpost. The husband coached her for a couple of hours, and then the two of them decided that since they had been in labor for six hours, it was time to get off to the hospital. Contractions were still five minutes apart.

But remember—for four of those six hours they really were not working much. They had been really *working* for only two hours.

Fortunately, they decided to take a picture of her all ready to walk out the door. Looking through the camera lens, the husband saw a confident *smile* and suddenly realized they were not as far along as they had thought.

This excellent coach very gently pointed this out. His wife took her coat off, and they worked at home for four more hours. *Then* they went to the hospital.

By then they were well established in the serious emotional signpost, with contractions four minutes apart and lasting sixty to seventy seconds. So, with four hours of easy labor and *six* hours of working labor behind them, they labored in the hospital for *another six hours before they had their baby.*

The coaching job during the serious emotional signpost is to get to work in earnest the minute she does. The laboring woman sets the pace. Take your cue from her. You match the intensity of your coaching to the work she is doing when she is serious. You should definitely not wait for this signpost to do things like pack the bag or take other children to the babysitter.

Get with the back rub, diligently, if she has backache.

Have a soft cloth ready to do it with. Get the ice chips ready and set up a bowl and a wet washrag. Begin coaching her gently in relaxation; remind her about breathing as well.

Don't wait for her to be desperate to start working with her. You don't suddenly turn into a birth team at the end of labor. So rub her back and talk her over and through contractions, concentrating intently on helping her to really let go and let her body sag. *The primary goal at all times is total relaxation.*

As soon as you start to work, run over Dr. Bradley's six needs of the laboring mother in your mind and be sure that all of them are being met.

The Third Emotional Signpost: Self-Doubt

Your uterus now shifts into high gear and speeds by the centimeters from seven to ten. You begin to wonder why you haven't reached your destination yet. You wonder if you are going to reach it. Are you really as far along as you thought? You are nearing the end of first-stage labor. *Your emotional response is self-doubt.*

At this point you will be quite absorbed in yourself and your body so that you may not even notice, but your coach sees that you have become uncertain, indecisive.

You don't know quite what you want to do, and even when asked you cannot say or explain. At this point, if you are asked any question, the most common reply is, "I don't know." You are not sure that you can do this, and may even say so aloud. This is the self-doubt signpost, and it really means that you are almost done.

Like a runner in a race who saves a burst of effort for the last part when the goal is in sight, the uterus will make a final surge to full dilation of the cervix, from six or seven centimeters to a completely open door. It may have taken you ten or twelve hours to get dilated to seven centimeters, and now you are about to go the last three centimeters in a fast half hour or two hours.

At this time your contractions may last seventy, eighty, or even ninety seconds, and your rest periods are usually one and a half to two minutes. (Most women will still get two minutes' rest.) You feel that the contractions are right on top of each other, but nature always does give you a rest.

If you have had backache it is stronger now as first stage is ending, but your coach should take care of most, if not all, of that for you with the back rub. Now, when you need it, that rub is fabulous.

What is happening at this point is just more of the same—contractions. But now your uterine muscles are working at their very best to open the door for you. You really feel that big bag of muscles working good and strong for you with a pulling, stretching or straining sensation around the cervix.

Many women will experience hot and cold flashes during this time and do a lot of burping. A few feel trembly; some actually shake as if they are cold or nervous. This is a physiological reaction which occasionally occurs, and although not seen too often it is within the range of normal. (Telling the laboring woman to relax does not make the shakes go away, but they usually disappear later as the pushing stage begins.)

A few women feel slightly nauseous; most do not. Very rarely will an unmedicated mother vomit. When she does it is often just because she had too much to eat too recently.

Do these physical sensations sound unpleasant or frightening? They are not when you really understand what is happening. Imagine yourself in some other kind of intense physical activity, like running a hundred yards at top speed or carrying a very heavy object upstairs without the chance to put it down along the way. When you stop you will probably feel slightly trembly. You might be quite warm with perspiration or slightly cold and clammy. You could feel nauseous.

Many women do not experience any of these physical sensations in labor, even during the last emotional signpost of first stage. Others feel one or two of them. The important thing to know is that they are within the range of normal.

Self-Help

Relax now, really let go. Listen attentively to your breathing. There is a tendency at this time to breathe too fast. Up to now you have mostly only observed your breath without having to control it; now you may have to think to yourself, "Breathe with a quiet, steady rhythm."

ERICK INGRAHAM

36. Third emotional signpost: Self-doubt, confusion; completely inward focus.

Concentrate, really concentrate on a super-limp, relaxed body. You know how. Permit the powerful sensation of the bag of muscles flexing to be there. It cannot "overpower" you because it is part of you, working to give birth to your baby.

You want to float over each contraction. You *think* your way through each contraction. This will be your hardest work, but it will be the shortest part of your labor.

COACHING THE SELF-DOUBT SIGNPOST

In this last emotional signpost, the laboring woman is uncertain; she doesn't know what she wants to do. She experiences self-doubt. Although to you she looks like she is doing a great job and dealing beautifully with the contractions, she may not be sure about that at all. She looks to you for support; she depends upon you for confidence and reassurance.

Remember, the only hurdle here is an emotional one. Physically what is happening is more of the same, contractions, but closer together and longer than they have been before. This is the very last part of the first stage of labor, the last half hour to two hours. It is the hardest part of the work, but the fastest.

My own first labor was a classic example of the self-doubt signpost. With my first baby (a sixteen-hour labor), we had been in the last sprint of first-stage labor for half an hour when I suddenly realized the contractions were quite close. I raised my head and said in a panicky voice, "They're coming right on top of each other. What do I do now?"

I didn't realize that they had been doing this for some time already. My coach, surprised by my concern, said, "You have been having them like this for the last half hour, and you're doing just great with them."

I really didn't believe him. I said, "Are you sure?"

My coach replied, "I'm positive. You've been doing just fine, just keep doing what you've been doing. You're practically done. You are doing just beautifully. Your concentration is great!"

After I was reassured that way, I said, "Oh, okay," put my head right back on the pillow, shut my eyes and continued as before. In another hour I was completely dilated.

This is what will help the laboring woman now:

Praise her for her efforts (she deserves it);

Encourage her to redouble her efforts (as almost every woman must for this short time);

Progress—let her know she's almost there (at this point she's right around the corner from the birth of her baby).

This is the most blundered and mishandled part of labor.

The laboring woman who needs emotional support and reassurance seems to frighten her medical attendants. Everyone runs for a hypo, a caudal, a spinal, or whatever—and WHAMMO, the rug is pulled out from under her, just when she is so close to giving birth after having worked so long and well with labor. She forgets she has only an hour or two to go.

She often takes the doctor's offer of medication as proof that she must not be doing well and that things are falling apart. Why else would he not praise and encourage her? Also, she can't understand why she feels so wishy-washy, unable to really decide what's best for her.

Here's another example. One of our students had been doing beautifully for ten hours or so. Her doctor came in when she was at eight centimeters (twenty minutes before this mother started pushing) and told her that if she would like to have an anesthetic he would have to give it to her now.

The mother looked up and said quietly and calmly, "Gee, I don't know."

Does that sound like a woman in pain or agony who

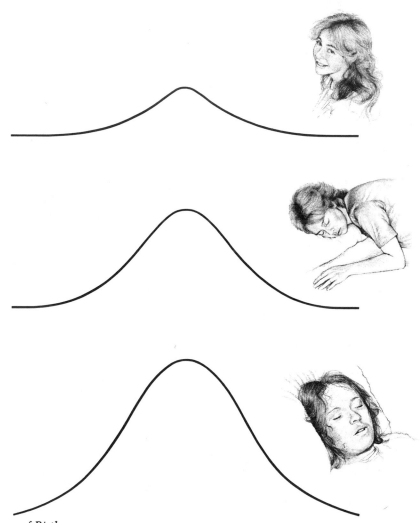

ERICK INGRAHAM

needed to be drugged and delivered? Medication has its uses, but it should *never* take the place of skillful support for the laboring woman. The woman who does not receive skillful support at this point in her labor and ends up with a caudal or a hypo twenty or thirty minutes before she starts pushing may be understandably bitter.

The first time I coached a woman in labor I frankly didn't have the confidence my husband had had when he was coaching me. I had very little experience behind me at the time, and I found myself thinking, "It worked for me, but will it work for other people?"

The woman I was coaching was doing a beautiful job. After she reached seven centimeters she turned to me with a tired look and quietly said, "I can't do this."

I experienced as much of a self-doubt emotional signpost as *she* did. I thought to myself, "Oh, my gosh, it's all over"—I panicked—"what do I do now? Everything's falling apart."

I sort of backed away from her for a few contractions, and then I decided I would have to bluff it and do just as my coach had done for me. I told her she was doing fantastic (and she was), and that she was practically in the birthing room. She sighed and put her head down on the pillow, and continued as well as she had before.

Three contractions later she was pushing. My reaction as her coach was—"Phew! And I almost blew it for her by three measly contractions."

The moral of this story is simple. As a coach you *cannot* also experience a self-doubt emotional signpost. You cannot back away from her. You are the only caring one there who can meet her needs, especially when she is experiencing this self-doubt.

Now, as a more experienced coach, I can hardly wait to see some of the emotions of the self-doubt signpost. I rub my hands together gleefully because then I know we're almost to pushing. I look forward to it!

Speedsters and Putterers

Speedsters skip the beginning emotional signpost along with the accompanying easy contractions. Quick birthers frequently get right down to work—no fooling around

In no time at all, their contractions are three minutes apart and a good sixty seconds long, with a very pronounced serious emotional signpost fast fading into doubt.

Our last fast couple labored about five hours. They started with contractions four minutes apart and forty-five seconds long which went to sixty seconds after just one hour. At the end of three hours the contractions were three minutes apart and eighty seconds, and she was already entering the self-doubt emotional signpost. The husband wisely decided that things were clicking along faster than the textbook, and they left for the hospital.

She was seven centimeters dilated upon arrival and ready to push after one hour in the hospital. Pushing also took one hour. They were there in plenty of time, because the husband was tuned into the emotional signs as well as into the closeness and duration of the contractions.

The putterer has hours of slow, nonserious labor. She is not working hard at all, but can fall into an emotional boobytrap if she is hung up on the passing time. She should simply enjoy the slow, nonserious part and not watch the clock.

It is important for the coach to point out to her that she is not really working hard yet. In fact, it is best not to count this as part of labor at all. Keep things light. It is foolish to get uptight when you're not even working hard. Also keep prepared for a possible twelve to fourteen hours of work after you do get down to business.

But some women can get *emotionally* exhausted by this kind of puttering labor before they even get started working. If the couple isn't focusing on the minutes left before going to the hospital, though, it may not become such a strain. Since the mother is not really even working hard, it is foolish to let this happen. RELAX AND ENJOY.

TO THE COACH: SUMMING UP THE FIRST-STAGE COACHING ROLE

During the beginning emotional signpost take care of whatever is left to get ready. Get your camera set and take pictures. Drop off any other children at the sitter's or in-laws' unless they are invited to be with you at the birth. (In that case you will want to ask your Bradley® teacher about the book *Children at Birth*, by Marjie and Jay Hathaway.) Now settle back and enjoy the excitement.

Do not dash off to the hospital before she has even started to work hard. Encourage her not to jump into bed the minute she starts feeling contractions, but to wait until she feels a need to lie down with contractions. If she starts late in the evening with slow labor, she should go to bed at the usual time to get as much rest as possible.

In the serious emotional signpost, get serious when she does. Coach her in relaxation and breathing. Remind her to go to the bathroom and turn over about every hour and a half. Give a diligent back rub if needed. Have all your props available: soft rubbing rag, wet washrag, ice chips, and so on. Plan to get as much as possible of the work of labor done at home.

Check Dr. Bradley's list of needs of the laboring mother and make sure you are meeting all of them.

One of the doctors we work for has this well figured out. As long as there is nothing unusual going on—no bleeding, nothing protruding from the vagina—he encourages his first-time mothers who live within a reasonable distance from the hospital to leave home when contractions are two or three minutes apart, lasting at least sixty seconds, with a very serious emotional signpost. Second-timers come in when contractions are four minutes apart and sixty seconds long, with a very serious emotional signpost.

It works out well. Most couples arrive when their labor is well under way and finish out anywhere from five to six hours in the hospital. No long, dragging twelve- and fourteen-or-more-hour stays.

When she experiences **the self-doubt emotional sign-**

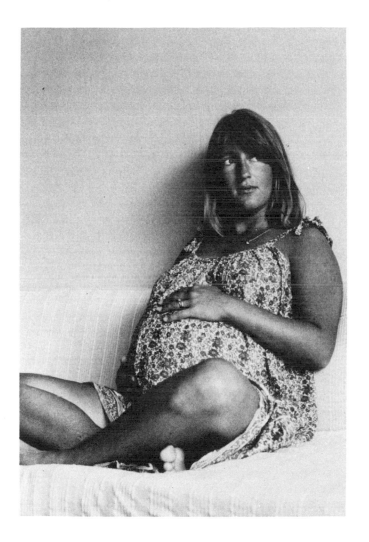

post, you, Coach, cannot. She is not sure she can do this, but you reassure her that she has been doing it all this time, that this is just more of the same thing but closer and longer, and that she is in the home stretch, almost there. Of course, if you are going to a hospital or birthing center, you are there by now.

Continue coaching in relaxation and breathing, rub her back, offer ice chips or sucks on the washrag for her dry mouth, and *praise* her for her efforts, give her *encouragement,* and let her know she's making good *progress.*

She's almost done. Never back away from her. Meet her needs!

How to Use the Emotional Map to Know Where You Are in Labor

The actual amount of dilation is the least reliable guide as to where you are in labor. How far dilated you are is not nearly as important as the emotional signpost, along with how far apart and how long the contractions are. Here's a classic, not at all uncommon example. Ed called me from the hospital at two in the morning. He said, "Susan, look, we've been in labor about fourteen hours, and Sharon is only four centimeters dilated and she says she can't do this anymore. They're about two to three minutes apart. She's really working hard. They're all about seventy seconds."

"Ed," I replied, "I think you'd better get right back there, it sounds like she's almost done."

Ed rushed back to see the baby's face emerging just one half hour later.

It didn't matter that Sharon was only four centimeters dilated. What mattered was *how far apart and how long the contractions were and the very clear self-doubt emotional signpost* she was showing Ed. Sharon was four centimeters, going on crowning. If you look at all three guides, the length and closeness of the contractions together with the emotional signpost, you will know more about where she is than dilation will tell you.

Here's another real example. Judy's contractions were three minutes apart, they were forty-five seconds long, and she was working lightly with them. She went to the hospital right away, thinking that since they were three minutes apart she would be fast. About twelve hours later she gave birth. How could she have known that? By looking at all three guides, not just one. Looking at how close the contractions were she thought she was going to go fast, but if she had also looked at her beginning signpost and the length of the contractions (only forty-five seconds), she would not have been fooled.

How far dilated you are, by itself, does not tell you the story as well as these other guides. Women should hardly be bothered with vaginal exams at all (once or twice during the whole labor is more than enough). No one can say, "Well, you're five centimeters so you will have your baby in five more hours." There is no way to predict the time.

What you almost always can tell is this: If she has been working at labor for hours, and her contractions are two and three minutes apart and lasting sixty to ninety seconds, *and* she has the self-doubt signpost, you can tell her with complete honesty and assurance that she is down to the end of her work. Still—never try to put a time on it, like "twenty more minutes" or "two more hours." If she goes fifteen minutes over the prediction, her will may crumble.

If you simply labor without being bothered by exams, and you feel strong contractions with hours ticking by and things getting closer together, you just naturally have a picture of steadily making progress—and of course you are.

chapter fifteen

Labor

There are ten different ways the first stage of your labor may begin. We will look at all of them before continuing with a final rehearsal of the whole process.

Opening Scene #1:   Textbook

You start with contractions several minutes apart. They are thirty-five to forty seconds long. You are having a textbook labor and it will last about fourteen hours.

The first emotional signpost is obvious to both of you. Your work does not begin for three or four hours and when it does, your excellent coach does not rush you off to the hospital the minute the working part begins, but settles you down for several hours of work at home.

The two of you leave for the hospital after getting a good number of hours of *working* labor behind you at home. You are extremely well established in the second emotional signpost and have been for a while before leaving. You arrive at the hospital and (of course, you don't know this) it will be five hours before you have the baby.

Opening Scene #2:   Mucous Plug

You notice the mucous plug coming out, either in little parts at a time or the whole thing at once. There is always an opening in the cervix, not much wider than a pencil, (called the cervical canal) and it is this canal that is stopped up with the mucous plug. It's about two inches long, naturally, since the cervix is about two inches long.

The plug consists of grayish white matter, sometimes slightly blood-tinged. The little amount of blood that may accompany it is from tiny blood vessels on the surface of the cervical canal. These little vessels are delicate and may bleed a bit as the plug comes away. It does not hurt. Parts or all of the plug may come out while you are on the toilet and so you may not notice it.

Please do not get all excited if you see some of the plug. *It is the most unreliable of all the signs.* I passed parts of the plug two weeks before labor with my first child, didn't notice it with the second, and noticed it a few hours after early labor contractions began with the third.

In other words, it's nice to know what it is, but if it puts you on the ceiling with excitement you're apt to be disappointed.

Opening Scene #3:   Water Breaking

Your bag of water breaks. Of course you are in the grocery store with a cart full of groceries, and you hear a distinct pop like a balloon popping. Water, water, everywhere!

Your contractions may start immediately or within several hours. Only rarely will a woman not start contractions soon after her water bag breaks. By the way, you will not have a "dry labor," since you constantly manufacture amniotic fluid. If labor still has not started after twenty-four to forty-eight hours (depending on the individual doctor's views), the doctor will probably induce labor.

Induction means forcing labor to start. This is rarely necessary as long as the woman is close to term and allowed a forty-eight hour span to start on her own. Unfortu-nately, one of the latest fads in obstetrics is to insist that a woman have her baby within twelve hours after her water bag breaks. For a more detailed discussion of this see Chapter Twenty-two.

Opening Scene #4:   False Alarm

You start with contractions several minutes apart as in the textbook labor. They are a mere thirty-five seconds long. You are not really working with them, but you are aware of them. However, instead of getting closer together and stronger, they get further apart and weaker. Things really never take off.

Real labor starts in a week or so. You are not upset by this because you realize that labor really gets going when you and your baby are ready. You do not bug the doctor by telling him how anxious you are to have the baby.

Opening Scene #5:   The Speedster

You start labor with contractions sixty seconds long and four minutes apart. You completely skip the first emotional signpost because your uterus starts right off to work. You are going to have a five-hour labor!

You stay home for two and a half hours. Your coach has noticed that your contractions are long (sixty to seventy seconds to the peak) and are now three minutes apart.

Your second emotional signpost is very serious and almost beginning to look a bit like the third signpost. Your coach knows what's going on or at least strongly suspects, and you go to the hospital. He was right, because you have only two and a half hours to go.

Opening Scene #6: The Puzzler

You start with contractions close together, three minutes apart but a mere twenty to thirty seconds long. You think you may turn into a fast labor at this point, but you don't really know that because although your contractions are close, they are not hard-working. *Fast labors usually work very hard!*

If you remember that anything less than forty-five seconds is nothing to get excited about, then you won't blow it and dash off to the hospital. You could have a very typical, textbook length of labor if it takes you several hours to work up to good working contractions of sixty seconds.

Opening Scene #7: Leaking

You start with the bag of water leaking, a little trickle (a teaspoon or two), three or four times a day. Not too much but enough to make you notice and wonder what's going on. (I'm definitely not talking about *gushes* of water, just an occasional slight leaking.)

Doctors have different opinions on what to do about this, and it's important to find out what your doctor says. A doctor who is calm about it and tells the woman to just continue as normal and let him know if anything changes seems to get the best results.

Very often a slight leak will seem to seal over and the pregnancy will continue undisturbed until the baby is ready and you simply go into labor. Women do much better when a slight leak is handled this way, rather than forcing labor to start now with drugs to make the uterus contract. Do not douche, do not insert a tampon, don't put anything into the vagina.

Opening Scene #8: The Putterer

Your labor starts with contractions only thirty to thirty-five seconds long. They are several to ten minutes apart. That's pretty far. Your labor may last about twenty-two hours or more and we hope that you decide to stay home for fifteen of those hours.

You feel confident about staying home, because you and your husband saw nothing but the first emotional signpost for the first nine hours of labor. It was obvious that you were not hard at work during this time.

You may have been lying down for some of this time, but only because it was late in the evening or you were simply tired of fooling around doing other things, not out of a *need* to work with labor yet.

You and your coach finally see the second emotional signpost and decide to get as much as possible of the working part of labor behind you at home. You do this for seven hours and arrive at the hospital with contractions sixty seconds long and four to five minutes apart (still on the early side).

You're certainly glad that you didn't come any earlier and that you understood the emotional signposts to guide you, because you find that you have eight hours to go in the hospital.

Opening Scene #9: Backache Only

You start with a backache. It gets stronger. It's recurring. It has a peak of strength, after which it drops off and several minutes go by before you experience it again. You start timing, and sure enough this is the real thing. A *few* women experience contractions only as a backache. If it is strong enough to stop your conversation and require that you lie down, plus it comes and goes and gets more frequent and stronger, then you should realize what's happening.

Opening Scene #10:   Any Minute Now

I commonly have students walking around who are four and five centimeters dilated. They are not in labor. Sometimes they are like that for three or four weeks. This is usually discovered on a routine office visit, and invariably the woman is informed that she is going to start labor any minute and certainly won't make it through the weekend.

The woman inevitably goes home emotionally very high and awaits her first contraction. Monday morning rolls around and she is still waiting. The next Monday morning she is still waiting. Weekends come and go and finally she is emotionally frazzled from all the foolish predictions.

Although this should be *the easiest possible labor*, it often ends up a disaster. Everything possible is done to get labor started. The woman is kept emotionally tense for the "any minute now" occurrence.

How foolish. This has to be the easiest possible way to dilate four and five centimeters and not even be aware of it. Most women have to work to dilate that far! When you force labor to start before it is ready, you are asking for a hard labor. To turn this type of extra-easy first stage into an extra hard one is the silliest thing you can do.

Be patient. Don't look for labor to start any second. You'll reach a point where you will *feel* contractions and have to get to work. Then, and only then, will you know what day will be your baby's birthday. This is not at all uncommon.

When you do start, chances are very great that you will bypass the first signpost and get right to work! Although you generally tend to have a shorter first stage, there is no consistent effect on second stage. It too may zip along or it may just as easily take a couple of hours.

TO THE COACH

More people get to the hospital way too soon rather than too late.

The surest way *not* to have a natural birth is to be psychologically beaten down and frustrated by a long stay in the hospital with all its routines and disturbances. Hospital personnel are accustomed to medicated mothers; they focus on complications, and these vibes come across with devastating effect on the laboring mother.

Coach, don't get a chip on your shoulder toward the hospital staff, though. They do not mean to hinder you. Certainly, they are not trying to make things difficult. You *must* develop good rapport with the staff. Never generate hostility because the laboring woman simply cannot relax in a hostile environment. There is no malice in hospital routines, but the fewer hours you are there the better your labor will go.

A Textbook Run-Through: The First Stage

Now that we've covered all the various ways your labor might begin, let's erase all that and start at the beginning of a *textbook labor* for our rehearsal so you will have an opportunity to think about and try out everything.

The pieces of the puzzle for first stage all fall together for you now. It is important that the two of you find a time when you can go through this entire section from beginning to end like a drill as well as adding Master Exercise II to your nightly practice routine.

You are ready for this rehearsal if you have carefully studied and put thought into the six needs of the laboring mother. You must know how to coach relaxation, breathing, and mental imagery. If needed, re-read some of the coaching exercises before starting the rehearsal.

Do not skip over anything in this rehearsal thinking you know it well enough already. If you do this rehearsal carefully and thoroughly, you'll have a good feel for labor. *Do it now*—tomorrow may be too late to practice!

MASTER EXERCISE II

Final Rehearsal of the First Stage

Your first contraction

You're standing at the sink doing dishes and you have your first contraction. Very minor really, only forty seconds long. You just sag your tummy extremely and breathe with a steady, slow rhythm way down low in your abdomen. *Right now, at the beginning, think of relaxing your tummy extremely to avoid a crampy sensation.* Try it now in a sitting or standing position. Your coach can time a pretend contraction.

Your contraction at this point: forty seconds long

Six to seven minutes have passed, and you have another contraction. Again, you simply sag your tummy extremely and breathe with a steady rhythm way down low.

Your contraction at this point: thirty-five seconds long

Anything from two to three hours to several hours has gone by now. You say, "I'm getting uncomfortable trying to stand or sit up with these. I really need to lie down with them." *Don't lie down until you have to.* Nothing is more boring than lying down concentrating for more hours than necessary. This is the beginning of the second emotional signpost.

Contraction begins: sixty seconds long, five minutes apart

COACH: Coach her from head to toe in relaxation and in quiet, relaxed abdominal breathing (see Chapter Eleven for review). Coach her in mental imagery (see Chapter Twelve for review). Rub her back if there is any backache at all. You should be serious and alert. Don't let tension build up. Be ahead of things.

Another contraction
COACH: Repeat the sequence above.

In between contractions
COACH: Offer her a wet washrag to take care of the dry mouth; wipe off her brow and the back of her neck, if she lets you. It can be nice too to have sweaty palms wiped. Continue to rub her shoulders in between contractions. Talk to her about relaxing. Do not let tension build up anywhere.

Another one-minute contraction
COACH: Coach her in everything.

In between contractions
COACH: About every hour and a half, remind her to go to the bathroom, and encourage her to turn over onto her other side.

(A contraction is not your enemy. It is just your own big bag of muscles flexing for you, to get the door open. As you feel the flex, think of opening and opening.)

Another contraction begins
Oops, no, it dwindled away before it got started.

Contraction begins: sixty seconds long, five minutes apart
Practice through it with your coach. Do not skip any practice contractions.

Contraction begins: sixty seconds long, four minutes apart
On this practice contraction, we are going to do a little play-acting and pretend that a contraction is starting to get away from you. You don't think you can relax, you tighten up a bit, maybe clench your hand, open your eyes, contract your tummy muscles slightly, and breathe rapidly. Respond to your coach *only* after he has coached you firmly!

COACH: Firm coaching does not mean harsh coaching, and, of course, you never criticize the laboring mother. Never tell her, "No, you're doing it all wrong!" If you say something like that her whole body will immediately go "twang" with tension. This is not helpful. Instead, look for tension, listen for frantic breathing. Give her specific coaching in whatever she needs help with, and continue to give it in an absolutely confident, warm, strong voice.

Many women never get off the track with a single contraction. Others lose one or two. If they do, it's not a big deal. It helps for both of you to remember what happens if she tightens up on a contraction. She just makes it last twice as long, and it's very painful for her to work against.

Breathing is the key to control: calm, normal breathing. The coach should jump on the breathing first because it's the simplest way to get her back on the track. It calms her immediately to slow her breathing down and get rhythmical once again, and encourages her that she indeed is able to respond and to help herself. But breathing is not enough. Breathing is the key to control, but *not* to comfort!

Relaxation is the key to comfort! Immediately after getting the breathing rhythm established (which occurs quickly simply by listening to slow it down), go right on to firm relaxation coaching.

Contraction begins: seventy seconds long, one and a half minutes apart

COACH: Use floating (whole-body) relaxation and mental imagery. Watch her breathing. Keep up the back rub.

In between contractions

COACH: use PEP (praise, encouragement, and assurance of progress). Give her the washrag or ice chips to suck on, and rub her shoulders.

Contraction begins: ninety seconds long

Some women feel as if they have to move their bowels as they feel the baby moving downward now and pressing against the rectum. If you do feel this at this point in the labor, it's the baby, and you will be pushing soon now.

Contraction begins: ninety seconds long

You are just now told that you are completely dilated. Ten centimeters. WHEW! You both feel a mixture of relief, delight, apprehension, and, of course, success.

This exercise should become second nature to you both. Plan to repeat it once a night from now until the birth, right after reviewing Master Exercise I on breathing and relaxation.

On to the Hospital or Birthing Center

If you're going to a hospital or birthing center, it's time to go when contractions are sixty seconds long and three minutes apart. (But for second-timers, the contractions should be sixty seconds long and four minutes apart as second-timers do sometimes tend to move along faster than first-timers from this point on.) Note this interruption when you practice Master Exercise II and read the sequence that follows so that you are both familiar with the disturbance and routine of getting to the hospital, and the need to get settled and back on the track with the contraction series.

Getting to the Hospital. When you decide it's time to go, it usually is a good idea to call the hospital and ask them to "pull your charts," so there will be no delay when you arrive. The coach should put everything in the car except the pillows. Run back and coach her through one more contraction, and then go to the car with your pillows.

What if she has a contraction on the way to the car? (This may have happened during a walk to the bathroom too.) The most comfortable thing is for the woman to put her arms around her coach's neck and simply slump against his body. If his hands are free he can even rub her back this way as he talks her through a contraction that will often be a short or light one. Then, on to the waiting car.

Get her as comfortable as possible in the car. We suggest she sit up with a pillow on her lap supporting her arms. What if she has a contraction? Usually this is no problem. Most women get "anxious" going to a hospital

37. Contraction while standing. Let your coach support your weight while you relax and breathe normally.

and start pumping adrenalin. This negates the hormone contracting the uterus, sufficiently impeding it so that the contractions are greatly reduced in strength or may stop altogether until she is in the hospital and settled down again. (If she is such a relaxed lady that her contractions continue in strength, then we're not going to worry about her at all.)

The coach should coach as he drives, keeping eyes on the road and hands on the wheel. The most helpful thing the coach can do is to drive slowly and carefully, no sudden stops, jerky starts or rough corners. You don't want to arrive at the hospital with an irritated teammate.

When you arrive at the hospital. You should have filled out all forms ahead of time so that you can just walk right in, sign your name, and get gowned up. This is very important to handle in advance. The red tape can easily take an hour otherwise.

When you first arrive at the hospital you may be examined before being admitted to determine if you are really in labor. If your coach has done his job, however, there shouldn't be much doubt about that.

Usually your blood pressure is checked, the baby's heartbeat is listened to, your pulse is taken. You may be asked to give a urine specimen, and be given a hospital gown to put on.

Some modern hospitals let the mother wear her own gown if it is short. A mother who has done this usually feels much better about it. Somehow she feels she's retaining her own identity this way, rather than becoming another cog on an assembly line. Her attitude toward the hospital in general seems to improve too.

Some doctors are still ordering "preps," although, for-

ERICK INGRAHAM

tunately, we find more and more doctors are abandoning this primitive initiation rite with natural-childbirth couples. **A prep** usually consists of a pubic hair shave and an enema. For more about "preps" see Chapter Twenty-three.

If you do have an enema, take your time and expel all of it before jumping back into bed. Otherwise, it can cause considerable discomfort. It may take fifteen or twenty minutes to do this. Be prepared for very strong contractions temporarily, until you are settled down once again.

Some hospitals still separate husband and wife for the prep. Coach, be sure that once you are reunited you get your wife back in stride with labor. *You alone are responsible for providing a warm, loving atmosphere for your wife to labor in. It is your very own specialty. Surround her with love and coach her diligently.*

Now, be sure to get back into the proper side position or, if she prefers, a sitting position.

If you have been working away for hours at home and you arrive at the hospital to find that you are even three centimeters dilated, that's terrific. That's almost halfway to seven, and dilation usually goes slowly only up to seven. Once you get to seven or eight centimeters you very often go the rest of the way in one-half hour to two hours.

A couple of hours go by, and you are now five centimeters dilated. Another hour goes by. You are again examined and told you are still five centimeters. You should never get discouraged if you SEEM to be stuck somewhere. When progress doesn't show up in centimeters, then you are making progress in another way if you are still having contractions requiring diligent work. Maybe the baby has dropped lower or you will jump a couple of centimeters all at once, very soon. If you were not being examined you would simply picture yourself making steady progress as your contractions get closer together and stronger, but since you are being examined it can be discouraging not to make progress in steady increments.

TO THE COACH: THE PRACTICAL SIDE

A well-meaning nurse walks in while you are coaching in the middle of a contraction, with a cheery "Hello." Your wife is the one having the baby and is the most important person during that contraction. Keep coaching. The nurse will realize that you take your work seriously and will respect your intentions. After the contraction be sure you show appreciation for her sensitivity and thank her for waiting for the contraction to end. It is up to you to create good communication and good will with the staff.

A couple of hours have gone by and you are now six or seven centimeters dilated. You are now seeing the third emotional signpost—*self-doubt*. She is really not sure she can do this. Remember Praise, Encouragement, Progress.

Step up your coaching now. Coach firmly in relaxation. Start using the floating technique or whole-body relaxation instead of simple muscle-grouping.

You are nearing the end of the first stage. Soon you will start pushing.

part III

The Second Stage of Birth

chapter sixteen

Pushing

In the last chapter we completed the first stage of labor: the cervix was open all the way. Now we will look at the next stage: pushing the baby out. The first stage was the major part of your labor. Now comes the exciting part. It took determination to stay limp and use skilled relaxation techniques during first-stage contractions. Now the second stage will be the exact opposite, both emotionally and physically. Instead of in-depth relaxation, this stage takes active physical effort. Pushing can be fun when you know what you are doing.

One of our students compared the urge to push to an undeniable need to sneeze. Your body just takes over. *You should know, however, that there are varying degrees of this urge to push. Some mothers feel it quite strongly, while others feel it only moderately and some don't feel it at all.* We will look at the ways second stage can begin in a later chapter.

At the end of the first stage your contractions will be close, about two minutes apart. Now, in the pushing stage where you will be exerting a lot of energy and effort, nature very kindly gives you more resting time. You actually get three to four minutes between pushing contractions. The exception is the woman who has a fast pushing stage. She does not need, and doesn't get, the longer resting periods between contractions. Once again, you will see how marvelously the body works for each individual.

Let's quickly review what is happening physically when you finally get to push. Since the cervix is open, the major action of the uterus now is the top moving down on the baby with each contraction to push him out of there. The uterus pushes, you increase the force by pushing with it, and you move the baby down the birth canal. Then the uterus rests, you rest, and the baby slides back a bit. This enables your soft tissues to draw back to their regular position and get ready for another downward push, rather than being pulled continuously downward and pinched or torn. Again, your body works in an intricately coordinated manner.

How long will the pushing stage take? With your first baby you usually push for some time before even seeing some head. You may push for, say, half an hour to an hour and a half and not see or feel any of the progress you are making. Finally, you see some of the head. First, "a dime's worth," then "a quarter's worth," and so on. The head appears just when you were thinking you really were not getting anywhere at all, so it is a needed and exciting boost. After a good number of pushes you work your baby past the coccyx bone (the tip of your spine) and under the pubic arch, so he no longer slides back between pushes. *Now things go much faster.* Each woman is different, and the pushing stage may take anywhere from a very fast half hour to an average two to three hours to a long four or five hours.

If you are a first-timer and giving birth in the hospital, you usually go into the delivery room with the head beginning to show. Second-timers usually go into the delivery room as soon as they are completely dilated, with or without any head showing at the outlet. Best of all, of course, are those hospitals where under normal conditions mothers give birth in the labor bed in the labor room and never go into the delivery room at all.

Once the head is clearly visible and the baby is not sliding back, things go very fast, and it is important not to let fear or panic detract from your enjoyment of birth. Don't get distracted. There will only be a few moments like this in your entire lifetime. Watch for the crowning sensation when your bottom feels numb and tingly. You will begin to feel your vaginal lips opening for your baby. You feel the stretching sensation momentarily. It may only take a few contractions after crowning and then your baby's head will be out.

Once the head is out, you usually have to give just a little grunt-push and the body wriggles right out. If you have not had a routine episiotomy or a tear, there will be little blood with the birth of your baby. There may be a lot of wetness from the bag of water, but little blood. People not used to natural birth are often surprised at this. Of course, later when the placenta comes out there can be a gush or two of blood.

Second-timers usually do not push as long before some head appears at the outlet, and the period when the baby moves forward and slides back is also usually shorter. Since the vaginal barrel has been stretched once, it simply stretches faster the second time. *But this is not a promise, since the length of the pushing stage can vary with the baby's position.*

The Pushing Position

The pushing position is actually a full squat, except that you are tipped back on your bottom to make it a sitting squat. Squatting is the best position for birth since the diameter of the pelvic outlet increases by as much as one and a half centimeters when the legs are flexed, making the birth easier.[1] This is quite a bit more room. You lose this extra space if you are on a delivery table with your legs up in the air in stirrups instead of flexed back against your chest in the squat position.

Look at pictures 38, 39 and 40 as we examine the sitting-squat position in detail. The bed or pillows are set so your back is propped up at a forty-five-degree angle. Labor beds in hospitals will crank up to this position. Your legs should be pulled back toward your chest by inserting your arms under your legs so the inside of the elbow and the inside of the knee are as close as possible, bringing the knees back all the way to the armpits. This is quite important if you want to imitate a squat and have the extra room in the pelvic outlet. (Sometimes it helps for the coach to hold one leg while the woman holds the other.) Your chin should be pointed down toward your chest or there may be a tendency to arch your back. (But, coach, do not hold her head down.)

Before going any further, try this position. The coach should check all the points. There may be some grumbling about the squashy feeling a pregnant woman gets in this

38. The sitting-squat position for pushing. Notice the angle of the back and the firm support.

39.

40. Sometimes it helps for the coach to hold one leg.

position. Actually, that is part of the benefit. Because the diaphragm is right against the top of the uterus, just taking a deep breath in this position puts pressure in the right place on top of the baby. When it is the real thing, however, you will feel a little less crowded inside because your baby will have dropped a bit into the birth canal. Right now, while you are practicing, your baby's navel is probably about where yours is, but once he has dropped into the birth canal his feet will be about even with your navel, so you will have more room.

If you are really quite uncomfortable while trying this position, check your angle. (See picture 41.) One of the most common errors is to sit too high, say at a sixty or seventy-five degree angle from the floor or bed. Try rocking a little further back. Your coach should check you from the side to help you get a good forty-five-degree angle. But remember that any lower than forty-five degrees is dangerous because it puts too much pressure on the large blood vessel behind the uterus. Also, if you find it quite uncomfortable to slip your arms under your legs, an acceptable alternate is to wrap your arms around the outside of your flexed knees so the knee rests against the inside of your elbow. This puts a lot of strain on your arms, though, and can tire you out more quickly.

Coach, be sure that she lifts her legs gently back toward herself. Do not push her down toward her legs. Look at picture 42 for a common mistake that is easily avoided. She should bring her legs back to her chest, not her torso down to meet her legs.

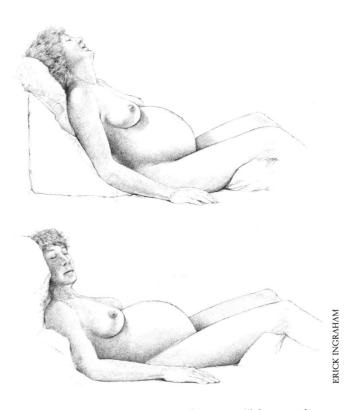

ERICK INGRAHAM

41. Top: Right.   This woman is at the correct 45-degree angle. Bottom: Wrong.   This woman's bed may be rolled up to a 45-degree angle but the woman's back is not. After pushing for a while you will want to check for this common error.

ERICK INGRAHAM

42. Top: Right. This mother brings her legs back to her. This is just like being in a full squat, but she is tipped back in a sitting position. Bottom: Wrong. Do not push her down to her legs. It is too compressed.

Breathing in the Pushing Stage

Now that you have tried the position, let's learn the breathing that will go with pushing. You will still be having contractions which start off slowly and build to a peak of strength. They work very well for you, with the uterus pushing down on your baby. When these contractions are just beginning, you certainly don't want to gulp a quick breath of air and hold it for several seconds, nor do you want to waste your efforts on the early part of the contraction. Instead, you should wait for these contractions to really get under way. Then you can put your best efforts behind them when your uterine muscles are also doing their most concentrated work.

How do you do this? Do you need a stopwatch to wait for the right amount of time to go by? No, nothing so complicated. You simply wait for the contraction to begin, then take a deep breath (like someone getting ready to swim under water) and let it all out without pushing. Then, take a second deep breath—just fill your chest and abdomen and exhale completely, still without pushing. Now, take a third deep breath. As you do, lift your legs *slowly* and *gently* back to the pushing position you have learned. This third breath is the one you will hold while you push down because by this time your uterus has really started to work. So you will be putting your best pushing effort behind the uterine muscles' best effort.

You will push as long as you comfortably can. When

you can no longer hold your breath, put your head back to open up your throat, exhale completely and take one more deep full breath. Now put your head back down toward your chest and push with this fourth breath as long as you can. Your contraction will now be over. The muscles have stopped to rest and you can too.

Perhaps you are wondering what to do if the contraction isn't over. This is not a problem because it simply does not feel good to lie back and do nothing during a pushing contraction. And since it does feel good to push with a pushing contraction, if it is still there you will get right back up in the pushing position with another breath and push. It is quite rare, though, to have a contraction that lasts longer than the four breaths. In three births, I have only had one contraction that was still working strongly when I quit pushing, and, of course, I responded automatically.

Sometimes a woman will look up after she has completed the four breaths of the pushing cycle and say, "Is it still there? Should I keep on pushing?" The best advice is to simply lie back and relax. This pushing technique will get you all the way through most contractions, and if it doesn't with one or two, you will also respond automatically and resume pushing. Instead this question tells you something important. If a woman has to *ask* if the pushing contraction is still there, it means *she can't even feel the contraction as long as she is pushing with it.* It hurts to do nothing during a pushing contraction. It feels good to do what the body is telling you to do.

Coaching the Pushing Stage

Of course, you knew the coach had an important role to play in the pushing stage as well. It starts with setting up the physical arrangements that will make her comfortable in this stage, like getting enough plump pillows and more ice chips, and continues into helping to set the psychological mood. And the coach will help talk the pregnant woman through the activity of this stage as he helped talk her through the relaxation of the last. The important thing to remember about the pushing stage is *not* to tell her to inhale, exhale, since you cannot know when one breath is done and another is needed, but to encourage her to take the next breath when she is ready. Now, read the following practice over once or twice and then set the book aside and try to repeat it in your own words before we try the actual exercise:

MASTER EXERCISE III

Pushing Contractions

As the contraction begins.

- Take your first deep breath, calmly and slowly. Everything is still relaxed and your arms and legs are still resting on the bed. Don't try to hold this breath.

- Now, when you are ready, take your second deep breath, calmly. There is no hurry. Fill your abdomen and chest completely and then exhale completely. Don't try to hold it. Just fill your lungs with air like a swimmer getting ready to plunge under water.

- Now, whenever you are ready, take a third deep breath and hold this one. As you do, gently lift your legs back to your chest, put your chin somewhat toward your chest, and push. Good.

- Now hold that breath as long as you comfortably can. Remember, your whole body is relaxed except for that breath of air pushing down on the top of your uterus. Remember, your legs are relaxed and apart. Concentrate on a loose, open vaginal barrel. Relaxed legs and a relaxed PC muscle go together. Push, down and out.

- Hold that breath as long as you comfortably can. You don't have to be a hero, but hold it as long as you can. Great. Now, when you are done with that breath put your head all the way back, open your throat, let the old, stale air out, and take another deep, full breath. No hurry, just take that fourth breath calmly and put your chin back down on your chest and push.

- Usually this fourth breath is the one that really moves the baby down and out. You are going to move the baby down and then he is going to slide back a little, so you want to really move him as much as you can with this push. Great. Concentrate on a loose, relaxed opening and push with your energy directed downward toward the pelvic floor.

- You are really doing great now. You will have that baby in your arms in no time at all. Nice, steady, even pressure. Down and out. Keep holding as long as you can. Good strong pressure.

As the contraction ends.

- Now put your feet back down on the bed with your heels close to your bottom. Let your arms hang limp at your sides. Relax your head back onto the pillow and relax deeply between contractions. You deserve it. You are really doing wonderfully.

Plan to practice this exercise a couple of times a week.

In between contractions.

Coach, make sure she relaxes out of the pushing position. Give her praise and encouragement, and note her progress (PEP). Wipe her off if she is sweaty. Have a clean damp rag or ice chips near by for her to suck on. Rub her shoulders.

Now, once you have that down in your own words, try a few practice pushing contractions. Please, no real pushing during practice contractions; just work on the position, holding your breath, and the coaching. Start with the woman in a contour-chair position with arms and legs relaxed and heels close to her bottom. This is important to avoid a jerky, over-energetic motion as you go into the pushing position. The woman sets the pace with her breathing, but the coach encourages her to take the first two breaths and hold the second two as long as she comfortably can.

TO THE COACH

Here are some things to watch for as she goes into the pushing position. Be sure she is not clasping her hands together under her legs (that would keep her legs together and restrict the opening). Watch that she is not holding her hands in fists. Make sure she is not hunching her shoulders or arching her feet back. Every part of her that is not part of the pushing process should be relaxed. And make sure she is not puffing up her cheeks and turning red in the face. It is better for her to take a deep breath and hold it by closing her throat than by merely keeping her mouth full of air. Her face should be relaxed; a wrinkled brow won't help get the baby out. All this takes is practice and you to remind her.

If there is a mirror mounted where you can watch during contractions, you will see progress with each and every contraction. (Often before any of the head is visible, you will be able to see the area around her vagina balloon out with each push, showing you how effective each push is.)

1. Take your first deep breath calmly and let it all out.

2. Take your second breath whenever you're ready, relaxing completely as you exhale.

ERICK INGRAHAM

3. As you take your third breath you gently lift your legs back to you, chin toward the chest. This breath you hold and begin to push as long as you comfortably can.

4. When you feel the need to, lift your chin, exhaling completely, and take just one more calm breath, chin once again toward the chest. Push downward and outward as you relax your legs and your bottom.

5. Think of pushing downward and outward. Relax your face and shoulders as you let all the energy go downward.

ERICK INGRAHAM

6. Rest now; the contraction is gone. Let your legs go and relax deeply.

The Full Squat

You may be wondering about using the full-squat position to push your baby out. Actually, this is the ideal position. It is what we are copying in the sitting squat. We use the sitting variation only because for most women in our culture, who are not used to squatting (or hunkering down, as it is sometimes called) for long periods, the sitting squat is more comfortable. But if you do a lot of squatting during your pregnancy and find it comfortable, you may want to use it for birthing. If you wish you can always try it for a

while and then use the sitting squat if you get tired. Or you may start with the sitting squat and go on to the full squat later in the pushing stage. The important thing is to talk over what you intend to do with your birth attendant and your coach so that you will not be pressured into a position that you don't want, something we will discuss in the next chapter.

It is not impossible to squat on a bed—as long as it is quite firm—but it is much easier to do on the floor. If you are birthing in a hospital and you have decided to use the full-squat position, you will need to bring your own mat and probably your own extra-firm, large pillows. (A triangular pillow is best, if you can find one.) Use the wall as a backrest and sit almost bolt upright with your heels

Dave and Debby doing a full squat instead of a sitting squat.

planted quite close to your body. Your coach will need to be in front of you, kneeling, tailor sitting, or squatting himself so he is quite close but does not block you as you come up into the full squat.

As the contraction begins, take your first two breaths while still sitting back against the wall on your pillows. You should put your arms around the coach's neck, intertwining your hands lightly behind him. The coach's arm should be around you under your armpits. As you take your third breath, your coach should lean back smoothly and help you rock forward with your heels as a pivot until your feet are flat on the floor. The coach continues to support you throughout the contraction, bringing his hands together behind you. As in the sitting squat, you push through the third breath, concentrating on a loose, relaxed opening, and then take a fourth breath and continue to push. When the contraction is done, your coach leans forward slightly and helps you to rock back on your heels until you are again in the sitting position against the wall and pillows. Your feet should be just about where they started. It is essential that you practice this motion on the floor with the pillows you will use until it is smooth. If you can't keep a good sitting-up position, the movement to the squat becomes a great, awkward commotion that is best avoided.

The full squat has some amazing advantages. You would be surprised to see how efficiently all the amniotic fluid drains out of the baby's mouth and nose when the mother is squatting and the baby's head first emerges. As she is pushing the head out, the mother can also move her pelvis more easily by tipping it back a bit as she wishes.

Mothers whose babies come out looking up instead of down often need to tilt their pelvis a bit, and in the squat it is easier to do this. I have seen a number of women birth in the full squat even in hospitals. Often they say they feel more centered and in better control of what is happening. Since they are physically and mentally focused inward it seems harder for others to distract or interfere with them.

The Emotional Map of the Pushing Stage

This is simple. In the average pushing stage you will probably see all three emotional signposts that occurred in the first stage of labor repeating themselves. She will start off with beginning excitement. She will again be chatty and alert between contractions. Something new is happening, and best of all, she gets to *do* things, not just relax deeply. Some birth attendants (particularly in hospitals) have time limits on pushing and begin to count from the first pushing contraction. But others know not to count this first emotional signpost of the second stage as part of the true pushing stage. One experienced midwife, quoted in Barbara Katz Rothman's good book, *In Labor: Women and Power in the Birthplace*, says, "I start counting when the woman begins to push and push in a directed manner, really bearing down."[2]

This is the beginning of the serious emotional signpost of second stage. The woman and the coach have gotten over the first few trial-and-error pushes, a pattern is established, and the pushing begins in earnest. The woman doesn't want to chat so much now, and the serious signpost gets progressively deeper as time goes by.

The self-doubt emotional signpost appears just before or sometimes just as the head begins to show at the perineum. As in the first stage of labor, this self-doubt is a normal progression that comes along as the stage is nearing its end. Coach, you take your cues from the laboring woman, responding to each emotional signpost. When she gets near the self-doubt signpost, the work is so intense she sometimes forgets to relax between contractions. She puts her feet back down on the bed but doesn't let go of her legs. Tell her to let go, drop her arms, sag back, and rest deeply. She may even be able to sleep between contractions. She deserves it.

What about the woman who is a speedster in the pushing stage? (It is possible to be a putterer in first stage and a speedster in second, and vice versa.) If a woman's pushing work is short and hard, you will not see an excitement signpost. She will go straight into seriousness and then may or may not have time for self-doubt. If she is a second-time birther, the pushing may be fast and easy and she may show almost all the excitement signpost and perhaps only a little seriousness with the last push or two. (Second-timers are not assured of a fast second stage, as we said before, since the position of the baby may slow things down.) In short, you expect to see the three signposts of first stage repeat themselves, but you must be certain to observe what actually happens in labor, and that is what the coach must respond to.

If a woman's pushing stage goes over two hours, it may not be her self-doubt that presents a coaching problem, but the doubts of the doctor or other birth attendants. A pushing stage that goes for three or four hours may not fit into the standard routine in most hospitals. In a later chapter we will discuss this in greater depth.

TO THE COACH

I once coached a mother who had an extra-long first stage, so that she was very tired even before she started pushing—and it showed. I propped up the bed correctly, put my arm around her, and said, "This is great, now you get to push your baby down and out and soon you will have that baby in your arms. Isn't that marvelous?" I said this with genuine enthusiasm because I know from experience that there is great joy in birth when the mother knows how to work with her body and when she has supportive, encouraging, helping people around her who know what she is doing. This mother immediately beamed. Her attitude changed from fatigue to "Great! I am ready. I'll just pace myself and get with this pushing."

It is entirely in the coach's hands to establish a good atmosphere. When your wife goes from first stage to second, be sure she hears the gentle enthusiasm in your voice. If the coach gets fatigued at any point and just drones, "Push, honey, push," in a dull, monotonous voice, then that is exactly what the laboring woman will reflect in her pushing—dullness and fatigue. Again, she is like a mirror. She will reflect whatever she sees in the people around her. If that is enthusiasm, confidence, energy, and anticipation with each and every contraction, that will be seen in her own work.

The pushing stage can be very hard, sweaty effort and at the same time quite exciting. Your wife will start off pushing cheerfully, but then she may push for some time without seeing or feeling any progress. Mistakenly, she believes that nothing is happening. A woman who has a long pushing stage must hear confidence, enthusiasm, and loving encouragement in her coach's voice.

Barbara and David

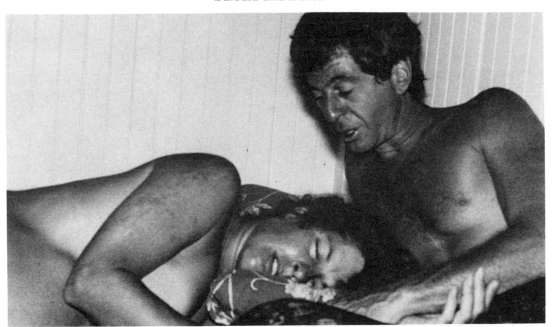

44. This is Barbara's first baby. Barbara is thirty-nine and is birthing at home. Here she is in the hardest part of her labor. She's labored about twelve hours and is seven centimeters dilated. David is coaching her through this contraction. Barbara described her labor as painless but hard work.

45. Barbara has just started pushing.

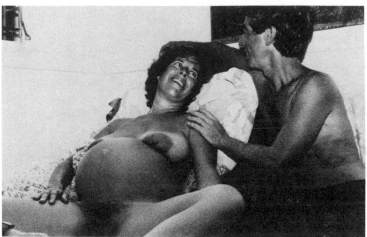

46. David asks Barbara how she likes the pushing and Barbara says, "Oh, I like this much better." She is clearly in the first signpost of her pushing stage. She gets about four minutes to rest between contractions. David keeps the atmosphere light as he chats with her, watching her mood.

47. Pushing is hard work. During the contraction you notice this is really an effort.

48. A friend calls to find out if Barbara has had her baby yet. Barbara takes the call and says, "No, not yet Bev, I'm pushing. Call back later." Everyone laughs. It is such a switch to see her working so hard and then carrying on this telephone conversation in between contractions.

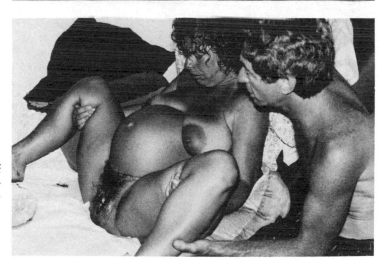

49. Back to work with another contraction. The bag of water has broken and you can see a little bit of the amniotic sac, the little shininess right at the outlet. Her pushing stage is really in earnest now and she has been working with it for some time.

50. Barbara's second emotional signpost. She is in between contractions and she is serious now. David wipes her off with a cool washrag and
rubs her shoulders to keep her from getting achy or tense in the neck and
shoulders.

152 *The Second Stage of Birth*

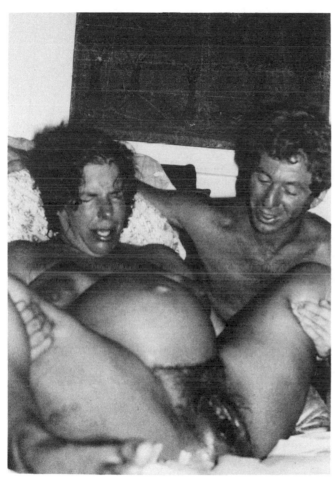

51. Notice the look of effort on Barbara's face as she really gets her baby's head down right at the outlet.

52. But look at her now. In between contractions, I asked Barbara, "How does it feel to have that much head down there?" She smiled and said, "Oh, that's fine." The ferocious look in the previous picture is from the effort of pushing, not due to pain from the baby's position. Barbara's pushing stage lasted three hours.

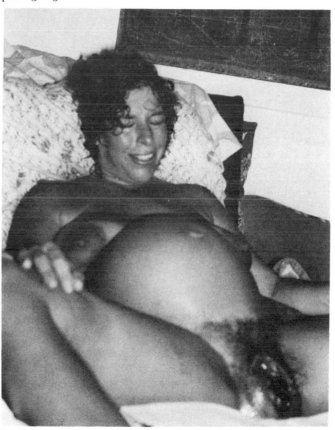

53. This part is hard, but just for a contraction or two as the midwife asks Barbara to stop pushing so the baby will come out gently. It's hard to just breathe when you want to push.

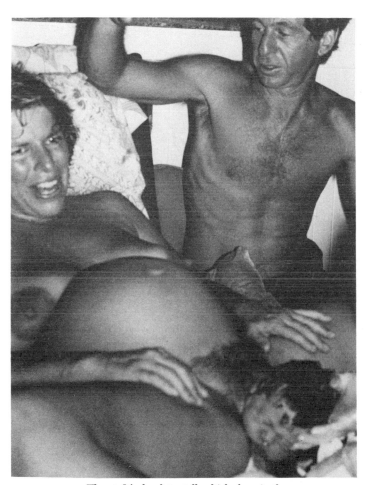

54. There! It's hard to tell which face is the more beautiful.

55. Barbara enjoys the peak of the emotional response following birth as her sensitive birth attendant hands the baby to her at once.

chapter seventeen

Alternatives in the Pushing Stage

You learned the basics of the pushing stage in the last chapter, but there are some other things you need to know. For instance, there are alternate pushing positions you may have heard about. And there are other positions the baby may be in that will affect pushing. Some of these variables will require choices on your part. As you know, it is essential to talk these choices over with your coach and attendant well before the birth of your baby.

In addition to the supine (on-the-back) position with

legs in stirrups that is still, unfortunately, used in many medicated births, there are two other less desirable positions that are sometimes used in natural births. Women are often manipulated into using their attendant's pet pushing position rather than the one they themselves decided upon ahead of time. So I recommend that you start off with a position that has a clear benefit for you and your baby, changing only if there is a good reason for doing so and it is *your* wish.

The Side Pushing Position

For this position, the laboring woman lies on her side with her upper leg cocked in the air, often supported by the coach. The drawback of this position is that it does not allow the extra one and a half centimeters of space at the pelvic outlet necessary to make birth easier. While one leg is pulled back and away from the body, the other is flat on the bed. Still, many nurse-midwives recommend this position out of tradition and a belief that it takes pressure off the perineum and prevents tears. (Dr. Kegel disagreed, however. He said the side position puts extra stress on one side of the vaginal barrel, which then gets an unequal distribution of pressure.) If you are being attended by a nurse-midwife, it is a good bet that you will end up in this position whether you intend to use it or not. The full squat or sitting squat has a physiological benefit by giving you maximum space in the pelvic outlet; the side position deprives you of some of this room.

I have found that women with back injuries sometimes will do better in the side position, and some women who are inhibited about sitting up and pulling their legs wide apart and open with other people around are genuinely better off in the side position since they feel less exposed and are better able to relax. These women may choose to use the side position. Some women also start off with a few pushes this way and then, when they become comfortable, roll over into the sitting squat or even the full squat.

Pushing on Hands and Knees

Some people, especially lay midwives, are fond of an "all-fours" position for pushing, with the woman on her hands and knees. A midwife urging you to try this would probably tell you it will be more comfortable for you to push this way. Again, the main drawback to the hands-and-knees position is that it leaves less room at the pelvic outlet than nature intended for you to have. And in the hands-and-knees position it is hard to feel really connected to your birth experience. After all, your head is looking one way and your bottom is pointed another. You can't see what is happening directly or in a mirror. And the birth attendant will certainly be the first to hold the baby, just so it doesn't fall to the floor.

In the sitting squat or full squat, as you have already learned, there is a greater feeling of being centered and in control of your body. And you can reach down at once to put *your* hands on the baby as he is emerging from your body. Again, be sure you and your coach have talked over what positions you want to use as a first choice and as a second choice (after you have tried four or five pushes) if you want to move on. If you want to start in the full-squat position, your coach should know your intention and that you are counting on him to coach you into it at the right time. Your coach should always help you follow through with your original plans, listening carefully, however, and being open to your desire to change.

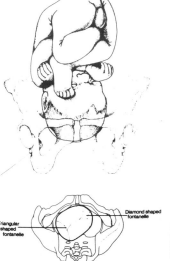

56. Front view of the "posterior."

Triangular shaped fontanelle

Diamond shaped fontanelle

ROBIN BURNINGHAM

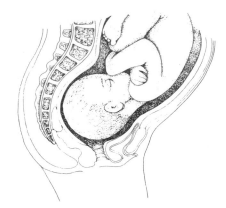

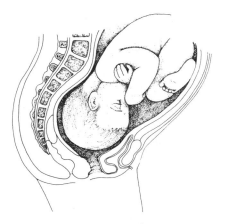

ROBIN BURNINGHAM

57. Side view contrasting posterior and anterior positions.

Posterior Births

So far we have only prepared you for pushing when the baby is in the most common position. But your knowledge of pushing is not complete until you have learned all about the posterior position. This occurs about twenty-five percent of the time, so it is certainly not rare. The physical sensations are going to be different, and the coaching requires some special tips, too.

Look at pictures 56 and 57 and notice the difference. In the anterior position, which you already know about, the baby starts off facing somewhat to the mother's side and then turns to face her spine as she is pushing the baby out. You can see that the baby in the posterior position faces more toward the mother's front, either slightly to the left or right. Most of these babies will also turn, like a key fitting into a lock, until they are facing their mother's spine as she is pushing the baby out. The posterior baby just has more of a turn to make. If your baby is posterior you will turn him with your pushing, and you will tend to do a lot more of it than the mother with an anterior baby. In a natural birth this is seldom a problem because the mother is quite capable of pushing well on her own, but in a medicated delivery this normal variation often turns into a complicated procedure.

The first stage of a posterior birth is the same as a regular birth, except that it may take longer to go from seven to ten centimeters because the uterus is already trying to do some of the work of turning the baby. And the woman with a posterior baby does not want just any old back rub in the first stage, but really strong pressure. "I couldn't believe how hard she wanted me to rub," one coach told me. "She kept telling me to push harder and I kept thinking that if I rubbed any harder I would push her right off the bed."

Now, instead of the backache disappearing as this woman switches over to pushing, the backache gets harder with each push, at least until the baby turns for her. So this woman may look quite distressed and uncomfortable during the pushing stage when she is well into it. My first and third children were posterior. The first one turned early on in the pushing stage and I had a pretty comfortable second stage that was just a lot of work. The third one took her sweet time turning, and with each push I experienced what I would call a damned uncomfortable backache.

How do you help yourself with a posterior birth? Push and think of moving the backache down and out. The better you push, the farther down you move it. Sort out the difference between the contractions and the backache. I found myself thinking, "Well, the contractions are okay, that's about the same as I have been doing all along. It is just the backache that is different, and I can work with that." Coach, it is important that you help her recognize that the contraction itself is something she has already been working with and handling well. Help her acknowledge the backache sensation and separate it from the contraction. This laboring woman needs a lot more direction to stay "on top" of the push. Your coaching, remember, should always match the intensity of the work as you take your cues from her. Although she still sets the pace, she may be quite distracted by the backache, and you must give her firm direction so she can just tune into your voice and follow. Remember, progress is often slow with a posterior birth, so don't stumble over the self-doubt signpost.

58. Here Debby has pushed for about an hour. She let one or two contractions go by without pushing so she could feel where the real working part of the contraction was happening. Having done that once or twice, she got a good sense of how the contraction worked and she synchronized her pushing effort with it. Here she brings a little more of the baby's head down. David gives her constant progress reports.

59. Notice how Debby puts her hands down and tips her pelvis back a little. This is the classic position to facilitate a posterior that doesn't turn. .

60. Fully crowning, the baby is about to emerge. Most posteriors turn, so they come out looking at the floor but Debby's baby turns to the pubis instead so he will come out looking up at his mother.

61. Debby cries out in surprise, "Oh look, it's face up, I'm looking right at a face!" Debbie described her labor as painless.

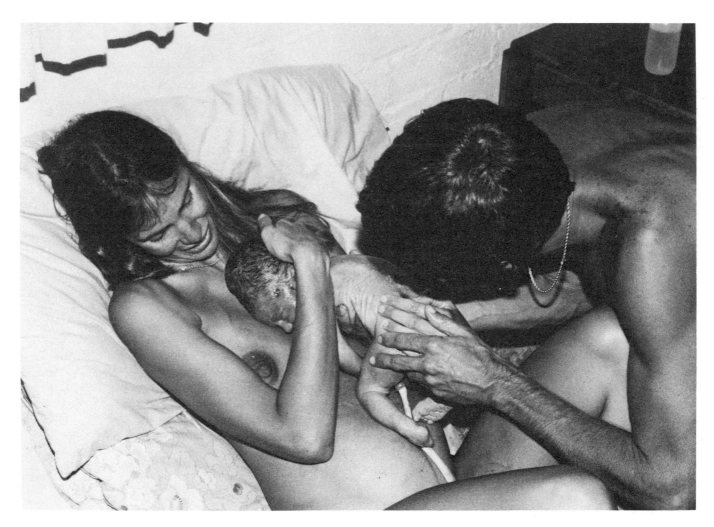

Twins

Twins occur about once in every eighty births, so they are not exactly a "common" variation. The big trick is to find a good doctor who has "caught" twins naturally. Most doctors are in a great hurry to get the second twin out. This can mean reaching inside you and attempting to extract the baby manually, or it can mean performing an episiotomy before the birth of the first twin and then taking you into the operating room for a caesarean surgery to get the second. Some doctors plan an automatic caesarean as soon as they learn that you have twins.

In the absence of a complication, the best thing to do is nurse the first twin as soon as it is born and wait for the contractions that follow, then push the second twin out. A number of my couples have had undiagnosed twins, and these have been some of our best twin births. Twins are rare enough that when they are diagnosed in advance the delivery room often gets crowded with other doctors, interns, and hospital staff wanting to watch the birth. That puts incredible pressure on the doctor to perform. With all these medical observers looking over his shoulder, you can bet he is tense. It is quite hard for him to just sit there and wait while the mother breast-feeds the first baby until the uterus adapts to the job of pushing the next baby out.

The most important thing you can do for yourself if you learn you have twins is to pick a doctor experienced in catching twins naturally. If you have to travel a bit to find

one, it may be well worth it. And you will want to study this book carefully or pay good attention in your Bradley® class, because the techniques you will use will be just the same. There is only one first stage, but once the door is open you will have two babies to push out, followed by the placenta or placentas.

Of course, your nutritional needs will be greater with twins and absolutely critical if you want to avoid low-birthweight babies and other nutrition-related problems in labor and birth. I urge you to read *The Brewer Medical Diet for Normal and High-Risk Pregnancy* by Gail Sforza Brewer with Tom Brewer, M.D., and I know you will enjoy the book *Having Twins* by Elizabeth Noble (Boston: Houghton Mifflin, 1980). And La Leche League will help you with breast-feeding twins, so be sure to contact them.

Breech Birth

Breech means the baby comes out bottom or feet first. This too is not exactly a common variation; it occurs about three times out of a hundred births. As with twins, you must pick a doctor who practices natural childbirth and has caught breech babies without intervention. Otherwise you will get routine caesarean surgery from a doctor who knows no other way to deal with a breech. I have seen a number of breech babies born vaginally with no problem. It is funny, but those were the ones that were not diagnosed in advance. Women say that the backache is often higher with a breech, but surprisingly they say their bottoms feel just the way we have described for when the head emerges first. There are two major differences in a natural breech birth. The attendant may wrap the baby's body in a blanket even before the head is born to prevent the cold stimulus from causing him to take a breath while the head is still inside, and the attendant may slide a finger up to the baby's nose while the head is still inside to make a passage for the baby to breathe through until the head is born. There are some risks with the breech position that you will want to know about if you are carrying breech, so that you can decide what's best for you (see Chapter Twenty-two).

The Pushing Stage Circus

The pushing stage is a bit more of a social affair than the first stage of labor, when you are left pretty much alone except for an occasional exam. But once you get to the pushing stage you suddenly find everyone involved. Having other people around for the pushing stage would not be so bad except that everyone wants to be a coach and gives different instructions. There are always a few "latest trends"—really just fads—in pushing. To avoid confusion and surprises when you are doing the real thing, we will look at these fads briefly right now.

- *"Don't push at all, just let the baby come out on its own."* This line of thinking shows extremely limited experience in birthing. Some second-timers might be able to give birth to a baby without pushing. But for the first-time birther, this technique often means an hour or so of very difficult contractions in which the laboring woman is denied the *relief* of pushing. This doesn't make a lot of sense, and in the worst circumstances the baby simply will not come out without those helping pushes. You know when your body is doing everything it can to get you to push; why would you not want to?

- *"Don't hold your breath more than five or ten seconds."* This technique goes back to the idea of getting more oxygen to the baby. But there are indications that natural hypoventilation (the opposite of hyperventilation) caused by holding your breath can play an important part in the initial breathing response of the baby at birth, since carbon dioxide and oxygen levels normally alter during the pushing stage.[1] Just as it is not wise to interfere with the laboring woman's urge to push, if she is inclined and able to hold her breath for a long time in pushing, do not stop her.

- *"Take an extra breath in the middle of the push."* This extra-breath approach is just another way to do the five-second push we have already discussed.

- *"Push with an open throat and let the air escape slowly during the contraction."* This is called "open-glottis" or "exhale" pushing and has been pretty thoroughly discredited, but the suggestion is still heard in some delivery rooms.[2] Doing this just decreases the intra-abdominal pressure that braces the uterus and helps to get the baby down and out. There has been one report comparing "exhale" pushing with long-breath pushing, and it found that exhale pushers took longer to get their babies out and their babies were in no better condition than those who held their breath and pushed longer.

- *"Let's move you into the delivery room. You will push better there."* What is in that cold sterile room to help you push better? Just a less comfortable table to lie on with less freedom to move around, and, of course, the physiological absurdity of stirrups. That's what awaits you in the delivery room.

- *"Grab this railing and pull on it. Push against the footboard. It will help you get the baby out."* These techniques may help you exercise your arms and legs, but they won't help get a baby out of your uterus. And they can wear you out.

A Word About the Episiotomy

There is a whole chapter ahead devoted to the controversial question of the episiotomy—the cut made in the outlet at the moment of birth in the overwhelming majority of hospital births. More and more women are deciding that they wish to avoid this routine surgery. If you do have an episiotomy, though, you will find that a pressure episiotomy works very nicely without medication before the birth. The pressure coming from the baby's head during crowning cuts off circulation and makes the perineum numb, so there is no pain and no need for pain-killing medication.

In a pressure episiotomy you do feel touch sensation. You are aware that someone is using scissors near you. But the actual incision feels like someone is cutting the seat of your pants, not you. There is no pain. Analyzing the sensation is the important thing. If you decided that having an episiotomy is not a critical thing for you, ask your doctor if he knows about the pressure episiotomy and if he would be willing to use that with you, *if he insists upon a routine episiotomy.* There are three prerequisites for having a pressure episiotomy:

- It should not be made until there is good crowning and the circulation in the perineum is cut off.

- The legs must *not* be in stirrups but pulled

back to the armpits. This is necessary to get sufficient pressure in the push, and since the sitting squat with legs pulled back is the most effective way to push, it does result in plenty of pressure at crowning.

- The woman must be pushing. Of course—how else could there be pressure?

Remember, Coach, it is your job to make certain the three prerequisites are met if your wife is to have a pressure episiotomy. Her legs must be pulled back—not strapped in stirrups; she must be crowning well; and she must be pushing to get pressure down there. At this moment the perineum will turn white as the circulation is cut off. If all the conditions are met, it works beautifully.

Doctors who are unfamiliar with pressure episiotomies whip out the little needle for a "local" or a very long needle for a pudendal block. This is at the last possible few moments before birth.

Pudendal blocks interfere with the bearing-down reflex, so here at the last moment you can end up with a forceps delivery. Any medication put in the mother's bottom now can and does reach the baby.

This is something you should have discussed with the doctor ahead of time, but even if you did you should be prepared to deal with it at the moment. Doctors tend to forget; after all, your wife is not his only patient. Simply remind him in a friendly way that you prefer to have no drugs.

chapter eighteen

Drugs During Labor

The Bradley Method® is an effective approach to natural, unmedicated childbirth. But why have an unmedicated birth? Because you want to do everything in your power to protect the well-being of your new baby. In an earlier chapter you learned about the dangers of drugs during pregnancy, many of them not known or recognized for years. You have come all this way eating carefully, exercising, and avoiding unnecessary risks to your baby. So you certainly do not want to give up now that you are in labor and your goal is in sight. Despite what you may have heard, the benefits of labor drugs in a normal birth do not outweigh the dangers. Actually, it is most often the medicated mother who talks about pain and being out of control during birth. And despite what you may be told, there are no drugs for labor that are without risks to your baby and to you.

For example, **Demerol** and **Seconal** are commonly used drugs, especially for the first stage of labor. Many parents are told in their "prepared-childbirth" Lamaze classes that "a little Demerol never hurt anything." But an article in the *Los Angeles Times* told of an eight-year-old girl whose cerebral palsy was attributed to improper care at birth—her mother was given Demerol at the wrong time. The court awarded $65,000 in damages.[1] Demerol did not help that mother have a more positive experience. The drug can cause depression of fetal breathing and decreased responsiveness in newborns.[2] The babies are less alert and are less vigorous in nursing.[3] And Demerol and other frequently used drugs have been detected in infants *several weeks after birth.*[4]

But some people think that natural, unmedicated childbirth is just for the sake of babies. It is for the baby, of course, but with natural childbirth both the baby and the mother have a better experience. *Drugs affect mothers too.* Choices disappear from the scene as soon as a woman is medicated. Drugs can affect the bearing-down reflex, and even though you want to push the baby out yourself, you end up with a forceps or vacuum-extraction delivery.

Sometimes women are told that they are going to be given "just a local" and that it won't interfere with pushing or get through to the baby. This is not true. The so-called "local" anesthetics all cross the placenta rapidly. Some examples of these drugs are: Xylocaine, Carbocaine, Novocain, and Pontocaine. They may depress the baby directly or indirectly by causing maternal hypotension if used for regional anesthesia, such as spinal or epidural anesthesia.[5]

Paracervical anesthesia (injections directly into the cervix) may interfere with the baby's blood supply by increasing the tension in the muscles of the uterus. A drop in fetal heart rate is not uncommon when the mother receives a paracervical block, and there is an increased incidence of a lower Apgar score for the infant. Dr. Avis Erickson warns, "Any drug which artificially changes the mother's blood chemistry or alters the intrauterine environment can jeopardize the fetus."[6]

Too often labor slows down or comes to a complete halt right after a woman gets "a shot of something." Then she has to wait for the drug to wear off to begin again where she left off. The work still has to be done, so the effect of giving her a shot is too frequently to prolong the labor. Sometimes, to counteract this common drug-caused slowdown, the mother will be given **Pitocin,** a drug which forces the uterus to contract. It is usually administered through an IV, an intravenous drip. As the original "shot of something" begins to wear off, the woman experiences contractions triggered by her own natural hormone. But now, in addition, she is having contractions triggered by the artificial hormone dripping into her bloodstream.

If the timing coincides, she has very intense contractions. If it doesn't, she experiences contractions more frequently than she should. Either way, the baby may be cut off from oxygen for longer periods than nature intended.

Drugs and medical technology can be enormously beneficial when used to take care of real complications, but too often they are abused when applied to women birthing normally. These women are thus subjected to unnecessary risks. The key to this problem is *informed consent,* an ideal too seldom realized. Informed consent means that no woman during pregnancy or labor should ever be deceived into thinking that any drug or procedure (Demerol, Seconal, spinals, caudals, epidurals, paracervical block, etc.) is guaranteed safe. Not only are there no guaranteed safe drugs, but many of them have well-known, recognized side effects and potential side effects.

Informed consent should mean that no woman would ever hear such falsehoods as, "This is harmless," or, "I only give it in such a small dose that it can't affect the baby," or, "This is just a local and won't reach the baby." These falsehoods would not be possible if consumers demanded that informed consent be practiced properly. I have seen women given statements to sign and told only, "Sign here, this is just a standard form." These statements sometimes give permission to use drugs or perform procedures on the woman and her unborn baby, stating that she has given her "informed consent." This must be the grossest misuse of the term possible.

Sometimes informed consent means that the laboring woman and her coach are told all the possible benefits of a drug or procedure in glowing terms but none of the possible negative outcomes. For example, before giving permission to use a fetal monitor, a woman is often told how valuable it will be to be able to tell when a contraction is about to begin (as if she can't tell very easily herself what her body is doing). She gets a sales pitch about how safe the baby will be because they will be able to tell at once if the baby is in trouble, and if so do caesarean surgery immediately.

What she is almost never told in this so-called informed consent is that the fetal monitor is known to increase the rate of infections and unnecessary caesarean surgeries, and, of course, there is a higher maternal mortality rate associated with major surgery. She is not told of a government-funded study indicating that electronic fetal monitoring is potentially dangerous and that effectiveness of such monitoring has not been proved scientifically.[7] She is not told that, in effect, she is consenting to unproved techniques and therefore allowing experimentation on herself and her unborn child. (We will look at fetal monitoring and unneeded C-sections in detail in a later chapter.)

The point here is that informed consent is not really being practiced in most hospitals today, beyond the "sign here" on a paper that means you have gotten a sales pitch with little—or more often no—information about potential hazards. Yet informed consent is essential as a cornerstone for parents to formulate intelligent decisions about drugs, routine procedures, and birthing.

chapter nineteen

Rehearsing the Second Stage

There are ten ways that labor might begin, but there are really only four ways to start the pushing stage. We will look at those and then take you through a rehearsal of the second stage that will go right on to the moment of birth.

Scene #1:   All the Way Dilated; An Urge to Push

You feel an urge to push, and it is impossible to continue to relax. Your coach asks the birth attendant (or, he asks one of the nurses) to check you. You are told you are com-

pletely dilated and ready to start pushing, so go ahead. Great!

Scene #2:   Hoquet Reflex; All the Way Dilated (With or Without Urge to Push)

You were seven centimeters or more in the last exam an hour ago. Your contractions have been close and strong. You feel relaxed and calm, and your coach is telling you that you are beautiful to watch. But now your fingers half close during a contraction, your shoulders seem to move downward, and your smooth breathing catches like a hiccup toward the peak of the contraction. You suddenly feel that you *cannot* relax. You are experiencing the *Hoquet* (ho-kay) breathing reflex, and you are actually entering the pushing stage. Your uterus is moving down powerfully to push the baby out, and the diaphragm actually bows downward as if to brace the uterus and force you to suck in air to push with. Of course you cannot relax. In the second stage relaxation does not work, *pushing* does. Women are often dismayed by this experience, thinking they have lost control when in fact they have not. They have simply slipped into another part of labor. It can be confusing for three or four contractions until someone figures out where you are in labor. Your birth attendant will now probably examine you and tell you to go ahead and push.

Scene #3:   All the Way Dilated; No Urge to Push

You are examined and discovered to be completely dilated. Although you do not feel an urge to push, you will probably be instructed to start. Your doctor may have the clock running on you, so it makes sense to try pushing even without the urge as long as you are having contractions. Better this than to let the time run out (in the doctor's head) and have him wanting to intervene.

I have seen some doctors, nurses, and nurse-midwives instruct the laboring woman to wait and see if she got an urge to push in a while, *as long as she was comfortable* with the contractions. In two or three hours the urge to push often establishes itself, and the woman begins to push. In this case she gets a nice rest between the first and second stage. These were birth attendants tuned in to the woman's body, not just to the clock. And they were not afraid to let some relaxed time go by to allow the picture of her labor to come into focus.

What if the time goes by and there is still no urge to push? Finally, the birth attendant will say, "Well, you got a nice rest anyway, now let's start pushing as long as you are having contractions."

But if you are going to begin pushing without a strong urge, you must start in a different position than you have learned so far, a position with legs extended. The most common reason a woman does not have the urge to push even when fully dilated is that the baby has not yet dropped low enough to press on the muscles that give her the feeling of having to bear down. This happens more often when the baby is in the posterior position.

In the first stage of labor, you recall, progress in dilation is measured in centimeters from one to ten. In the pushing stage, progress is measured in stations. Look at picture 62 to see where those stations are. Your birth attendant can determine the baby's station during an examination. When the attendant's fingers bump into the baby's head and find it even with two bony points known as the ischial spines that protrude from the pelvis, the baby is said to be at zero station. Before that, the baby is at a minus station. Generally, when a woman has an undeniable urge to push, the baby will be at a zero or lower—that is, plus—station.

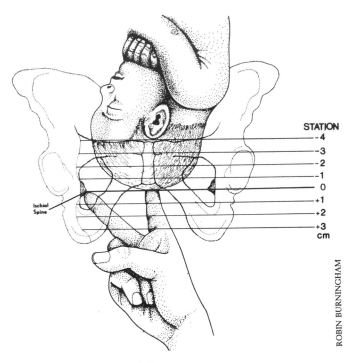

62. What station is this baby at?

So, if you have no urge to push but have been told to begin by your birth attendant (especially one who sets a time limit on the pushing stage), it would be a good time for your coach to ask what station the baby is at. If the answer is a minus station, you do not want to start right away in the full or sitting squat. Why? As you know, squatting opens up the bottom part of the pelvis at the outlet by

making it up to one and a half centimeters wider. But to gain that room at the bottom, it is lost at the top or inlet to the pelvis. If the baby is high, then by squatting the woman is decreasing the space at the top of the pelvis and slowing down or stopping the work of the pushing stage.

If the baby is at a minus station and the birth attendant is telling you to push but you do not have an urge to, you should not push with your leg's flexed back as they are in a squat. You can push lying on your side with legs extended, or you can push standing up and leaning on your coach or bent over the bed for support. This leaves the upper part of the pelvis open to its maximum and allows you to begin effective pushing. As soon as you either get an actual strong urge to push or are told the baby has dropped into a zero or plus station, you can move into the sitting- or full-squat position and begin to really move along with the work of pushing your baby out. It would be great if all birth attendants knew to start women who do not have an urge to push in the legs-extended position (and even better if no birth attendant had a short, arbitrary time limit on a normal pushing stage). But this is not the case. You may want to talk over in advance how your birth attendant would handle this situation. But it will still probably be up to the coach to remember—if the woman has been told to push but has no strong urge—to ask what station the baby is at and to recommend a pushing position accordingly.

Scene #4: Not All the Way Dilated; A Strong Urge to Push

You have a very strong urge to push. You can't wait to get started. You are examined and told you are eight or nine

ROBIN BURNINGHAM

centimeters dilated and you should not start pushing yet. The rationale here is that you may tear the cervix. You should be prepared for a short but difficult time now. It is quite impossible to relax with genuine pushing contractions. The uterus is pushing anyway, cervix complete or not, and of course this is what gives you the pushing urge as the baby drops lower.

To deny the mother the comfort she gets from pushing when she has a strong urge is very hard on her. Fortunately, some doctors feel that if the cervix is very soft—that is, thin and pliable—it is all right to push anyway. The result is almost always a completely dilated cervix in a short time, usually four or five pushes. I have seen this happen many times, and the doctors reported no damage to the cervix. In my experience, doctors who do this get the best results and women are happiest for it. The criteria are that the cervix should be soft, thin, and pliable and that the urge to push should be undeniably strong. It should be very difficult for the woman not to push. This definitely does *not* describe the woman who says, "Oh, I *think* I have to push," or one who has a slight urge to push in the middle of the contraction only.

The final test is that when the mother does give a good, strong, fearless push, it feels right. It should not hurt. The birth attendant waits to hear this. This applies, of course, *only to a labor proceeding without obstetrical intervention.* It does not apply to an induced labor, one started by stripping the membranes or by an IV drip with Pitocin, or any other unnaturally started labor. It also does not apply when the bag of waters is artificially ruptured during labor. Any form of intervention can create real problems. When labor proceeds naturally without any obstetrical interference, you can pretty well count on your body to give you the right cues.

The other side of the coin is the doctor who will not allow the mother to push until she is "complete," in spite of her overwhelming desire to bear down. The woman is told she will cause the cervix to swell if she pushes. What often happens here is that after two or three hours of the mother's fighting a tremendous urge to push (and having a most difficult time), her uterus just sort of quits, as if it has done the work necessary to expel the baby and is now too tired to continue. I have seen this happen several times. This seems a much rougher course of action (or inaction) than simply allowing her to try several good pushes.

I have also seen numerous other women eight or nine centimeters dilated (or having so little cervix left that it is referred to as a "lip" or "rim") who were told to hold off on the strong urge to push, again resulting in great discomfort. Twenty minutes to an hour or so later, these women were *crowning.* Obviously, the uterus was pushing away, and the mother was being denied the comfort of pushing with it. This is most dissatisfying. In such a situation, we can only hope you have a *flexible* birth attendant. You should talk this over with your attendant (and of course, your coach) and decide ahead of time how you would want each of these situations handled. You will not be able to make decisions at the time, in the midst of it.

A Textbook Run-Through: Second and Third Stages

You have learned the four ways that the pushing stage begins, so we will continue this rehearsal of the textbook labor from that point right through the moment of birth and after. If you need to, before you begin, you should review the pushing contractions Master Exercise from Chapter Sixteen. For this exercise, we will say that you have an urge to push, and, after being examined and found to be fully dilated, you are told to push.

MASTER EXERCISE IV

Final Rehearsal of the Second Stage

In a hospital birth the coach will now roll up the bed to a forty-five degree angle and arrange the pillows, helping the laboring woman into a contour-chair position with her feet planted close to her bottom and her hands at her side. (In a home birth it is just a matter of setting up the birthing place and pillows as you have practiced, and you may want to put a waterproof mat beneath you.)

Pushing contraction begins: one and a half minutes

If you need to, go back to the pushing chapter and review the pushing technique. Do this contraction now before going further.

In between contractions

In a hospital, you should already be gowned up by this time—If your hospital requires this.

COACH: Use PEP (praise, encouragement, and assurance of progress). Wipe her off. Massage her shoulders. Give sips of water or ice chips. Tell her to rest. Wait three or four minutes before the next practice contraction.

Pushing contraction begins: one and a half minutes

Do this contraction before going further. Use either the sitting or full squat position.

In between contractions

COACH: Keep the atmosphere cheerful and light if she is still chatty. If she feels that she is not doing this right, remind her that she's just starting and it takes several contractions before she feels that she has it together. Rest at least three or four minutes before practicing the next contraction.

Pushing contraction begins: one and a half minutes

During real pushing you will want to try this. Back off from one pushing contraction; don't push, just let it happen and sense where the power of the contraction is. Perhaps you could just push when the contraction feels overwhelming to you.

In between contractions
Rest. Talk over what the contraction was like. Was it powerful at the beginning or more so toward the middle or at the end? Was it a mild, moderate, or overwhelming urge to push? Did you gain any new knowledge by tuning into your body this way that you can now use to synchronize with your pushing technique?

Pushing contraction begins: one and a half minutes

In between contractions
Rest. With this next contraction be sure that you try out at least one alternate way to push from the basic sitting squat.

Contraction begins: two minutes
In your mind's eye, see a "dimes worth" of the baby's head.

If you are moving into a delivery room
COACH: Go right with her. Take your washrag. Remind everyone that she wants to use the forty-five-degree backrest. Do not stand around gawking, you are not a tourist. Put your arm around her, be close; maintaining touch or close eye contact is important.

Procedures to expect in a delivery room
The mother's perineal area is usually swabbed with an antiseptic solution, her blood pressure checked, the fetal heart rate listened to. She may or may not be "draped" in hospital gray or green sheets to give the doctor a "sterile field." Doctors accustomed to medicated deliveries tend to drape from neck to toe with only the woman's face and perineum showing. It is quite difficult to see much of what is going on. In fact, it is difficult for the laboring woman to feel mentally or physically connected to the birth of her child. Doctors accustomed to natural-childbirth couples these days drape very little, and some not at all. A tubelike pillow case on the legs is about the most used.

In between contractions
COACH: Remind her that at this point, the baby is trying to come under the pubic arch. Here, for a few contractions, she may have to push beyond what she thinks she can. After a few more contractions the baby's head clears the pubic arch and then you feel the crowning sensation beginning.

Crowning
This can be startling. It feels stretchy, burning, stingy, or it may just feel like funny tingles as it is becoming numb. Do not panic and react emotionally—simply analyze what it feels like. Although this can be scary at first, you soon realize that your perineum is fanning out nicely for you. Picture in your mind the exciting pictures of crowning that you have seen in this book.

COACH: Watch for a startled reaction if the head comes down quickly. Direct her to analyze what she is feeling and not just react to it. Remind her what it is.

Pressure episiotomy
COACH: If your wife is having a pressure episiotomy, be sure to remind her that she will feel something like someone cutting the seat of her pants but not her, that she will feel touch sensation.

Stop pushing

If you are asked to stop pushing, all you have to do now is stop holding your breath and breathe, calmly and evenly. It is difficult to get any oomph behind a push when you are breathing regularly. Do not pant. It is dangerous for the baby and quite unnecessary. Simply breathe. This works better and holds no hazards for the baby.

COACH: Your coaching here is essential. Plan on repeating the birth attendant's instruction to her to stop pushing. She has been tuned into your voice for hours and may not even hear the birth attendant tell her to stop pushing. Nothing fancy is needed here, and nothing should detract from this moment of birth. Plan on saying, "Stop pushing now, just breathe, nice and steady with no panting."

Birthing

The head is emerging.

COACH: Remind her to open her eyes and look. Hopefully you're practically cheek to cheek and sharing the same great view over the tummy. Share it and enjoy it. This moment is intense.

Some babies breathe right away with just their heads out, but more of them wait for their bodies to be born, and others wait for the umbilical cord to stop pulsating.

With the next push or two, the baby's body is born, slippery, wiggly, and wet. It may be covered with a substance like cold cream called vernix caseosa which can be rubbed right into the baby's skin. This is a wondrous moment. You feel so unbelievably empty just afterward. One minute ago you were so tired, but this minute you feel exhilarated.

Practice both Master Exercises III and IV several times a week. By now you should be doing the advanced PC exercises.

---

63. Red and Elizabeth birthed their first baby at Kahuku Hospital. Here they are chatting as they wait for a pushing contraction. Elizabeth described her labor as very hard pain.

DAVID HOGG AND AMBER MATHEWS

DAVID HOGG AND AMBER MATHEWS

64. The pushing contraction begins.

DAVID HOGG AND AMBER MATHEWS

65. Elizabeth takes two deep breaths and as she takes the third, Red rocks her forward to a full squat.

66. Red supports her as she pushes and he is encouraging her, saying, "Nice steady pressure. Relax. Just open up while you push."

DAVID HOGG AND AMBER MATHEWS

67. Contraction gone. Red rocks her back gently to lean against the pillows to rest and wipes her off with a damp washrag, saying, "That was good, Elizabeth."

DAVID HOGG AND AMBER MATHEWS

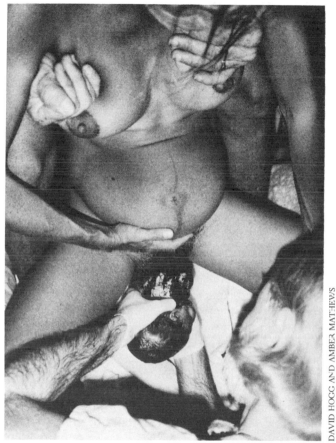

68. Elizabeth preferred a half squat for the actual moment of birth, with Red's hands under her armpits to support her. Dr. Branch, ever obliging, came in and said, "Oh, this is how you're doing it, all right." He sat down in front of her and caught the baby.

DAVID HOGG AND AMBER MATHEWS

69. Dr. Branch handed the baby to Elizabeth with no delay. The cord is still attached and pulsating, and it's a bright blue.

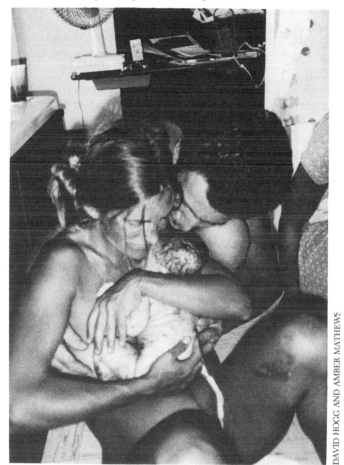

DAVID HOGG AND AMBER MATHEWS

Third Stage: Nursing and Expulsion of the Placenta

This is pure anticlimax. Skin-to-skin contact and nursing the baby at once will help cause the uterus to contract efficiently and loosen the placenta in one piece from the uterine wall. Coach, ask the birth attendant if you can clamp and cut the umbilical cord yourself, and then stall a bit to make sure the baby gets all its cord blood. You will know this has happened when the cord turns white and stops pulsating completely. If you notice the doctor tugging on the cord to see if the placenta is loose, say something like, "Is it time to push the placenta out, doctor?" This reminds him the mother wants to push the placenta out herself and would rather not have it pulled out or her tummy mashed. Usually a few pushes will expel the placenta. It normally takes from five to ten minutes, but can take up to forty-five minutes. Sometimes it helps to get into the full squat to expel the afterbirth, which you can do if you are birthing at home or in a labor bed.

An artificial hormone may be injected at this time to contract the uterus and expel the placenta. But sometimes the effects of this hormone shot can actually trap the placenta inside the uterus. The mother then has to be put under sedation while the doctor goes in after the placenta and scrapes it out of her. Second-time mothers can have unnecessarily violent postpartum contractions with this hormone that are often reported as more uncomfortable than labor. How much simpler if everyone would just wait a few minutes and let labor take its course!

Be sure the mother is again at a forty-five degree angle for nursing. It is nearly impossible to do so lying flat. If the baby is not interested in nursing right away, the mother should squeeze the nipple gently to express a little milk. Often the smell of dinner is enough to get the baby started. Nursing immediately after birth is beneficial to the baby as well as the mother. At that time the milk has colostrum, which is high in immunity factors that are important to the baby—especially if he is going into a central nursery to be exposed to unfriendly forms of bacteria. It also has a laxative effect on the baby and helps get that system working quickly. While the mother is putting the baby to the breast, the doctor will stitch up the episiotomy if he has performed one. He will inject novocaine into her bottom, but now that drug no longer matters, the baby is born. The new mother should have the baby for *at least* half an hour at this time, even if it is to go to the nursery, since it takes a while to establish nursing. Surely weighing the baby and the like can wait a bit. It is far better for the two of you to have the baby with you completely for the first few hours so the three of you can get acquainted as a family. This is another decision you probably made when you chose your doctor.

Next the nurse will want to put drops in the baby's eyes, a legal requirement in most states to prevent blindness from venereal disease. Ask your doctor or birth attendant to avoid using silver nitrate, which burns the baby's eyes and causes some squinting and tears when you want a quiet time with your new baby. Where we live, parents may request tetracycline or erythromycin to be substituted. See what is available where you live. As for a warming crib, which may be suggested at this time, the medicated baby's metabolism is not functioning normally at all, and so the newborn may have a definite need to be in a warming crib. The normal, natural-birth baby, on the other hand, does not need one and may possibly find it detrimental to normal responses at birth. An initial cold stimulus may play an important role in the onset of breathing. And studies have also shown that heat loss in the mother's arms is insignificant.[1]

Many Bradley Method® couples are able to walk out of the birth room together holding the baby. This is only possible if they have had a normal and totally unmedicated labor and birth. If you would like to leave together, and the mother feels up to it, be sure that she nurses the baby immediately after birth and that she drinks a glass of orange juice to restore her depleted blood sugar. The new mother will find that she feels fantastic after a totally unmedicated labor and birth. (The coach is probably showing more fatigue than she is.) Many Bradley® mothers go home within a few hours after the birth. If you are planning to go home at once, you should talk this over with your pediatrician during your pregnancy. Make it clear that if the baby checks out fine, following a normal, unmedicated birth, you may like to go home within a few hours. Some doctors are more accustomed to this than others, and your pediatrician's attitude is important.

When you go home early you should be prepared for the baby's first bowel movements. They are black or blackish-green. This is just the meconium, which plugs up the bowel tract when the baby is in the uterus. He clears this out first. Then the stools quickly turn a liquidy yellow. This is a typical breast-fed baby's stool and not diarrhea. Beyond this you will have to depend on other books for the care of your baby. Two of the best for getting started are *Nursing Your Baby* by Karen Pryor and *The Womanly Art of Breastfeeding*, published by La Leche League, which has groups meeting in almost every community in the country that are extremely helpful to new parents.

Having the Baby on the Way

So, Coach, after all this you're worried about having the baby in the car? (It's in the back of every coach's mind.)

It happened to Marty and Judy. Judy was a second-timer who had had a very bad, medicated, forceps delivery the first time. She was going to the hospital on a medical plan, which made it difficult to get agreements with the doctors about the upcoming birth. So, as Judy told me later, she decided she was going to wait until the last second to go to the hospital. Did she ever!

As Marty was driving her to the hospital in their van, Judy said, "Marty, I feel like pushing."

"Okay," he said. He stopped the van, flagged down a passing motorist to take the wheel, and got in back with Judy.

She was definitely pushing! A little head showed at the vaginal outlet. Marty put his arm around her and said,

"Okay, honey, you are doing great. I think you're supposed to stop pushing now. Just breathe."

But with the next contraction the baby's head did not come forward, so he told her to go ahead and push a little more. Now he could see a lot more of the baby's head and, wondering if this was enough to call crowning, told her again to stop pushing.

She did, and the baby's head was born gently. With the next contraction and another push the entire body slipped out with a gush of amniotic fluid. (The bag of water was already broken; this was the water remaining in the bag behind the baby's shoulders.)

As Marty told the class later, "He breathed and then he let out a small cry. I cried a lot and Judy laughed and said she couldn't believe it!"

They put the baby to breast, and at first they were worried he wasn't going to nurse. Then he latched on and really went for it.

When they arrived at the hospital, Marty helped unbutton and rebutton Judy's bathrobe so the cord could protrude between the buttons. (The placenta was still attached.) Judy and Marty got out of the van and headed for the front door.

Just as they got there, they heard a great racket. They turned around to see the total stranger who had driven them to the hospital, jumping up and down and hollering, "HOORAY!"

The placenta came out about fifteen minutes later, and Marty went to the cashier's window for a bunch of dimes to make some quick, happy calls. Guess who was right in front of him in line to get dimes? The stranger, of course.

Another of my couples, Jan and Don, had their baby in the car, too. They had left for the hospital with contractions at three minutes apart, sixty seconds long, and a definitely serious signpost, after many hours of labor at home. They had called me to compare notes, and I agreed it certainly sounded like time to go. When Jan arrived at the hospital she was examined (after waiting for about half an hour) and told she was only one centimeter dilated and probably in false labor. She was never admitted because no one believed she was in labor. (Relaxation techniques can sometimes cause attendants to underestimate how much work you are doing.)

But as they drove back home, the contractions got to be about two minutes apart and seventy to eighty seconds long. Jan told Don, "If this is false labor, I'm never going to be able to do this!"

Don said, "You are not supposed to have a third emotional signpost in false labor." Then he heard her grunt as she felt an overwhelming urge to push. They looked at each other, and Don turned the car around to head back to the hospital. They birthed as they pulled into the parking lot.

Neither one of these was a "blitz" labor. One couple stayed home past all the signs they knew to look for because that was the way they wanted to do it. The other couple went to the hospital at the perfect time after a number of hours of labor at home, but the staff looked only at how far dilated she was rather than how much work she was doing or how close and how long the contractions were.

Neither of these couples was in an emergency situation. Simply having a baby outside the hospital does not constitute an emergency. This is just birthing. So here is what to do with the unexpected birth outside the hospital.

Do

Have the baby. Don't try to hold it back if it's ready to be born. Don't keep your legs closed. Don't pant.

When you can feel yourself stretching open and the baby's head is quite definitely right there at the outlet (you have that numb, tingly, burning, stretching feeling), stop pushing! Just breathe and let the head be born gently. This is important to avoid an unnecessary tear; it usually only takes two or three contractions.

If the cord permits, put the baby to breast. If not, perhaps if the mother tries a tailor-sitting position the cord will be able to reach without any pulling so the baby can nurse.

Do Not

Do not pull on the baby's head.

Do not get in a big hurry. The baby is still connected to the placenta and getting oxygen via the cord. And normally there is a pause now with the head out and the body still in. With the next contraction, push the body out.

Do not pull on the cord. This can pull the placenta off the uterine wall before it is ready and cause bleeding. It can also invert the uterus.

You don't have to worry about cutting the cord. If the placenta is still attached and you go on to the hospital, then you may want to use Marty and Judy's trick of weaving the cord between buttons. If the placenta comes out, just wrap it up with the baby. After all he's been floating around beside it for nine months; he won't mind a bit.

Go on to the hospital to have them check the mother and baby, but I think you will be happiest if you can get right out of the hospital again. Otherwise your "contaminated" baby (who has been in touch with the real world outside) may be isolated from the nursery and from you!

part IV

Controversies in Childbirth

chapter twenty

The Episiotomy

The episiotomy is the most common surgical procedure done in the United States today, except for the cutting of the umbilical cord.

How common is the episiotomy? *Very.* It is done in *at least* ninety percent of first-time births in hospitals and again in most second or later hospital births.

How often is it really needed? A Maternity Center Association record of home births shows that out of almost 5,000 home births, there were only twenty-two episiotomies (and only one third-degree tear). That's an episiotomy rate of about one out of every two hundred women, or half a percent![1] (It is also interesting to note that in most European countries, the episiotomy rate is only twelve to fifteen percent of hospital births.)

What is an episiotomy? Typical birth books describe it as a "small incision" made at the time of birth through your perineum to "get the widest part of the baby's head through the opening of the vagina."

This incision, made with scissors inserted into your vagina as the baby's head is crowning, can be two to four inches long. What's that? You say that doesn't sound like a "small cut"? You don't think that you have two to four inches around your vaginal outlet to cut?

Well, you will at birth. When the baby's head

crowns, the perineum fans out, the thick, springy muscles flattening and spreading as they are designed to. At that time you easily have two to four inches between your vaginal opening and rectum spreading out for the surgeon's scissors. But once the baby is out, your perineum is no longer fanned out. It will return immediately to its thick, muscular form, meaning that the cut you are left with is about two inches on the outside, with the rest going up into your vaginal barrel.

70. Crowning

ROBIN BURNINGHAM

That is a pretty serious bit of "minor surgery." And it is so frequently performed (at least in the U.S.) that you would expect a lot of research has been done on its usefulness, wouldn't you?

Quite the contrary. Drs. David Banta and Stephen B. Thacker's research into the medical literature about episiotomy found that "there were little scientific data to support the widespread use of episiotomy. Indeed, if one restricts the definition of scientific data to that which is obtained from a randomized, controlled, clinical trial, there were *no* data to support widespread use of episiotomy."[2]

Considering the significant risks associated with the episiotomy, these medical doctors say that the episiotomy rate in the U.S. could easily be cut in half without causing harm to either mothers or babies. That is probably conservative.

These risks include *pain*—swelling, burning, and aching in the perineum that stays for weeks, months, or longer, often interfering with sexual relations—and they include infection, which can lead to more serious complications.

Why is the episiotomy rate so high with no evidence that it is needed or useful? Banta and Thacker say, "Many physicians feel that clinical experience provides an adequate basis for good practice . . ." In other words, doctors say that this is the way they were taught and this is the way they do it; it works for them and they don't know any other way—and, frankly, it doesn't hurt them a bit.

This may seem a cold, harsh indictment of physicians. Yet as Drs. Banta and Thacker point out, "While many obstetricians perceive it to be a minor problem, many women regard post-episiotomy pain as quite a serious matter." That pain can be severe for as many as sixty percent of the women who undergo the procedure.

In my classes I have seen many women who have a deep and sincere dread of the episiotomy. It is, after all, a serious surgical procedure performed on the most intimate part of their bodies. They want to know if the episiotomy is necessary, and they want to know how they can avoid it.

Some mothers who return to the class after their birth to share their experiences echo and intensify this concern. They say that there were things they didn't *like* (the enema, the shave, the IV), but that the *worst* thing about their birth experience was the episiotomy and its aftermath of pain and discomfort.

This is not a pleasant subject. This was probably the hardest chapter in this book to write. But let's look a little more closely at the episiotomy.

The history of this surgery goes hand in hand with the shift to hospital deliveries and the development of new methods to intervene in what should be a natural, normal process.

When anesthetics first appeared on the scene, women were really "put under" for birth, completely "zonked out." Obviously, it was impossible for mothers to push their babies out in this condition. The baby still had to come out, though. If the mother couldn't push, then the doctor had to get it out. This was the real beginning of the "routine" forceps delivery, and with it came the "routine" episiotomy.

Speed was the watchword whenever the mother was completely put under because the baby was in great danger. It was necessary to get the baby out quickly, or it would be exceedingly difficult to get him to breathe. You could get a baby out faster by cutting the mother's perineum open and extracting the infant with forceps. So it was speed and efficiency (made necessary because the mother was medicated) that made the episiotomy and the forceps delivery the norm rather than an unusual form of delivery. The routine episiotomy is a legacy women bear of the history of intervention in childbirth.

As you know, an episiotomy need not be painful at the moment it is given because the baby's head cuts off your circulation and makes your bottom numb. This is the so-called pressure episiotomy that we discussed earlier and that requires no anesthetic. After your baby is out, an anesthetic will be needed as the obstetrician stitches up your sexual organ. When this wears off, the pain begins.

Episiotomy can do permanent harm to your PC muscle and set you up for future health problems.[3] It also creates scar tissue in the perineum and leaves a numb spot in this sexually responsive part of your body. Psychologically, this intense, unnecessary pain associated with birthing can make women feel victimized, abused, and bitter.

Many women who are left with lingering pain (which may last several months and even return occasionally in twinges years later) have difficulty piecing together their expectations of being a mother (and a woman) and the reality of the ache in the very core of their sexual organs.

And I have seen women burst into tears over the physical pain and frustration of trying to care for their baby during the prolonged recovery that often goes with the unnecessary loss of blood and the pain.

I had a mediolateral episiotomy with my first baby and decided having babies was great but episiotomies were not! I went on to have two more babies with no episiotomy and no tear. I simply forbade my OB to do an episiotomy, and I was amazed that after the birth there was nothing to recover from but a lost night's sleep.

This is not nearly as uncommon as women think it is. I have seen many babies born without tears or episiotomies, including some nine- and ten-pound first babies!

Three Kinds of Episiotomy

The original episiotomy was the bilateral, a cut made sideways out toward the leg. This episiotomy is now obsolete. It has been abandoned due to excessive scarring, poor healing, and extreme pain. But at one time, women were told it was perfectly safe.

The three most common episiotomy techniques used at this time are: the mediolateral; the median, or midline; and the relatively new "hockey stick." We will look at them one by one.

Mediolateral Episiotomy
This incision is a slanting cut to one side of the perineum. It cuts through nerves, muscle, and tissue. This may be the most painful episiotomy. The fact it is so painful should

alert both the woman and the doctor that the perineum is a highly sensitive, sexually responsive area.

But—besides the perineum—Dr. Arnold Kegel (who as you'll recall invented the PC muscle exercises you have been doing) made an entire film to document the permanent harm the mediolateral episiotomy can do to your PC muscle. One of the main reasons doctors say they give every woman a routine episiotomy is to prevent "stretching" of that PC muscle. The doctor who gives you this reason believes stretching will cause your muscles to sag permanently and your inner organs to fall downward. He believes the episiotomy preserves the muscles in good condition and prevents this future problem. But Dr. Kegel's film clearly shows that the mediolateral episiotomy does *not* prevent this problem and, in fact, can be a major factor contributing to it.

The reason for this is that the PC muscle is wrapped around the vaginal barrel. This muscle extends down toward the perineum as the baby moves through the vaginal barrel. When the cut is made in your perineum, the PC muscle, which can't be seen, may be included. It is usually not completely severed but it frequently may be partly cut. Since it can't be seen, it is not sewn up as the perineum is after the cut. This results in permanent damage to your supportive muscle that was caused, not prevented, by the episiotomy.

Women who have had mediolateral episiotomies and suffered this damage can feel for it and find it if they know what to look for. Simply insert two fingers into the vagina and press firmly right at the outlet, around in a circle. You will feel the damage. Where you were not cut, the perineal

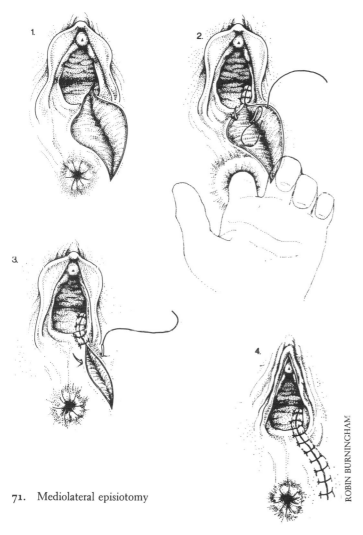

1.

2.

3.

4.

ROBIN BURNINGHAM

71. Mediolateral episiotomy

muscles feel thick and springy against your fingers. Where a cut was made, your fingers will not feel that counterpressure, but instead will feel no support. It will feel as if this part is a thin, not a thick, muscle.

You can also use a mirror, and you may notice that the tissues surrounding your outlet are slightly bulgier on one side than on the other. This is the musculature trying to compensate by overdeveloping on the unharmed side.

The Median or Midline Episiotomy
So what if your doctor says not to worry, he hardly ever does a mediolateral episiotomy. Instead he uses a median or midline episiotomy.

The median goes through connective tissue, rather than nerves, straight down the middle of your bottom toward the rectum. It is less painful than the mediolateral and does not include the PC muscle, but this one has many other problems.

The biggest and rather frequent problem is that it tends to tear right on through the rectum. The perineum is stretched thin like a piece of cloth at the moment of birth. Cutting the perineum now is like cutting a piece of cloth and adding pressure. Anyone who sews knows what happens. It tears straight on through.

When this happens, of course, you are right back to facing a long, painful recovery; and in addition, your sphincter muscle has been severed and permanently weakened.

This happens much more often than any doctor I've ever known cares to admit. After having my student couples go to a hundred or more different doctors through the

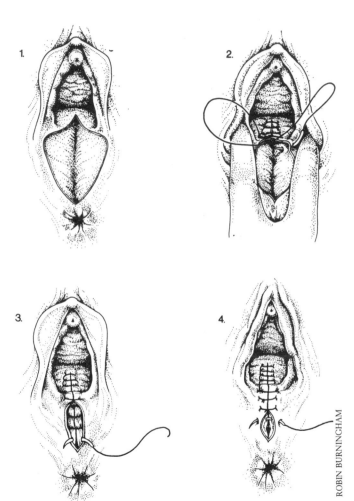

years, it has become apparent to me that the doctor's skill as a surgeon does not prevent this from happening.

The Hockey Stick

This episiotomy goes straight back toward the rectum like a median and then veers off at the end like a mediolateral. The fact that this one was invented makes it quite clear that doctors are aware of the dangers of both of the other kinds of episiotomy.

So somehow this technique is at one and the same time an admission of the hazards of both median and mediolateral episiotomies and a compounding of the problems of both.

I have seen women be given this "compromise" technique and then tear in both directions, through the rectum *and* off to the side. Where you cut into the thin-stretched perineum, you are risking an extension into a longer tear. The hockey stick solves nothing and risks the dangers of both the episiotomies in one.

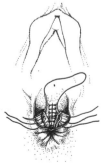

73. Extended episiotomy tear

ROBIN BURNINGHAM

72. Median episiotomy

Tears

I have never seen a tear happen when no incision was made that was as bad as an episiotomy. I have seen some bad tears *with* episiotomies. But when no cut is made, most tears (if they occur at all) consist of the following: (1) A little split in the *surface* of the skin inside the vaginal barrel; (2) A small tear in the perineum, usually less than a quarter of an inch long. (Much less than an episiotomy.)

The word "tear" strikes fear into the hearts of most women, but when you take a close look at what a tear usually consists of, and what an episiotomy consists of, it is the episiotomy that should make women more apprehensive.

An episiotomy is a complete severing of all the layers of tissue, muscle, and nerves *and is no guarantee of not tearing.* In fact, it can contribute to a much more serious extension. Again, to quote Drs. Banta and Thacker, who reviewed all the available medical literature, "These studies give no clear indication that episiotomy prevents third-degree lacerations. It is also evident from these data that episiotomies sometimes tear further and can extend into the rectum."[4]

I have seen doctors very nonchalant about this complete surgical severing and yet very upset about a surface split in the skin or a quarter-inch tear.

Why? Because among a doctor's colleagues episiotomy is acceptable. It is considered proper obstetrical technique; but a tear is considered careless. Imagine the pressure this puts on the young doctor, new and anxious for his peers' approval. Even when he wants to help women out with this, there are strong forces pressuring him to conform to "prevailing standards of practice."

It is sometimes said that it is better to cut the perineum than to risk the possibility of a tear up by the clitoris. This hardly ever happens, but even when it does, I challenge the idea that the clitoris is more important than the perineum. This is a male concept.

The perineum itself is a highly sexually responsive area, and it is certainly difficult to enjoy intercourse with the penis directly rubbing a cut, stitched, and scarred area in the very organ that holds it during intercourse.

Other Reasons Given for Episiotomy

When women question doctors about episiotomies, they are often told about tearing, but this is not the rationale that most physicians are themselves sold on. It is just the one women accept the most readily. It pushes all the fear buttons and ends the questioning.

The reasons given in obstetrical texts, however, include:

1. To shorten the second stage.
    Yes, it does shorten second stage by all

of *several to sometimes a dozen contractions* (say fifteen minutes). This is a kind of cruel joke from the woman's point of view, since she has just experienced perhaps a couple of hundred contractions.

2. To prevent the baby's head from pounding on the perineum.

   Pounding on the perineum? This is really reaching to support the "routine" episiotomy. The perineum is hardly a brick wall. Any baby that just came through the cervix, which took ten to fourteen hours to dilate with much more work, is not going to have any difficulty with the vagina and perineum.

3. To prevent overstretching of the muscles that support the inner organs, preventing uterine prolapse (uterus dropping down into or even out of the vagina), and incontinence (leaking of urine).

   We already know what Dr. Kegel had to say about this, so suffice it to say that scar tissue does not make for strong muscles. Exercise does that.

4. To make repair easier. A clean cut is said to be easier to repair than a jagged tear.

   But somehow doctors manage to repair the many tears caused by midline episiotomies without much hassle about it. There would be far fewer tears and less serious tears to repair in the first place if we gave up episiotomies.

Are Women Able to Give Birth Without Episiotomy?

There are physicians sensitive to the trauma of surgery performed on a sexual organ. I have the highest regard for them. My own faith in the normality and simplicity of birth is reaffirmed each time I accompany a mother to see her give birth with no episiotomy and no tear.

At a teacher-training workshop in the Bradley Method®, Dr. Victor Berman, who practices obstetrics in Los Angeles County, reported on a mother who gave birth to a thirteen-pound baby with no tear and no episiotomy. (He humbly spoke of catching the baby rather than delivering it.) Why do we expect it to be otherwise? Birth is a normal bodily function and women are designed for it. Most women *can* give birth without an episiotomy or a tear if they are allowed to assume a proper position for pushing, given adequate training to help them prepare the muscles involved in actually giving birth, and, most importantly, told when to stop pushing.

A woman must also have a doctor who is not in a hurry, who does not use his fingers to stretch her apart and grasp the baby's head to hasten its birth. All this hurry-up technique does not allow your tissues a chance to stretch gradually as they should.

To Avoid an Episiotomy

Be sure you have selected your doctor carefully. Get one who *seldom* does episiotomies.

Prepare yourself by doing lots of squatting. Remember that a muscle in good tone has a much greater stretch ratio. You squat to make the perineum more flexible and to get into good tone.

Prepare yourself by doing your PC contractions. Again, you increase the stretch ratio of this muscle too. You also get to know what it feels like to consciously relax and let go with this muscle.

Do not have a pudendal block or any "local" anesthetics. You can't tell when you are letting go or contracting the muscle.

Avoid anesthetics! Spinal, caudal, and paracervical anesthesia interferes with pushing and can lead to an episiotomy to hasten the end of the anesthetic-slowed pushing stage.

If you don't want to do anything that would increase the likelihood of a tear or an episiotomy, then don't take drugs that interfere with the way your body works.

And finally, you absolutely cannot be flat on your back to give birth. This position puts too much pressure on the perineum when the head is emerging, and at the same time makes it difficult to relax the perineum. A flat-on-the-back position *creates* the need for an episiotomy.

The physician who sees bad tears invariably also has the mothers in this position or is *hurrying the birth with manipulation*. Perhaps the reason I have never seen a bad tear when no episiotomy is performed is because I have attended births with physicians who do not require the woman to be flat, who do not hurry, and who do not use anesthetics which interfere with the perineal reflex.

The episiotomy is one of those unpleasant, unnecessary things which happens to a woman at birth that is being questioned more and more by those concerned about women's health issues. We may not be able to revolutionize the practice of obstetrics in this country during the nine months of your pregnancy, but you can take steps to avoid having this initiation ritual of motherhood performed on you.

In the next chapters we will look at some of the other risks that you face when going to the hospital to have your baby.

chapter twenty-one

Caesarean Surgery

Last year, the United States had the highest rate of caesarean sections in the world . . .

Washington Post, Sept. 25, 1980

Fifteen years ago when I started teaching, your odds of having caesarean surgery were thirty to one. Today, your odds are four to one. The caesarean section rate is now so high that even Congress has investigated it.

You don't really need to know what your hospital's C-section rate is, but you certainly *do* need to know your

individual doctor's rate, because that will be the risk you personally run of having your birth turned into major surgery. Your independent Bradley® teacher—not a hospital's or doctor's childbirth instructor—is your best source of information when you are seeking to reduce this risk.

I have actually had the experience of working for one group of doctors with a three-percent surgery rate while working at the same time for another group with a forty-percent rate. As I worked for the two groups of doctors, I clearly saw the impact of a high group-practice surgery rate on the health of mothers and babies. I had taught for years with so few problems that at first I thought perhaps statistics were catching up with me, as four out of ten women from one doctors' group had their babies via major surgery. The difference was incredible, not just in rates of caesareans but in the condition of the mothers and babies. I had never seen so many washed-out, pale women with dark rings under their eyes. Many of them had to be rehospitalized to treat infected uteruses (rather common after caesarean surgery) and had to leave their nursing babies at home. Some of them came back to the class to tell their stories without their babies, since the babies were still hospitalized to recover from breathing difficulties and other problems common to caesarean delivery. And, of course, all of these mothers had to deal with more than their share of pain and frustration. Meanwhile, women who went to the doctors whose caesarean surgery rate was only three percent rarely had infections, experienced fewer days of hospitalization, and were far more successful at breast-feeding. Those mothers were simply happier and healthier—and so were their babies.

Almost half of all caesarean patients in a survey of 4,000 who had this surgery from 1959 to 1976 had one or more operative complications, "including a respectable number of severe complications which compromise future childbearing or are potentially lethal," according to L. T. Hibbard writing in the *American Journal of Obstetrics and Gynecology*.[1]

What are these complications? Almost all women experience gas and pain. Until recently almost all women who had caesarean surgery had to have repeat sections for later children, although now the VBAC (vaginal birth after caesarean) movement is growing. Infection is fairly common: intrauterine infection occurs in thirty-five to sixty-five percent of cases if the mother had internal electronic fetal monitoring and in twenty to forty percent of cases without monitoring. Other categories of infection include cystitis, peritonitis, abscess, gangrene, and generalized sepsis.[2]

The list goes on and on. In a declining order of frequency it includes things like: hemorrhage, accidental reopening of the wound, subsequent uterine rupture, injuries to adjacent parts of the body like the bladder or bowels, complications with blood transfusions including hepatitis, aspiration pneumonia, anesthesia accidents, and even cardiac arrest. Death occurs for the mother after caesarean surgery about once in every thousand operations.[3] This is about ten times more often than in vaginal births.

It stretches credibility beyond reason to really believe that twenty or thirty percent of all women need major abdominal surgery in order to have a healthy baby. In this caesarean-section chapter, unlike the class taught in the hospital, we won't prepare you for your highly likely caesarean surgery with no questions asked, but will teach you to know how to carefully pick your doctor to make a C-section highly *unlikely* and also help you get information before you give your informed consent to anything.

First of all, your doctor's rate of C-sections should be no more than three to five percent—not fifteen, not twenty, not thirty percent! But how do you know which C-sections make up the unnecessary increase and which fall into the necessary-three-percent category? We will take a look at some necessary C-sections, but first let's move in for close scrutiny of the reasons most commonly given for many of those unnecessary C-sections, and how you can avoid them.

The three main categories into which the dramatic increase of unnecessary C-sections falls are:

1. *THE FETAL MONITOR C-SECTION.* Alias: Fetal distress, or inefficient or nonproductive uterine contractions.

2. *THE PUTTERER C-SECTION.* Alias: Failure to progress, or prolonged labor, or uterine inertia (lazy uterus); or it may even be called CPD (cephalopelvic disproportion).

3. *THE "YOUR TIME'S UP" C-SECTION.* Alias: Failure to progress, or CPD. Differs from the putterer C-section in that it occurs in the pushing stage.

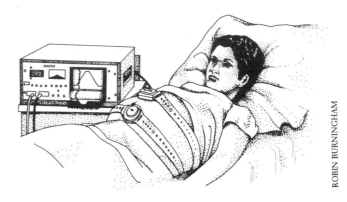

74. External fetal monitor

The Fetal Monitor Caesarean Section

We need to start with a little vocabulary. **EFM** means "electronic fetal monitoring." Let's take a look at the electronic fetal monitor and at the evidence stacked up against it as hazardous to the health of the mother.

With the external fetal monitor, two belts with sensors are strapped around your waist. One directs sound waves (ultrasound) at your baby, and as the sound waves

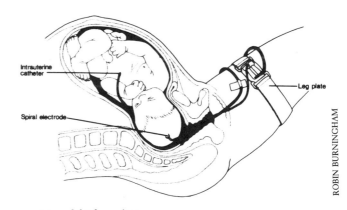

Intrauterine catheter

Spiral electrode

Leg plate

75. Internal fetal monitor

are bounced back your baby's heart rate is recorded. The other belt with sensor records your uterus contracting. Already two hazards have been added. Lying on your back for this monitoring increases risk to the baby, and ultrasound has not been tested for long-term side effects.

With internal monitoring, a catheter is pushed into your vagina and up into your uterus (which increases the risk of infection). The catheter is then filled with water and connected to a pressure sensor which records the contractions. In addition, an electrode is inserted into your vagina with a thin spiral-wire ending that is screwed into your baby's head, recording his heart activity. Both tubes are strapped to your leg. Often this means rupturing an intact bag of waters just to insert the spiral electrode into the baby's scalp.

Many doctors believe that every woman in labor should be monitored electronically and are doing just that. Most are using the internal monitor, but sometimes a woman is put on the external monitor early in labor and on the internal monitor later.

It looks pretty unappealing. If it made a difference for your baby you would probably put up with it anyway. But the fact is that out of five scientific studies (randomized, controlled trials) of fetal monitors, four showed no differences in outcome for the babies whether the fetal monitor was used or not.[4] Only one showed an improved outcome for the babies, and that study has been severely criticized for poor scientific methodology.[5]

Dr. A. D. Haverkamp of Denver told the Central Association of Obstetricians and Gynecologists in 1975 that research showed no difference in the health or survival rate of babies when internal electronic fetal heart monitoring was used to manage deliveries. But the big difference, he said, was in the caesarean-section rate. It was 16.5 percent in the group of women who underwent electronic fetal monitoring but only 6.8 percent in the group whose births were managed by frequent use of the stethoscope to check the baby's well-being.[6]

Clearly, repeated scientific studies show that the baby does not benefit when the mother is electronically monitored. These studies show that the major difference in outcome when the fetal monitor is used is for the mother. *The caesarean surgery rate is as much as tripled!*

More women undergo the trauma and risks of major surgery, the days of pain afterward, the dual difficulties of recovering from a major operation while also trying to learn how to mother a new baby, and for what? When so many studies tell us that we only get more women having major, high risk surgery, then don't you think it's time to say the risks outweigh the benefits?

Let's take a look at the scenario of the fetal-monitor C-section. This is how it happened for Sharon and Tom with their first baby.

SHARON: "When we got to the hospital, I was seven centimeters dilated. I was elated. Tom had to go down for the admittance papers. We had filled out everything we could ahead of time, but it still took about twenty minutes before he returned. We'd looked over the Xeroxed handouts of various studies in our birth classes and, if it didn't make things better for the baby, I didn't want to be attached to a machine and wires. But when I turned the monitor down, they told me that everyone had to have it, it was a rule, and my baby would be much safer with it. I just couldn't argue. When Tom got back I know he was surprised to see me attached to the monitor. He knew how I felt about it. Well, we just kept working and I went really quick to ten centimeters. We'd only been in the hospital for two hours."

TOM: "But the doctor didn't like what he saw on the fetal monitor printout. He told us the baby's heart rate was dropping periodically and that he would have to deliver it right away if we wanted to avoid brain damage. Brain damage! I didn't know what to do. Sharon and I both sure didn't want a brain-damaged baby, but I knew she was thinking the same thing I was—all those studies that showed more caesarean sections for nothing. We wished we hadn't allowed the fetal monitor. I kicked myself for not being there to help her refuse it. We would have felt more confident of the decision to do the caesarean if Sharon had only been monitored with a stethoscope."

SHARON: "Our baby came out in perfect shape. He breathed right away and was a nice pink. I was relieved, but at the same time it was hard to see what he had been saved from. We had been told the baby was in trouble and we were willing to do whatever was necessary to protect our baby, but neither of us could see that our baby had been saved from anything."

What happened to Sharon and Tom is a daily occurrence, repeated across the country. How can this be? How can the fetal monitor show a "distressed baby" and yet after cutting the mother open the doctor pulls out a baby who is clearly in no trouble?

Some doctors claim that when you see a "nonreassuring pattern you do a caesarean right away and you prevent a problem from developing." This argument is supposed to explain how they can cut a mother open and find a baby in no trouble after all. But we now know beyond a doubt that this argument is not true. The controlled studies have shown us that mothers who are not monitored do not have more babies in trouble.[7]

The problem is that we have a machine that gives us the beat-to-beat variations of the baby's heart rate. We are getting more information about what's going on with the baby, but the results make it clear that *we don't really understand just what this additional information means.*

"That reliable recording could be done seems to have blinded most observers to the fact that this additional information will not necessarily produce better outcomes," say Drs. Banta and Thacker in their review of EFM. "This is not surprising, given the lack of precision of EFM for the diagnosis of fetal distress, and the general difficulty of separating normal fetal stress during labor from fetal distress."[8]

The studies show us that the stethoscope, tested side by side with EFM, will pick up *sustained* distress of a serious nature—meaningful distress that requires action. The bottom line is this: the stethoscope is a valued diagnostic tool for well-defined fetal distress. It will not miss the baby in real trouble.

So, how to avoid the fetal-monitor caesarean section? Sharon and Tom feel they have the answer. When they have their next baby, they are absolutely not going to be on a fetal monitor. They're convinced that it is essential to *stay off the monitor* if you want to avoid unnecessary caesarean surgery. As Tom says, "What can you say when the doctor says, 'Brain damage if I don't do a C-section.'? How can you deal with that? You can't say, 'That's all right, Doc, we'll take the chance.' Who would say that? Once you're in that situation it's all over, it just isn't possible to deal with it when it happens. The trick, I'm convinced, is to just stay off the fetal monitor in the first place. When we have our next baby we'll certainly allow monitoring with the ordinary stethoscope occasionally. We do want a healthy baby; what we don't want is another unnecessary C-section."

If you go to a doctor who uses the monitor with the idea that you will just refuse the procedure (which, of course, you can do), remember, he really believes that it works and that you are being stubborn by refusing it. The result is you may become the recipient of a lot of ill will. *This is definitely not a good laboring situation.* Bad feelings generated by others can seriously inhibit your labor! My advice is, don't put yourself in this situation. Instead, find a doctor who doesn't use the monitor.

There is one other important consideration. Birth is an incredibly safe and successful journey for ninety-nine babies out of a hundred, but there will be about one out of every hundred babies who will die. This inevitable death occurs whether a woman is on the monitor or not. Although these are terrific odds, if you have the one that dies, the experience is one hundred percent for *you.* If you go to a doctor who uses the monitor regularly and you refuse it, and if you happen to have that one baby out of a hundred, then you might be told that you caused your baby's death because you wouldn't allow the fetal monitor. Could you really cope with that? Although there are plenty of studies

to prove you denied your baby nothing, this is not what you will hear from a doctor who believes otherwise.

When you have found a doctor who does not use the fetal monitor, you have eliminated the risk of an unnecessary fetal monitor C-section. Your physician will listen to the baby's heartbeat regularly with a stethoscope and you are far less likely to get a false alarm.

The Putterer Caesarean Section

You already know that each woman will produce a baby at her own speed, and that this can vary from the "speedster" to the "textbook" labor to the "putterer." There are two kinds of putterers. One is the on-again-off-again putterer, whose labor actually stops and starts, stops and starts.

My own third birth is a perfect example of a putterer birthing normally, the on-again-off-again variety. I labored from 4:00 P.M. to midnight in light to moderate labor, four nights in a row. Gruesome? Not at all. I wasn't working hard yet. I got a full eight hours sleep each night, had a whole day off from labor, and started again the next evening doing light to moderately hard work. False labor? Hardly. I was dilating a little more each night. On Monday morning when labor had stopped, my husband went to work and I went to the grocery store and stocked up on labor snacks and things I could make and freeze. On Tuesday morning when labor stopped, I baked the "birthday cake." On Wednesday I went to one of my student's births. When labor stopped Thursday morning, I was five centimeters dilated. Thursday night labor took off, and then I labored moderately hard to quite hard. The doctor attending my home birth arrived about midnight, and I began pushing at four in the morning. Then I pushed for two hours of hard work, turning Polly from a posterior position to the more usual one, and birthed her around 6:00 in the morning. There was a lot of work in this labor, not all jammed together but nicely spread out over the week (which I think is precisely the reason the uterus behaved this way). If I had birthed Polly in a hospital, my labor pattern would not have been allowed. The putterer's pattern is labeled "prolonged labor," "dystocia" (abnormal labor), "uterine inertia" (lazy uterus), "failure to progress," and finally "**CPD.**"

Currently, out of every 2,500 births, at least 100 women have their babies removed surgically due to CPD.[9] **Cephalopelvic disproportion** means the mother's pelvis is too small for the baby's head to fit through. Now the FDA has published a booklet that lets obstetricians know that "the incidence of a truly 'small' pelvis in patients selected for pelvimetry was as low as one or two cases in 2,500. Furthermore . . . the effects of molding of the fetal head and expansion of the maternal pelvis during labor may render pelvic diameter measurements meaningless."[10]

So what have all these women been having caesarean surgery for? These are the putterers. As the term CPD becomes largely invalidated, it will become an embarrassment to those obstetricians with high surgery rates, and I have no doubt it will become a worrisome problem for such obstetricians as malpractice suits are filed for this un-

necessary surgery. The term CPD will not be used much five years from now, as the FDA publication gets around, but putterers will continue to have their babies surgically removed for uterine inertia, failure to progress, dystocia, or prolonged labor.

The woman who has the putterer pattern spread out over a couple of days is most in danger of unnecessary caesarean surgery. *The mere passage of time by itself, without evidence of trouble, is not a medical emergency.*

The second type of putterer is the one whose labor never stops but takes its sweet, slow time all the way up to about six or seven centimeters. She may have nine to twelve hours of mild to moderate contractions before she really gets down to business. So at the end of this time, say twelve hours, she's really just beginning. It is important that you do not fall into the emotional booby trap of getting exasperated as the time goes by; keep it in perspective by looking at the amount of work you are doing, and don't count the work until it begins to demand your utmost concentration. And if, after all is said and done, you still arrive too early at the hospital, be prepared to turn around and go home. Diony Young and Charles Mahan, in their booklet *Unnecessary Caesareans: Ways to Avoid Them,* give a piece of advice that is worth memorizing: "Plan to stay at home until active labor is well established. Return home if you get to the hospital and are less than four centimeters dilated and the baby is well . . ."[11]

If a woman enters the hospital, she is treated as a medical problem if her labor stops or doesn't move fast enough. If the same woman had stayed at home during that time and later mentioned it to her doctor, he would just say, "Oh well, that was just false labor," while everyone waits for the "real thing." In fact, she has experienced the real thing, but it does not have to take off and go all the way on the same day. Once you enter the hospital, though, you have declared yourself to be in labor, and labor must continue according to the hospital's timetable.

The putterer, birthing normally, is the most bungled, mishandled labor pattern in a hospital birth. Since you are in control of the decision on when to enter the hospital, this is one unnecessary caesarean section it is clearly in your power to avoid. This is why we made such a fuss back when we discussed the emotional map of labor about not going to the hospital in the excitement signpost, nor at the beginning of the serious signpost, but instead waiting until you get some of the hours of serious working labor behind you at home. Those doctors who give instructions to come in when contractions are three minutes apart and one minute long are, in my experience, the ones with the healthiest outcomes for mothers and babies. (Second-timers should be going at four minutes apart and a minute long by these doctors' recommendations.) And the emotional signpost you want to see is absolutely dedicated seriousness, aggravation at having to move, and wondering if in fact she even can. (She can, of course—she only thinks she's made of glass.)

If it is your first baby and you think you have nothing to compare contractions with to know what is hard and what is not, call your teacher; she knows, and she will spot your emotional signpost.

The woman having prolonged labor, dystocia, uterine inertia, or failure to progress is too often just the putterer,

and no one is allowed to putter in the hospital. In fact there is a chart that says you are supposed to dilate about a centimeter an hour. Few women dilate in equal increments. Caesarean surgery for puttering accounts for as many as twenty percent of all C-sections.

Remember that the mere passage of time itself does not constitute a medical emergency situation, and that you should have a doctor who is interested in intervening only when there is an indication to do so.

The "Times Up" C-Section

This one takes less time to explain than the putterer, but is no less important. When you get to the pushing stage in a hospital birth, the clock is running. Many doctors will set it for two hours, and then your time's up! You end up with caesarean surgery (or, if the baby is quite low, a forceps or vacuum-extractor delivery). Some doctors set the clock for three hours. This means that many women whose babies are in posterior positions will end up as C-sections or other operative deliveries. Many posterior positions will require a good amount of pushing time. Other women get a rest in the pushing stage, and their contractions will begin again a while later. But their time may have run out before then. Why should it be okay to push for two hours but not two hours and twenty minutes? Why can't you wait for the uterus to begin again when it's ready? An article in the *American Journal of Obstetrics and Gynecology* further questions this two-hour limit: "Elective termination of labor simply because an arbitrary period of time has elapsed in the second stage is clearly not warranted. Rather, the practice of subjecting patients to potentially traumatic operative procedures merely because they have not delivered within two hours after second stage had begun should be decried."[12]

One of the ways not to "run out of time" is to stall the pushing stage as long as you can. I mean back before you begin pushing in the first place. How? Well, if your last exam revealed that you were, say, six or seven centimeters dilated or more, stall the next exam for as long as you can. The clock begins to run in the pushing stage once someone "officially" knows that you are completely dilated, whether you have an urge to push or not. So even if you think you may be in the pushing stage, hold off that exam as long as possible and buy yourself some time. Allow the extra time to let the pushing urge become so well established that you can no longer reasonably hold off.

As we discussed earlier, nurse-midwives who have had home-birth experience have a far better idea of the range of normality here than their counterparts who have been limited to hospital birth experiences only. Two hours is often the hospital time limit for pushing in second stage, and hospital birth attendants do not get to see what happens if it goes longer. In fact they are scared of it. Barbara Katz Rothman sheds some real light on this in her book, *In Labor: Women and Power in the Birthplace*. She tells us that some nurse-midwives working in a hospital deal with the challenge of not letting the clock get started by a tech-

nique known as "not looking for what you do not want to find. They are careful about not examining a woman who might be fully dilated but doesn't have the urge to push for fear of starting up the clock" sooner than necessary.

Some nurse-midwives have taken this a step further and redefined second stage itself. Rather than saying it starts with full dilation—the "objective," medical measure—they measure second stage by the subjective measure of the woman's urge to push. Most women begin to feel a definite urge to push and begin bearing down at just about the time of full dilation.

But not all women have this experience. For some, labor contractions cease after full dilation. These are the "second-stage arrests," which medicine treats by the use of forceps or caesarean section. Some nurse-midwives now think "second-stage arrest" may just be a naturally occurring rest period at the end of labor, instead of a problem requiring medical intervention. . . .

In the medical model, once labor starts, it cannot stop and start again and still be "normal". . . . But a nurse-midwife can call the "hour or so between full dilation and when she starts pushing" as *not* second stage. This is more than just buying time for clients: this is developing an alternative set of definitions, changing the way she sees the birth process.

Midwives who did not know each other, who did not work together, came to the same conclusion.[13]

The Repeat Caesarean Section

The repeat caesarean section requires more information than I can do justice to here. If you had a C-section the first time or have a friend who had a C-section the first time, go straight to *Silent Knife* by Nancy Wainer-Cohen and Lois J. Estner. This is an absolute must for anyone approaching a repeat C-section. "Once a C-section always a C-section" is not necessarily true at all.

Some Necessary C-Sections

Bleeding
This one is pretty commonsense, isn't it? Bleeding can be life-threatening for both mother and baby, and in such an instance a caesarean can be appropriate and life-saving. I don't know of anyone who has had trouble realizing this at the time.

Cord Prolapse
This is so rare that it is a less-than-one-percent occurrence (.3 to .6 percent). The umbilical cord can slip down before the baby's head, even protrude from the vagina, and the head then presses down on it, cutting off the baby's oxygen supply. Again, when this rare accident has occurred, I have never known of anyone who had difficulty realizing that a caesarean might be in order to save the baby.

Fetal Distress
Yes, of course there is such a thing, and as we have already discussed, the stethoscope or fetoscope will pick up the real thing, sustained, meaningful fetal distress that may require a C-section to save the baby in trouble. What we have objected to here is not the validity of fetal distress as a reason for doing a C-section but the inaccuracy of the electronic fetal monitor in identifying fetal distress.

Herpes
An open lesion in the birth canal at the time of labor is thought to increase the chances of the baby being infected. A C-section will probably be done. Recurrent herpes attacks have not been conclusively shown to cause this problem, and studies on this will bear watching.

CPD
Yes, there is also such a thing as CPD, the baby's head not fitting through the pelvis. But it is astoundingly *rare*, as noted—only about one or two cases in 2,500.

How can a doctor know when CPD is for real? There is only one way, a good trial of labor. A second stage in which there is a series of intense contractions and a uterus that stops, gives another thrust forward, and stops with no progress is the only way to be tipped off to this. An arbitrary two-hour limit does not allow time for the many posteriors or putterers to birth. To do caesarean surgery before allowing this to come clearly into focus puts hundreds of women and their babies at the risk of surgical complications.

Some Frequently Asked Questions on Caesareans

Q: I can't understand why there is such a gap between the evidence and the way doctors practice. In spite of the information available on the inefficiency and hazards of fetal monitoring, most women continue to be monitored. In spite of the fact that there are three times as many caesarean sections that do not result in better odds for babies, women are still getting surgery at these increased rates. Why?

A: Dr. Marieskind gives us the answer in her book *An Evaluation of Caesarean Surgery:* "Habits and beliefs are already formed and the specter of suits for past unnecessary interference [is] too great."[14]

Q: My doctor says he just uses the fetal monitor for high-risk pregnancy. If I'm high-risk will my baby benefit, and am I less likely to have one of those unnecessary caesareans?

A: Two of the five controlled trials *were* with high-risk pregnancies and showed no differences in outcome and triple the C-section rate, so I don't understand the rationale for thinking that it should be used on high-risk mothers.

Q: My doctor says there are studies that show the fetal monitor and the C-section have made big improvements in the infant mortality rate and that there are studies of hundreds of thousands of babies that prove this.

A: Articles in journals and books by physicians appear all the time (*Safe Delivery* by R. Freeman and S. Pescar is a perfect example) that claim the fetal monitor and the rising rate of C-sections have reduced infant mortality and refer to studies of hundreds of thousands of babies. In fact, studies cited in these articles and books do not use the accepted scientific method of randomized, controlled trials. They are retrospective studies. I have found that these statements often compare infant mortality in a given hospital with the same hospital's mortality rate for the 1950's and 1960's. But in the 1950's we couldn't do much for *premature* babies. Even in the late 1960's we lost most premature babies. Today 50 to 75 percent can survive.

It is true that our infant mortality rates have improved, and it is also clear that the improvement has come mainly in the area of saving prematures. We must not lose sight of the fact that we still rank low in relation to other industrialized nations in terms of overall infant mortality. There are still many other countries where it is safer to have a baby. Sweden, for example. Kathleen Newland tells us in *Infant Mortality and the Health of Societies* that Sweden has a lower infant mortality rate than the United States because fewer premature babies are born there, not because the Swedes save more of their vulnerable infants.[15]

Many women come back to class to tell me that their doctor claims the fetal monitor and the caesarean section are improving our infant mortality statistics, and women stumble over this as they struggle to decide whether or not to allow a monitor or whether to change doctors. For this reason it is important that you have an understanding of what *is* happening today to improve our statistics. We have not improved them by doing more C-sections and electronic fetal monitoring. We have, first of all, improved our ability to keep the premies alive. In addition to this, birth control has allowed mothers to space children and build up their own strength and nutritional reserves. Women are also now less likely to limit their weight gain. Finally, the return to breast-feeding has been an important factor. To promote the high caesarean surgery rate and the use of the fetal monitor as the reason for low infant mortality is not telling the whole story.

A Solution

Every woman *should* be able to easily find out her doctor's C-section rate before she hires him. Unfortunately, it will probably take an act of Congress (or something stronger) to require that obstetricians be accountable to their clients by publishing their annual statistics for C-sections, forceps deliveries, and use of drugs in labor as a ratio of their total births.

Just as the Occupational Safety and Health Administration has businesses post their accident and injury record annually where workers can see it, OBs should be required to post their total births attended and number of C-sections and other procedures performed annually.

Consumers have a right, even a parental responsibility, to get this information. I have worked for a number of doctors and have known their C-section rates firsthand. But I have watched women ask what the doctor's rate is and be given dishonest, "reassuring" answers.

Women should be protected from this misinformation and lack of information. Like anyone else selling a service, OBs should be accountable to consumers.

Controversies in Hospital Birthing

Risk. Risk. Home-birthers confront risks; the home-birth dangers must be faced and put into perspective. So the home-birther learns about birthing and plans for good prenatal care which will screen her out of a home birth for obvious problems. The home-birther finds a skilled birth attendant to watch for problems that are not obvious, and a medical backup to be in readiness. With no drugs used and a mother who will nurse after birth, the home-birth risks are statistically small. The California Department of Health studied 1,146 cases of *planned* home birth and found that the perinatal mortality rate for home birth remained lower than the state average. The key seems to be planning, which means adequate prenatal care, plenty of knowledge, and a good birth attendant. (If you are planning a home birth you will find much useful information in Rahima Baldwin, *Special Delivery* [Berkeley: Celestial Arts, 1979]).

The major risk to the mother in home birthing is unexpectedly heavy bleeding *after* the birth. A midwife or other attendant must know what to do in this most unlikely life-threatening event. Bleeding *before* birth is rarely sudden. In almost every instance there are preliminary signs of bleeding that are not severe enough to threaten life, but are ample warning to go to the hospital. Most other kinds of problems have to do with the baby not coming, and in that event it is always possible to move to the hospital.

Next, the home-birther needs to consider risks to the baby. The attendant should know ordinary resuscitation techniques, but there will be no intensive-care nursery minutes away to help a baby born with severe problems. (Some small hospitals don't have them either.) There are problems the baby may have that cannot be handled in a home birth. But if you are healthy, have had prenatal care to screen out toxemia or other predictable problems, and have selected an attendant (usually a midwife) who is competent, then you have confronted the risks of home birth and reduced them to a minimum. Still, home birth is not the choice of most people. You should only consider it if you can confront these risks and feel totally comfortable with your decision.

What the home-birther does, the hospital-birther must do also: get to know the risks; weigh them deliberately, consciously, and knowingly; decide whether or not they are acceptable; and then go about the business of reducing all risk to a minimum. The hospital-birther can be falsely lulled into thinking that the hospital birth is one hundred percent safe with a guaranteed perfect outcome because *no one talks about hospital-birth risks* as they do about home-birth risks.

So this chapter is especially for the hospital-birther. It is provided so you, too, will get to know the risks in the hospital birth you are planning and be able to reject those that are not acceptable.

This process of learning the risks so that you can reduce them to the barest minimum is just as necessary for the hospital-birther as it is for home-birther.

Intravenous Drip (IV)

What is an intravenous drip? A hollow tube is inserted into a vein in your arm so that fluids can be dripped directly into your bloodstream, and you have taken your first giant step away from birthing normally.

I have watched bottle after bottle being dripped into a woman's arm during labor. After the nurse hooks up an IV she will often say, "You may notice your contractions slowing down." Isn't it just common sense that dripping fluid into an open vein is going to dilute the bloodstream that carries oxygen and nutrients around the body, as well as the hormone the body produces to make the uterus contract? No wonder an estimated thirty to forty percent of women in labor have so-called uterine inertia or dystocia and then need some artificial hormone added to the IV to force the uterus to contract. Having caused the problem with the intervention of a routine IV, it is necessary to solve it with a drug that has numerous known side effects and risks.

Women who are given IVs are often not allowed to eat or drink and are told the IV will replace the food and water they may need in labor. (The obstetrician is a surgeon who may already be thinking in terms of surgery later and preparing for it by inserting the IV and withholding food.) But the denial of food and water can make a woman's contractions weak and ineffectual in a long labor. Her ability to work with pushing contractions may be affected if she has just gone eighteen to twenty hours without anything to eat.

Glucose is often dripped in for energy. Many natural-childbirth mothers prefer to suck on oranges or drink fruit juices, but simple solutions are not the approach taken in most hospitals. Almost every woman in labor is now told she is dehydrated and hooked up to an IV when she arrives at the hospital. A little test is done on her urine, after which, with absolute authority, she is told this is so.

Or she may be told it is necessary to have an open vein in case of bleeding that requires a transfusion. (Not only is this rare, but an IV can be hooked up at that time if needed.)

A harmless procedure? Think again. When almost every woman in labor is declared to be dehydrated, we should begin to be suspicious. There is an important process going on here that we don't know much about. We don't know enough about what constitutes "normal" for the laboring mother to start instituting corrective measures, en masse, for all laboring women. As one doctor pointed out, the normally low concentrations of serum glucose in the human fetus may contribute to its capacity to withstand asphyxia. This suggests that if, for any reason, there is a temporary reduction of oxygen to the baby's brain, the baby can survive that condition better when the mother's serum-glucose level is low.[1]

So here we are, doing our misguided best to raise the woman's serum-glucose level by hooking her up to an IV and dripping the stuff directly into the vein.

Postmaturity

Postmaturity is one of the most common reasons parents are given for inducing (forcing) labor. Postmaturity is a theory which assumes that if you go past your "due date" the placenta gets old and starts to deteriorate.

This is supposed to result in a tiny baby who has lost weight in the womb. (It does not mean a baby who was allowed to grow too long and is getting too big, a common misconception women have when their doctors mention postmaturity.)

But there is another theory that the deteriorating placenta may be one of the natural triggers of labor.

Dr. Bradley makes it quite clear in *Husband-Coached Childbirth* that he doesn't believe in trying to second-guess nature. Although he has occasionally had to induce a labor for medical reasons, he has never induced any woman merely for going past her so-called due date.

Dr. Bradley says that an obstetrician who thinks he can tell when the baby is ready to be born is fooling himself and will occasionally "pick a green apple."

This has happened to several of my students. One went four weeks over her calculated due date. She was told her baby would be postmature if they waited any longer. After her forced labor was over, the pediatrician diagnosed her three-pound baby as *premature*. The first year of this baby's life was extremely expensive for the parents, both financially and emotionally.

Another student, induced for the same reason, discovered that her labor simply would not get going in spite of the induction. Since her membranes (bag of waters) had been ruptured artificially, in an attempt to force labor to start, she couldn't be sent home from the hospital. Something had to be done, so she had a caesarean section.

This problem is not at all uncommon in induced labors. It is one of the recognized risks of induction: that it might simply not work. A C-section will then be done. Few women realize that once they start this procedure, there is no turning back if it doesn't work.

I will never forget the student who was told her labor would have to be induced because she was so far past her due date that labor would never start on its own. Have you ever heard of a permanently pregnant woman?

I could go on and on. The majority of our students choose not to have a labor induced for postmaturity reasons. They do so with confidence in Dr. Bradley's book. His chapter "When Will the Baby Come?" is a must for any couple past their "due date."

Ultrasound is often used to tell if the baby is ready to be born—if he is mature enough or the right size. But ultrasound is not adequate to the task. It can be off by five to six weeks![2] That is not a reasonable margin of error.

At Dulwich Hospital in London in 1980 a study was done of 142 women who had been pregnant forty-two weeks or longer. In following up the courses of these so-called overdue mothers' deliveries, researchers found that women whose labors were induced ended up with caesarean surgery far more often than the women allowed to start labor normally; in fact, the surgery rate tripled for the forced-labor mothers. Even more significantly, the infants born in both induced and non-induced groups showed similar Apgar scores and were evaluated in every way as equally healthy. The induced group of babies had no advantage, and yet their mothers were subjected to the higher risks of surgery without benefit to their babies.[3]

Stimulating or Stripping the Membranes

There is a little trick to get labor started. The procedure is to separate the amniotic sac from the uterine wall, sort of "reaming" the cervix. The woman is usually told she will probably go into labor over the weekend, but she rarely does. It's not a very effective technique.

But it can produce some unwanted side effects. Every once in a while, I'll get a call from a student who will tell me her back is just killing her and it has been for a couple of days. She is not in labor. She's not talking about any ordinary backache. She's close to tears, practically breaking down over the phone.

My first question is, "Did your backache start right after a visit to the doctor?" Too often the answer is yes. Next question, "Were you given an internal exam and did it seem more uncomfortable than usual?" Again, the answer is yes.

Invariably, the mother's membranes were stimulated

without her knowledge or consent. It is a procedure that can be performed on her during what she thinks is a regular exam. It is most likely to be done if she happens to be a week or two past her "due date" or happens to be dilated one or two centimeters.

Women are much more comfortable when they are left alone to begin labor at the proper time.

Inducing Labor

Inducing labor means forcing it to begin. It is sometimes necessary when the continued pregnancy itself is a threat to the mother's life, as in the case of a diabetic mother whose pregnancy is too stressful, aggravating the diabetes into a life-threatening situation.

This would be a medical reason and the proper use of induction. But such cases are rare.

The majority of inductions are done today for what can only be termed "frivolous" or very questionable reasons. The induction for convenience (of the mother or the doctor) is frivolous, and the induction because the woman has gone past her "due date" with no other medical reason indicating induction is highly questionable.

Forcing labor to begin is usually a rough business for the woman. An artificial hormone, a second-rate copy of the hormone that naturally contracts the uterus, is dripped into her arm intravenously.

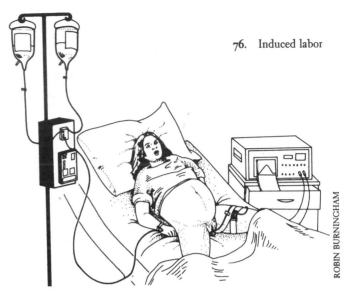

76. Induced labor

ROBIN BURNINGHAM

I say "second-rate" because the effect it can have on the uterine muscles is alarming. Your own hormone contracts the long muscles of the uterus progressively from the top downward toward the cervix in a wavelike action. The contraction builds slowly to a peak of its strength.

The second-rate copy can cause violent "tetanic" contractions which make the muscles contract all over at once. It feels just like a big CRUNCH! It feels stronger, and it cuts the uterus off from circulation longer than nature intended. That blood supply to the uterus is also the baby's oxygen supply.

A forced labor is an extremely hard labor. It is difficult for the two of you to work with. It is certainly not the labor we have described in this book.

The woman in a forced labor often starts with a self-doubt emotional signpost and stays that way for the entire labor. She is apt to feel overwhelmed. If both of you are looking forward to an unmedicated, enjoyable labor experience, then you should know that an induced labor makes your goal difficult to achieve. Most women feel it is an extremely painful experience.

Induction is a risky business, and yet not only is it widely used, but those labors that start naturally are often hurried along with the same drug just to speed things up.

There seems to be a very real question of legal vulnerability here. In a *Journal of Legal Medicine* article titled "Will Common Delivery Techniques Soon Become Malpractice?" the specific techniques in question were: the induction of labor or the speeding up of labor by drugs, rupturing the bag of waters artificially, and the supine (flat-on-the-back) position for delivery.[1]

It's not too surprising that induction leaves a doctor open to the possibility of malpractice. The *known hazards of induction* are:

Prematurity. This is what Dr. Bradley is referring to when he talks of physicians fooling themselves when they think they can tell when a baby is ready.

Prolonged latent period with intrapartum infection. This means having a lot of trouble getting labor to take off when it is induced—an extra long time for the mother which can wear her out. And, since the bag of waters is often ruptured, she is exposed to increased possibility of infection.

Uterine spasm with possible separation of placenta. This means the placenta separates too early, before it is supposed to, jeopardizing both the mother's life and the baby's by causing serious bleeding by the mother.

Tumultuous (violent) labor. This is dangerous to the baby, since it cuts him off from oxygen too long.

Amniotic fluid embolus. Amniotic fluid entering the mother's bloodstream.

Lacerations of the cervix and birth canal. Forcing the baby out so fast that the cervix and birth canal do not have a chance to stretch and open, so instead they tear.

Postpartum hemorrhage. Heavy, life-threatening bleeding.

Uterine rupture. The uterus "explodes" or tears apart in one out of a hundred induced labors. The infant usually dies; the mother is in extreme jeopardy.

Fetal distress due to anoxia and intracranial hemorrhage. Can lead to brain damage. Too much pressure on the baby's head caused by forcing it down and perhaps through the incompletely opened cervix.

Failure of induction to work. Usually resolved by caesarean section.

The point you should be very clear on is this: by far, the majority of forced labors are *elective inductions* with no clear medical indications requiring them. Informed parents accept induced labor when it is medically necessary, but avoid elective induction.

Rupturing the Membranes (Amniotomy)

Rupturing the membranes means breaking the bag of waters. This is most commonly done with the idea of speeding up labor. But does it?

After studying the matter, Dr. Robert Caldeyro-Barcia, a past president of the International Federation of Obstetricians and Gynecologists, has determined that breaking the waters speeds up the average labor, as previously discussed, by thirty to forty minutes. He condemns the practice of rupturing the membranes to speed up labor and also for the sole purpose of using an invasive fetal monitor.

The amniotic sac is filled with fluid that surrounds the baby like a hydraulic cushion. It is protective. When the bag of waters is ruptured, the walls of the baby's house close in on him and he experiences direct pressure on his spine, neck, and head. The bag of waters acts as a buffer for the infant's head. Says Dr. Caldeyro-Barcia, "Premature rupture of these membranes can produce massive

tears in brain tissue due to misalignment of the yet unfused bones of the skull."[5]

When the bag of waters remains intact during labor, it serves the mother as well as the infant. Part of it can protrude before the baby's head through the cervix when there is enough dilation. This is called the forewaters. The

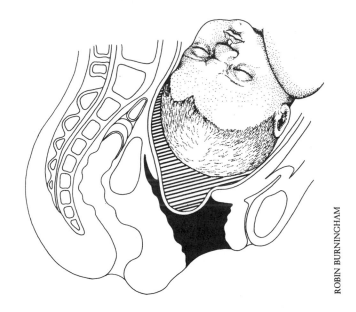

ROBIN BURNINGHAM

77. Bag of waters intact. The forewaters acts like a wedge to help open the cervix, gently and evenly.

216 *Controversies in Childbirth*

forewaters acts as an efficient conical dilator of the cervix. It is gentler than the hard head, so the mother is apt to be more comfortable when it is left intact. When the sac is intact, pressure from the forewaters during a contraction helps to spread the cervix back and to dilate it more evenly.

Forceps

The forceps is an instrument used to pull the baby out of the woman's vagina. The traction and force required to pull the baby out of you would quite surprise you. It is not a gentle art.

Your broad ligaments may be torn, and the damage may not be discovered at birth. It may not be diagnosed until you have gone through years of great pain with intercourse. Then, if you are lucky, you might find a doctor who can identify the problem.

Women who suffer this damage are often told they are frigid. Masters and Johnson have seen five cases of women with damaged broad ligaments (not all due to forceps extraction) who went many years being told they were frigid. Finally, they found their way to doctors who knew what was wrong and corrected it with major surgery.

The forceps puts a great deal of traction on the baby's neck and spine and often results in some bruising of the baby's head. Forceps extraction may also be implicated in our cerebral palsy rate. Occasionally, a facial nerve is paralyzed by the use of forceps, and the mother's pelvic tissues can be accidentally torn.

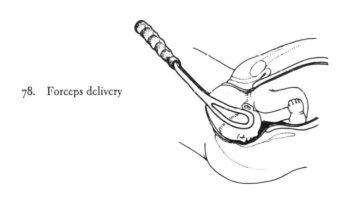

78. Forceps delivery

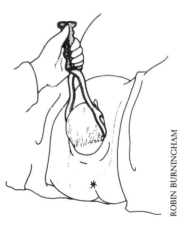

ROBIN BURNINGHAM

Controversies in Hospital Birthing **217**

Most doctors will tell you that they only use "low forceps" or "outlet forceps" to control the birth of the head. This is supposed to be easier on the baby's head than the mother pushing.

But, obviously, the mother's body parts are soft, and nature intended for the baby to be pushed from behind, not tugged and pulled out by the head and neck with hard metal instruments.

Women tend to think that the forceps is something rarely used, but many doctors use it most of the time. It is used almost always when the woman is given a regional anesthetic because she is unable to push properly; the pushing reflex becomes ineffective.

If you select a doctor who believes in controlling the head this way (instead of simply telling the mother when to stop pushing), then you will probably end up with a forceps extraction of your infant.

I don't think you will be pleased with the experience. Most women describe it as quite painful and requiring some powerful anesthetic. An episiotomy is practically mandated when drugs and forceps are used.

Vacuum Extractor

This is something like a vacuum cleaner. A caplike cup is attached to the baby's head and suction pulls part of the scalp into the cup. Then the doctor grasps the handle and pulls and tugs the baby out of you. It can cause severe molding of the cranial bones, and you still risk the traction damage to the broad ligaments.

Like the forceps, it's an experience I think you will be less than pleased with, and it is not without some of the

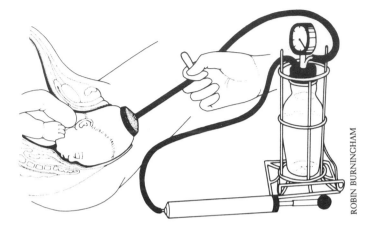

ROBIN BURNINGHAM

79. Vacuum extractor

same hazards to you and your baby that were described with forceps delivery.

Stress Test

You're nine months pregnant. Your doctor suggests that you check into the hospital for the afternoon and he will connect you to an IV with Pitocin in it to force your uterus to contract three or four times, so that he can see on the chart how your baby is going to take contractions. Of course, your baby isn't ready for labor or you'd be in labor, so you are risking recording a baby who is not ready for labor. This is another road to caesarean surgery. There is a high "false positive" rate with this test, as you might expect. In other words, there are a good number of babies who appear as though they are going to have trouble in labor and then don't have trouble.

There is also a *non-stress* test. This one is called non-stress because no drug is used to force contraction. Instead, the baby's heart is listened to whenever you feel him move during the test. This, too, has a high false positive rate. Both of these tests are far from reliable and yet caesarean surgery may be performed as a result of either.

Breech Babies

A breech baby (one who will be born feet or bottom first) does not have to mean automatic caesarean surgery. If your doctor tells you it does, he or she hasn't kept up with the latest on the subject, contained in a 1981 report from the National Institutes of Health, Task Force on Caesarean Childbirth. It recommends that "vaginal delivery of the term breech should remain an acceptable obstetrical choice" under certain conditions, the most important of which to you is that the doctor you choose be experienced in this kind of birth.[6] If your baby is breech, you will need to know more, and the best place to look is Nancy Wainer-Cohen and Lois Estner's *Silent Knife*.

ROBIN BURNINGHAM

80. Breech birth position

Inducing Labor
When the Water Bag Breaks

Physicians have become extremely aggressive in the last few years about forcing labor to start soon after the water bag breaks, instead of waiting for you to start contractions on your own. They are afraid you and your baby will get an infection if you don't have your baby soon. What is soon? It used to be forty-eight hours, then twenty-four, and recently I have had a few students who were told they would have to come into the hospital and be induced immediately, and if they didn't have their babies in twelve hours, they would have caesarean surgery.

Frankly, infection is most often the result of vaginal exams. It takes only one vaginal exam after the water bag breaks for the examining fingers to carry potentially bad organisms up into the uterus. In fact, one doctor reporting on a study involving women with ruptured membranes tells us that mere time passing is not related to infection rates. As a result of his study, he tells us "there would appear to be no real basis for the stimulation of labor in patients with premature ruptures of the membrane, especially before thirty-two weeks of gestation, since *the risk of infection was unrelated to the duration of membrane rupture*" (italics mine).

He goes on to state that only a "hands-off" policy will reduce the chances of infection. Sometimes a culture is taken and women are put into a state of alarm by being told they have bad organisms in the vagina. In fact, the same experienced researcher says cultures often show such organisms but have very little use in predicting whether or not the woman will get an infection. The mere presence of bad organisms is not the same as succumbing to them. For example, throat cultures often show bad organisms in people who are not sick.

Three women in my last class of ten couples started with the water bag breaking. One of these six birthed within or at forty-eight hours, and two birthed one week later. All of them received good advice from their birth attendant. They were told not to put anything whatsoever in the vagina—no tampons to stop the leaking, no douche—and not to have intercourse, and were asked to take their temperatures regularly and report immediately if there was any rise in temperature. There were no infections. There were also no vaginal exams.

chapter twenty-three

More Questions for Your Doctor or Birth Attendant

Near the beginning of this book you learned that a lot of decisions about the kind of birth experience you have are made at the time you choose your doctor or other birth attendant. The problem was that at first you did not know just what to ask a prospective doctor or how to interpret his or her answers. Now you know a lot more about the controversies in childbirth. You can decide what is really important to you and what matters less. And you can now ask more specific questions and understand what the answers mean.

This chapter will give you a list of questions you may want to ask a prospective birth attendant. The way you ask them and the way you listen to the answers are important. Try to avoid the questionnaire, clipboard, and pencil routine. If you are checking out a new doctor in a face-to-face interview, you may want to make notes about what to ask, but we advise against bringing in a long list of written questions.

Doctors do not like to feel they are being interrogated. Try not to challenge the doctor on the procedures he or she uses. But do not make it easy for the doctor to just reassure you by answering with what you want to hear. Ask questions that draw out a matter-of-fact explanation of what the doctor thinks is the best in birthing, and compare that to what you have come to look for.

As discussed in Chapter Four, if the doctor's or birth attendant's answers are at odds with your ideas on points that are quite important to you, don't think you will be able to convince that person to change later on. Move on to find a birth attendant who already thinks the way you do on the main points and seems at least adaptable on the points that are less critical to you. Now, here are some further questions.

What do you think of the fetal monitor and a routine IV in labor? If the doctor thinks that everyone should be hooked up, you have quickly found out that he or she does *not* support birthing normally. This doctor is not experienced at natural childbirth. His or her caesarean surgery rate will be an unnecessary risk that you should avoid. And you took a shortcut with this question to get directly to this doctor's view of birth.

What would you do if I were nine months pregnant and the bag of waters broke, but no contractions followed? If the answer is that you must produce your baby within twelve hours, this may not be the doctor for you. A reasonable answer to this would be something like: "Well, I would want you to report immediately if you started running a temperature. In the meantime, no tampons or anything should be put in the vagina and you would probably start labor within the next

forty-eight hours. It is rare not to start labor within that time span, so it is highly unlikely you would need to be induced."

As long as everything is normal—I am fine and the baby is fine—how long will you let me push? If the doctor answers two hours (or less), this may not be the doctor for you. You are looking for a doctor or birth attendant who says something like this: "Well, as long as there are no problems with you or the baby, you can continue pushing as long as you are willing to."

What do you think about episiotomies? "Well, I don't do them routinely but I find most first-time mothers need them or they tear." This answer tells you two things. Either this doctor does a routine episiotomy every time (otherwise he or she would know by experience that most women do not tear), or the doctor hurries the birth by forceps, vacuum extractions, or by holding onto the baby's head so it won't slide back. The hurrying causes tears. The answer you want to hear is rather something like: "I rarely do an episiotomy because most women don't need them. Sometimes there is a small tear but it is usually minor."

How do you feel about women birthing in a labor bed rather than in a delivery room? If the answer is, "We have an alternative birthing room and a lot of women are opting for that," it is a good sign. But you want to go a step further and ask, "Do you leave the bed like it is or do you 'break' it open like a delivery table with stirrups at the time of birth?" If the answer is that the doctor prefers to use the stirrups and you say that *not* using them is quite important to you, this may be a subject for further discussion. If the doctor is adamant about the stirrups, which defeats one of the purposes of staying out of the delivery room, he or she may not be the doctor for you.

How do you feel about letting the new mother nurse the baby immediately and, as long as there are no problems, wait until the placenta is out before the cord is clamped and cut? You want a birth attendant who knows about the advantages for mother and child of putting the baby immediately to breast and who will make every effort to make this possible. Beware of a doctor who tells you about all the many reasons why babies often have to be whisked away from their mothers at birth.

Do you have a time limit for producing the placenta before you feel that you must take measures like mashing on the stomach or going into the uterus after it? You want a doctor or attendant who is willing to let you nurse peacefully and wait up to a half an hour or even longer to produce the placenta as long as there are no indications of problems. Patience and a willingness to stay out of the picture are sometimes rare traits in doctors and other birth attendants. You want someone who realizes the importance to you of this special time and has no arbitrary time limits for the placenta to be delivered.

If you have gotten satisfactory answers to the questions so far, it sounds like you are on the right track. If the answers to these important questions have not been satisfactory up to this point, you have probably already left the office, hung up the phone, or started to look for another birth attendant to interview. The questions that follow have more to do with things that are really up to you to handle during labor. But it is a good idea for your birth attendant to know that they are important to you so he or she can help you make your choices happen.

How do you feel about the routine prep (the hospital admission routine that usually consists of shaving the pubic hair and administering an enema)? Many doctors have dropped this procedure, or leave it up to the patient, but there are a few things you should know about it. The shave was thought to decrease the chance of infection, but research has clearly demonstrated that it does not accomplish this at all. In fact, in one test, the infection rate was slightly higher in the shaved group of mothers.[1] Some hospitals now do a "mini" shave of only the perineal area, rather than all of the pubic hair. When the entire pubic area is shaved, it's terribly itchy as it grows back.

As for the enema, most women have a painless sort of diarrhea immediately preceding labor, and of course, the trained relaxed mother is quite capable of going to the bathroom during labor. Many mothers give birth without having had an enema and rarely is there any fecal matter left at birth. However, Dr. Bradley makes the important point that some women are inhibited in their pushing if they have not had an enema. They tend to worry about it and unconsciously hold back. This is something the woman herself should consider. Some deal with it by administering an enema themselves, at home.

How do you feel about purposely breaking the bag of water during labor? I really don't want this done. This should be just a simple matter of declining the procedure, but talking about it ahead of time alerts the birth attendant that you do not want to be "surprised" by having the waters broken without being asked.

What if I get to the hospital too early and find that I am less than four centimeters dilated and my labor is just poking along? I

would rather go back home and continue to labor normally rather than being induced or speeded up. Would you support me in this? The best birth attendants know that a hospital is not the best place to pass the early hours of first stage labor and will encourage the laboring couple to return to the familiar comforts of home if labor has not progressed as far as expected.

Do you know about the pressure episiotomy in the unlikely event that cut should be necessary? I don't want a little shot of anything in the bottom at the last moment before birth when I am crowning. I understand there is sometimes a misunderstanding about this, so I want to be quite clear. Of course, if I need a few stitches after the birth then I would be happy to have a local anesthetic shot at that time. You should already feel that your doctor will help you give birth without an episiotomy if that is important to you, but this question will make it clear that you want no medication before the birth of the baby.

How do you feel about the use of a routine shot of Pitocin after birth to force the uterus to contract after the placenta is out? Your doctor or birth attendant should already know that you expect to nurse immediately so the uterus will contract naturally. A shot of pito-

cin can give the woman a painful "double whammy" of artificial contractions on top of natural ones. This is just an unnecessary nuisance that can be avoided.

Finally, if you have gotten this far with satisfactory answers and good feelings between you and your prospective birth attendant, you may want to sum up your expectations for this birth ahead of you. You might say something like this: "What I am really asking you is to refrain from anything that is a routine procedure unless you see a situation that requires special treatment. I hope that both of us are ready and eager for things to go normally and naturally and that you do not plan on using any drugs or procedures designed to take care of problems unless those problems clearly develop."

If you find your prospective birth attendant agreeing wholeheartedly with this statement, you can feel confident you have found the right person. The responsibility for having the kind of birth you want still rests with you and your coach, of course, but you can feel assured that your birth attendant will be a help, not an obstacle to your plans.

Now you know the major birthing issues and the techniques needed to go after the safest and most fulfilling birth experience. Be decisive and don't hesitate to act on your decisions. We have, through these pages, done what we can to help you help yourself to a great birth. Our last word to you is, "Don't give your birth away."

references

Chapter One: An Introduction

1. Cole, K. C., "Can Natural Childbirth Survive Technology?" *Maternal Health and Childbirth*, Resource Guide 4, (Washington, D.C.: National Women's Health Network, 1980), p. 21.

Chapter Two: What Is the Difference Between the Bradley Method® and Lamaze?

1. Bing, Elisabeth, *Six Practical Lessons for an Easier Childbirth*, rev. ed. (New York: Bantam Books, 1982), p. 13.
2. Pritchard, J., and Macdonald, P., eds., *Williams Obstetrics*, 16th ed. (New York: Appleton-Century-Crofts, 1976), p. 453.

3. Hughey, M. J., McElin, T. W., and Young, T., "Maternal and Fetal Outcome of Lamaze Prepared Patients," *Obstetrics and Gynecology, Journal of the American College of Obstetricians and Gynecologists* 51, no. 6 (June 1978), p. 645.
4. Bradley, R. A., *Husband-Coached Childbirth*, 3rd ed. (Harper & Row, 1981), p. 15.
5. Feldman, Silvia, *Choices in Childbirth* (New York: Grosset & Dunlap, 1979), pp. 108, 109.
6. Motoyama, E. K., et al., "Adverse Effect of Maternal Hyperventilation on the Foetus," *Lancet* 1 (1966), pp. 286–288.

7. Soentgen, Mary Louise, quoted in "Practically Everything Transmitted by the Placenta," *OB GYN News* 7, no. 10 (May 15, 1972), p. 36.
8. Bing, *Six Practical Lessons*, p. 120.

Chapter Three: How to Choose Your Childbirth Teacher

1. Feldman, *Choices in Childbirth*, p. 103.

Chapter Five: Nutrition: How Does Your Garden Grow?

1. Ebbs, J. H., Tisdall, F. F., and Scott, W. A., "The Influence of Prenatal Diet on the Mother and Child," *Journal of Nutrition* 22 (1941), p. 515; Burke, B. S. et al., "Nutritional Studies During Pregnancy," *American Journal of Obstetrics and Gynecology* 46 (1943), p. 38; and Montagu, A., *Life Before Birth* (New York: New American Library, 1977), p. 25.
2. Ebbs, Tisdall, and Scott, "The Influence of Prenatal Diet," p. 515
3. Shneour, E. A., "Nurture Needs of the Unborn Baby," in *Expecting*, a special enclosure in *Parents Magazine* (Fall 1974), pp. 12, 26; and Rene Dubos of Rockefeller University quoted in "Progress in Prevention of Birth Defects," *Leaders Alert Bulletin*, no. 27 (New York: The National Foundation/March of Dimes), p. 1.
4. Brewer, Gail S., and Brewer, Tom, *The Brewer Medical Diet for Normal and High-Risk Pregnancy* (New York: Simon & Schuster, 1983), p. 220; Brewer, Tom, *Metabolic Toxemia of Late Pregnancy: A Disease of Malnutrition* (New Canaan, Conn.: Keats, 1982); and Tompkins, W., "The Significance of Nutritional Deficiency in Pregnancy: A Preliminary Report," *Journal of the International College of Surgeons* 4 (1941), pp. 147–54.
5. John Dobbing of the University of Manchester, England, quoted in "Crucial Time for Brain Growth," *Woman's Day*, November 1970, p. 44.

Chapter Six: Drugs During Pregnancy

1. Okuda, S., "Yale Researchers Establish Link Between Drug, Birth Defect," AP domestic wire, AM Cycle, December 16, 1982; also printed as "Anti-Nausea Drug, Birth Defect Linked," Honolulu *Star-Bulletin*, December 24, 1982, p. A-10.
2. "Aspirin Use During Pregnancy Linked to Birth Complications," *Los Angeles Times*, September 5, 1975, Part I, p. 25; and "Physician Warns: Aspirin Can Be Harmful," *Health Insurance News* (Washington, D.C.: Health Insurance Association of America, April 30, 1983), p. 1; and Stuart, M. J. et al. "Effects of Acetylsalicylic Acid Ingestion on Maternal and Neonatal Hemostasis," *The New England Journal of Medicine* 307, no. 15 (October 7, 1982), pp. 909–12. Also reported in *New York Times*, October 7, 1982, sec. 1, p. 20.
3. Ibid.
4. Hazell, L. D., *Commonsense Childbirth* (New York: G. P. Putnam's Sons, 1969), p. 129.
5. Bracken, M. B., et al., "Exposure to Prescribed Drugs in Pregnancy and Association with Congenital Malformations," *Obstetrics and Gynecology* 58, no. 3 (September 1981), pp. 336–43.
6. Yaffe, Sumner J., et al., American Journal of Pediatrics Committee on Drugs, "Stilbestrol and Adenocarcinoma of the Vagina," *Pediatrics,The Official Journal of the American Academy of Pediatrics, Inc.* 51, no. 2 (February 1973), pp. 297–99.
7. Brody, Jane E., "Shadow of Doubt Wipes Out Bendectin," *The New York Times*, June 19, 1983, p. 7, sec. 4.
8. Ibid.
9. Bracken, "Exposure to Prescribed Drugs," pp. 336–43.

10. Bross, I. D. J., and Natarajan, N., "Leukemia from Low-Level Radiation: Identification of Susceptible Children," *New England Journal of Medicine* 287, no. 3 (1972), pp. 107–10; and MacMahon, B., "Prenatal X-Ray Exposure and Childhood Cancer," *Journal of the National Cancer Institute* 28 (1962), p. 1173.

11. Kelly, K. M. et al., "The Utilization and Efficacy of Pelvimetry," *American Journal of Roentgenology: Radium Therapy and Nuclear Medicine* 125, no. 1 (September 1975), pp. 66–74; and U.S. Department of Health and Human Services, Food and Drug Administration, Bureau of Radiological Health, *The Selection of Patients for X-Ray Examinations: The Pelvimetry Examination* (Washington, D.C., 1980), p. 3.

12. MacMahon, "Prenatal X-Ray Exposure," p. 1173.

Chapter Seven: Sexuality and Birthing

1. Haire, D., and Haire, J., *Implementing Family-Centered Maternity Care with a Central Nursery* (Milwaukee: International Childbirth Education Association, 1971), pp. III-1–III-25.

2. Nelson, Harry, "Decreased Drug Use in Pregnancy Urged," *Los Angeles Times* 92 (March 15, 1973), Part II, p. 5 (reported also by Dr. Edward J. Quilligan at the California Medical Association's 102nd annual meeting in Anaheim).

Chapter Sixteen: Pushing

1. U.S. Department of Health and Human Services, *The Selection of Patients for X-Ray Examinations: The Pelvimetry-Examination*, p. 24.

2. Rothman, B. K., *In Labor: Women and Power in the Birthplace* (New York: W. W. Norton, 1982), p. 267.

Chapter Seventeen: Alternatives in the Pushing Stage

1. Motoyama, E. K., et al., "Adverse Effect of Maternal Hyperventilation on the Foetus," *Lancet* 1 (1966), pp. 286–88.

2. Barnett, M. M., and Humenick, S. S., "Infant Outcome in Relation to Second Stage Labor Pushing Method," *Birth* 9, no. 4 (Winter 1982), p. 221.

Chapter Eighteen: Drugs During Labor

1. "Improper Care at Birth," *Los Angeles Times*, April 28, 1972, p. 2.

2. Caldeyro-Barcia, R., "Effects of Labor and Delivery on the Fetus and Newborn," in Caldeyro-Barcia, ed., *Oxytocin* (New York and Oxford, England: Pergamon Press, 1967).

3. Brackbill, Y., et al., "Obstetric Premedication and Infant Outcome," *Obstetrics/Gynecology* 118 (1974), p. 377; and Kron, R. E., et al., "Newborn Sucking Behavior Affected by Obstetric Sedation," *Pediatrics* 37 (1966), p. 1012.

4. Bernal, J., and Richards, M., "Effects of Obstetric Medication on Mother-Infant Interaction and Infant Development," paper presented at the Third International Congress of Psychology of Medicine in Obst./Gynec. (London), April 1971.

5. Haire, D., "The Cultural Warping of Childbirth" (special issue), *International Childbirth Education Association News* (1972), p. 23; and Nelson, H., "Anesthetic Held Danger to Baby During Delivery," *Los Angeles Times*, March 11, 1970, sec. II, p. 2.

6. "Hazards of Paracervical Block Anesthesia," *Modern Medicine*, June 1, 1978, p. 123; Stimeling, Gary, "Will Common Delivery Techniques Soon Become Malpractice?" *Journal of Legal Medicine* 3, no. 5 (May 1975), pp. 20–21; and Shnider, S. M., and Way, E. L., "Plasma Level of Lidocaine (Xylocaine) in Mother and Newborn Following Obstetrical Con-

duction Anesthesia: Clinical Applications," *Anesthesiology* 29, no. 5 (September–October 1968), pp. 951–58.

7. Banta, D. H., and Thacker, S. B., *Costs and Benefits of Electronic Fetal Monitoring*, Department of Health, Education, and Welfare Pub. No. (PHS) 79-3245 (Washington, D.C.: National Technical Information Service, U.S. Dept. of Commerce, 1979).

Chapter Nineteen: Rehearsing the Second Stage

1. Dahm, L. S., "Temperature Regulation in the Delivery Room," *Contemporary OB/GYN* 3, no. 5 (May 1974), pp. 55–58; Notelovits, M., "Commentary," *ICEA Review* 2, no. 3 (Summer 1978), p. 6.

Chapter Twenty: The Episiotomy

1. Wessel, H. S., *Natural Childbirth and the Christian Family* (New York: Harper and Row, 1963), p. 196.
2. Banta, D., and Thacker, S. B., "The Risks and Benefits of Episiotomy: A Review," *Birth* 9, no. 1 (Spring 1982), p. 26; Thacker, S. B., and Banta, D., "Benefits and Risks of Episiotomy," in Young, D., ed., *Women and Health* 7, nos. 3/4 (Fall/Winter 1982), p. 165.
3. Kegel, Dr. Arnold, untitled film on the pubococcygeal muscle, documenting the permanent damage often caused by the mediolateral episiotomy; a copy was given to the American Academy of Husband-Coached Childbirth for teaching purposes.
4. Banta and Thacker, "Risks and Benefits," p. 27.

Chapter Twenty-one: Caesarean Surgery

1. Hibbard, L. T., "Changing Trends in Caesarean Section," *American Journal of Obstetrics and Gynecology* 125 (July 1976), p. 798.

2. Enkin, M. W., "Having a Section Is Having a Baby," *Birth and the Family Journal* 4, no. 3 (Fall 1977), pp. 99–105.

3. Marieskind, H. I., *An Evaluation of Caesarean Surgery in the United States* (Washington, D.C.: U.S. Dept. of Health, Education, and Welfare, 1979), p. 1.

4. Haverkamp, A. D., et al., "The Evaluation of Continuous Fetal Heart Rate Monitoring in High-Risk Pregnancy," *American Journal of Obstetrics and Gynecology* 125, no. 3 (June 1976), pp. 310–20; Haverkamp, A. D., et al., "A Controlled Trial of the Differential Effects of Intrapartum Fetal Monitoring," *American Journal of Obstetrics and Gynecology* 134, no. 4 (June 15, 1979), pp. 399–412; Kelso, I. M., et al., "An Assessment of Continuous Fetal Heart Rate Monitoring in Labor—A Randomized Trial," *American Journal of Obstetrics and Gynecology* 131, no. 5 (July 1978), pp. 526–32; Renou, P., et al., "Controlled Trial of Fetal Intensive Care," *American Journal of Obstetrics and Gynecology* 126, no. 4 (October 1976), pp. 470–76; and Wood, C., et al., *American Journal of Obstetrics and Gynecology* 141, no. 5 (November 1981), p. 527.

5. Marieskind, *Caesarean Surgery*, p. 14.

6. Haverkamp, A. D., quoted in "Criticism of Electronic Monitoring," *Ob Gyn News* 10, no. 24 (December 15, 1975), p. 1.

7. Murphy, J. R., et al., "The Relation of EFM to Infant Outcome," *American Journal of Epidemiology* 114, no. 4 (October 1981), pp. 539–48.

8. Banta and Thacker, *Costs and Benefits of Electronic Fetal Monitoring*, p. 18.

9. Ibid., p. 7.

10. U.S. Department of Health and Human Services, Food and Drug Administration, Bureau of Radiological Health, *The*

Selection of Patients for X-Ray Examinations: The Pelvimetry Examination p. 3 (for sale by the Superintendent of Documents, U.S. Government Printing Office, Washington D.C. 20402).

11. Young, D., and Mahan, C., *Unnecessary Caesareans: Ways to Avoid Them* (Minneapolis: International Childbirth Education Association, 1980), p. 10.

12. Cohen, W. R., "Influence of the Duration of Second-Stage Labor on Perinatal Outcome and Puerperal Morbidity," *Obstetrics and Gynecology* 49, no. 3 (March 1977), pp. 266–69.

13. Rothman, B. K., *In Labor: Women and Power in the Birthplace* (New York: W. W. Norton, 1982), p. 268.

14. Marieskind, *Caesarean Surgery*, p. 19.

15. Newland, Kathleen, *Infant Mortality and the Health of Society*, World Watch paper no. 47 (Washington, D.C.: World Watch Institute, December 1981), p. 23.

Chapter Twenty-two: Controversies in Hospital Birthing

1. "Doubt Is Raised on Wisdom of Giving Glucose in Labor," *Ob Gyn News* 11, no. 24.

2. Marieskind, p. 15.

3. Gibb, D. M. F., et al., "Prolonged Pregnancy: Is Induction of Labour Indicated?" *British Journal of Obstetrics and Gynaecology* 89, no. 4 (April 1982), pp. 292–95.

4. Stimeling, Gary, "Will Common Delivery Techniques Soon Become Malpractice?" *Journal of Legal Medicine* 3, no. 5 (May 1975), pp. 20–21.

5. Caldeyro-Barcia, Robert, quoted in Anderson, Sandra F., "Childbirth As a Pathological Process: An American Perspective," *MCN, The American Journal of Maternal Child Nursing* 2, no. 4 (July/August 1977), pp. 240–44.

6. "Caesarean Childbirth: The Final Report of the Consensus Development Conference," (Bethesda, Md.: National Institutes of Health Office of Research and Reporting, 1981), p. 14.

Chapter Twenty-three: More Questions for Your Doctor or Birth Attendant

1. Haire, Doris, "The Cultural Warping of Childbirth," *International Childbirth Education Association News*, special edition (1972), p. 14; and Newton, Niles, "Niles Newton Speaks for Women," *Preparation for Parenthood News* 14, no. 6 (June 1971), pp. 1–4.

further reading

Every student in our classes borrows these essential books from our lending library.

Husband-Coached Childbirth by Dr. Robert A. Bradley (New York: Harper & Row, 1981)

This is a classic. Pay particular attention to the chapter entitled "It's Not Nice to Fool Mother Nature." And Dr. Bradley's chapter "When Will the Baby Come?" is essential reading for all birthing parents.

Commonsense Childbirth by Lester Hazell (New York: G. P. Putnam's Sons, 1969)

Lester Hazell's introduction and her chapter called "The Choice Is Yours" are very important reading. Birth is not just one day in a woman's life. The experience will stay with you for many years. Hazell does an excellent job of pulling women into this reality.

Immaculate Deception by Suzanne Arms (Boston: Houghton Mifflin, 1975)

Writer and photographer Suzanne Arms gives you a close-up view of what birth is like when you pick an unhelpful birth attendant or passively approach the experience expecting others to take care of things for you. She alerts you to the experience of mechanized, high-tech, depersonalized childbirth. Through her interviews you will be able to pick up on attitudes that tell you whether a birth attendant will be helpful or not. This will help tune your ear for when you are interviewing your own prospective attendant.

The Brewer Medical Diet for Normal and High-Risk Pregnancy by Gail Sforza Brewer with Tom Brewer, M.D. (New York: Simon & Schuster, 1983)

There is no book equal to this one on nutrition in pregnancy. If you think it is a boring subject, this book will pleasantly surprise you. Reading chapters like "Forty Weeks, Forty Problems: Situations Most Likely to Interfere with Your Diet," you will find yourself thinking, "How do they know so much about me?"

Children at Birth by Marjie and Jay Hathaway (Sherman Oaks, Calif.: Academy Pubns., 1978—can be ordered through your Bradley ® teacher)

If you are planning to have your other children with you at the birth, this book is an essential part of the preparation for you and your children. It is full of practical advice in chapters such as "How to Decide If Your Child Should Be at a Birth" and "How to Prepare Your Child." The book includes the experience of birth through the eyes of children who have been there.

How to Relax and Have Your Baby by Edmund Jacobson, M.D. (New York: McGraw-Hill, 1965)

This book is dated in many ways, and Jacobson thinks women should be totally obedient to the physician. It is also enormously aggravating that he believes women do not need to know anything about labor and birth, only relaxation. Still, he is an expert on relaxation, which is of major importance in labor, and his great wisdom is his understanding of how to acquire the ability to relax as a skillful tool. Ignore his idiosyncracies and read this small book to get that wisdom.

The Womanly Art of Breastfeeding by La Leche League (local chapters are listed in phone books)

This is one of the first and still one of the best books on nursing. It is a fast read, completely practical and to the point. I recommend purchasing a copy (that way you also support a worthwhile organization) to read before the birth and to have on hand for quick reference after.

Nursing Your Baby by Karen Pryor (New York: Simon & Schuster, 1976)

This is THE BEST book on breast-feeding. Though not as quick and easy to use as La Leche League's book, it contains all of the practical information and much more. If you want your reading detailed and referenced, this is the one, but both these breast-feeding books are valuable to read and have.

For the avid reader who wants more, we recommend:

Childbirth Without Fear by Grantly Dick-Read, M.D. (New York: Harper & Row, 1978)

This is an oldie-but-a-goodie by the "father" of modern natural childbirth which always offers some valuable insight that has been temporarily lost in the art of birthing.

Silent Knife by Nancy Wainer Cohen and Lois J. Estner (South Hadley, Mass.: Bergin & Garvey, 1983)

This book is the latest word on caesarean surgery and is especially useful to the mother who has had a C-section but wants a vaginal birth next time around.

In Labor: Women and Power in the Birthplace by Barbara Katz Rothman (New York: W. W. Norton, 1982)

A new book that looks at the sociology of childbirth and especially at the re-emergence of the midwife.

A Woman in Residence by Michelle Harrison, M.D. (New York: Random House, 1982)

This is a personal account by a woman doctor who tried to buck the medical birth establishment from the inside.

Directory of Alternative Birth Services and Consumer Guide ($5.95; available from NAPSAC, Box 428, Marble Hill, MO 63764)

The Five Standards for Safe Childbearing (Marble Hill, Missouri: NAPSAC International, 1982)

NOTE: If you have difficulty finding these books, they can be ordered from the Birth and Life Bookstore by writing to:

Lynn Moen
7001 Alonzo Avenue N.W.
P.O. Box 70625
Seattle, WA 98107
206/789-4444

Protein Counter

Food	Quantity	Grams
DAIRY PRODUCTS		
Cow's milk, whole	1 cup	8
Cow's milk, skim	1 cup	9
Milk, powdered,		
whole	1 cup powder	27
skim, instant	1⅓ cup powder	30
skim, non-instant	⅔ cup powder	30
Yogurt (of partially		
skim milk)	1 cup	8
Custard, baked	1 cup	13
Ice cream	1 cup	6

Food	Quantity	Grams
Ice milk	1 cup	9
Cream, light or		
half-and-half	½ cup	4
heavy or whipping	½ cup	2
Cottage cheese		
creamed	1 cup	30
uncreamed	1 cup	38
Cheddar or American cheese	1 in. cube	4
Cheddar, grated	½ cup	14
Cream cheese	1 oz.	2
Processed cheese	1 oz.	7

Food	Quantity	Grams
Swiss cheese	1 oz.	7
Eggs		
yolks only	1	3
whole	1	6

MEAT AND POULTRY

Food	Quantity	Grams
Bacon	1 slice	2
Beef, chuck, pot roasted	3 oz.	23
Hamburger, ground lean	3 oz.	24
Roast beef	3 oz.	16
Steak, sirloin	3 oz.	20
Chicken,		
thigh, leg, or breast	3 oz.	25
Chicken liver	3 oz.	22
Turkey	3 oz.	27
Lamb, chop	4 oz.	24
leg	3 oz.	20
shoulder	3 oz.	18
Pork chop	3 oz.	18
Ham, cured	3 oz.	16
Pork roast	3 oz.	21
Pork sausage, bulk	3 oz.	18
Veal cutlet	3 oz.	23
Chili con carne, with beans	1 cup	19
without beans	1 cup	16
Sausage, bologna	2 slices	7
Frankfurter	1	7

FISH AND SEAFOODS

Food	Quantity	Grams
Clams, steamed or canned	3 oz.	12
Cod	3½ oz.	28
Crabmeat	3 oz.	14
Fish sticks	2	7
Flounder	3 oz.	30
Haddock	3 oz.	15
Halibut	3 oz.	26
Salmon, canned	3 oz.	17
Sardines	3 oz.	12
Scallops	3½ oz.	18
Shrimp	3 oz.	23
Swordfish	1 steak	17
Tuna, canned	3 oz.	25

VEGETABLES

Food	Quantity	Grams
Artichoke	1	2
Asparagus	6 spears	1
Beans, green snap	1 cup	1
lima, green	½ cup	4
lima, dry, cooked	½ cup	8
navy, with pork	¾ cup	11
kidney, canned	1 cup	15
Bean sprouts	1 cup	15
Broccoli	½ cup	1
Brussels sprouts	1 cup	1
Cabbage (as coleslaw)	1 cup	1
steamed	1 cup	2
Carrots	1 cup	1
Celery	1 cup	1
Corn	1 ear	3

Food	Quantity	Grams
Cucumbers	6	0
Eggplant	1 cup	0
Lentils	½ cup	7
Lettuce	¼ head	1
Mushrooms	½ cup	2
Onions	½ cup	1
Parsley	1 T.	1
Peas	1 cup	5
Peppers, pimientos	1 pod	0
raw, green	1	1
stuffed with beef and breadcrumbs	1 med.	9
Potato chips	10	1
Potatoes, baked	1 med.	2
french fried		0
Soybeans	½ cup	11
Spinach	1 cup	3
Squash, summer	1 cup	1
Sweet potatoes	1 med.	2

FRUITS

They have 0 to 1 or 2 grams.

BREADS, CEREALS, AND GRAINS

Biscuit	1	3
Bran flakes	1 cup	3
Bread, cracked wheat	1 slice	2
rye	1 slice	2
whole wheat	1 slice	2

Food	Quantity	Grams
Corn bread	1 serving	3
Corn flakes	1 cup	2
Corn meal, yellow	1 cup	9
Crackers, graham	2 med.	1
soda	2	1
Flour, soy, full fat	1 cup	39
wheat, all purpose	1 cup	12
wheat, whole	1 cup	13
Macaroni	1 cup	5
Noodles	1 cup	7
Oatmeal or rolled oats	1 cup	5
Popcorn	2 cups	3
Puffed rice	1 cup	0
Puffed wheat	1 cup	1
Rice, brown	1 cup	15
white	1 cup	14
Rolls, breakfast	1 large	3
Shredded wheat	1 biscuit	3
Spaghetti with meat sauce	1 cup	13
Wheat germ	1 cup	26
Wheat germ cereal	1 cup	20

SOUPS, CANNED AND DILUTED

Bean	1 cup	9
Beef and vegetable	1 cup	6
Bouillon, broth	1 cup	5
Chicken or turkey	1 cup	4
Clam chowder without milk	1 cup	5

Food	Quantity	Grams
Cream soups	1 cup	7
Noodle, rice, and barley	1 cup	6
Split pea	1 cup	8
Tomato with milk	1 cup	6
Vegetable	1 cup	6

DESSERTS AND SWEETS

Food	Quantity	Grams
Candy, caramels	5	0
plain fudge	2 pieces	0
Chocolate syrup	2 T.	0
Cupcake	1	3
Doughnuts, cake type	1	2
Hard candies	1 oz.	0
Honey, strained	2 T.	0
Jams and jellies	1 T.	0
Marshmallows	5	0
Milk chocolate	2 oz. bar	2
Molasses	1 T.	0
Pie, apple	1 slice	3
cherry	1 slice	3
Sugar, white	1 cup	0
brown	1 cup	0

Food	Quantity	Grams
Syrup, maple	2 T.	0
Tapioca pudding	1 cup	10

NUTS AND SEEDS

Food	Quantity	Grams
Almonds	½ cup	13
Cashews	½ cup	13
Peanut butter	⅓ cup	12
Peanuts	⅓ cup	13
Pecans	½ cup	5
Sesame seeds, dried	½ cup	9
Sunflower seeds	½ cup	12
Walnuts	½ cup	7

BEVERAGES

Food	Quantity	Grams
Alcoholic drinks		0
Carbonated drinks		0
Coffee, black	1 cup	0
Tea, black	1 cup	0

SUPPLEMENTARY FOODS

Food	Quantity	Grams
Desiccated liver	½ cup	28
Brewer's yeast, powdered	½ cup	13

SOURCE: Department of Health, State of Hawaii, plus additional nutritional information.

index

Note: Page references to illustrations are in *italics*.

Abdomen
 breathing into, 91–95, *92, 95*
 crampy sensation in, 89–90
Adrenalin, 130
Afterbirth. *See* Placenta
Altered breathing (in Lamaze method), 7–8,
  10–11, 18, 91
American Academy of Husband Coached Child-
  birth (AAHCC)®, x, xii, 18, 19
 feedback form for, 242
American Academy of Pediatrics, 36, 38, 40
American College of Obstetricians and Gynecolo-
  gists, 30, 33
American Institute of Family Relations, 3
American Society of Psychoprophylaxis in Obstet-
  rics (ASPO), 8, 17–18
Amniotic fluid embolus, 215
Amniotic sac. *See* Bag of waters

Amniotomy, 216–17
 See also Bag of waters, breaking of
Anesthesia. *See* Drugs
Antihistamines, 36
Apgar, Virginia, 11
Apgar score, 11, 168, 213
Apnea in babies, 11
Arms, Suzanne, 231
Aspirin, 34–35

B vitamins, 33
Baby
 anemia in, possible cause of, 46
 at birth, 54–58, *54–58,* 136, *153–55*
  from hyperventilated mothers, 11
  no need to cry, 58
  union with mother, 10, 19, 58, *155, 181,*
   182–83, 223

date of birth of, 48, 75–76
drops in eyes of, 182 83
drugs' effects on, 10, 166, 168
first bowel movements of, 183
forceps damage of, 217–18
going home with, 183
heart problems in, possible cause of, 46
home-birth risks to, 211
mother's nutrition and, 29–33
in uterus, 45–48, *47*
Back injuries, side pushing position for mothers
  with, 157
Backache
 in breech births, 164
 contractions as, 125–26
 exercises for, 65, *65*
  back rub for, 87–89, *87, 93,* 114–15, 120
 in posterior births, 164

Rothman, Barbara Katz, 146, 206, 232
Round ligament ache, 89–90, 89

Seconal, 167
Self-doubt (in labor), 115–19, *118*, 120–21, 131, 147
Self-massage in Lamaze method, 11
Seriousness (in labor), 112–15, 120
Sexual organs, description of woman's, 41–48, *42–44, 46, 47*
Side position, 78–83, 79, 80, 90
  alternations in, 105
Sleep, appearance of, in labor, 106
Sleeping in pregnancy, side position for, 79
Solitude, mother's need for, 104–105
Sonograms, 40
Speedsters, 49, 112, 119–20, 124, 147
Squatting
  exercises for, 62–65, 63, 64, 66–67, 197
  in pushing. *See* Pushing, positions for
Stirrups, use of, 21, 137, 156, 223
Stress tests, 218–19
Successful outcomes in Bradley® vs. Lamaze methods, 8
Sweden, 208

Tailor sitting, 60–62, *61*, 66
Teachers. *See* Childbirth teachers
Tears, episiotomies and, 195–97, 222
Textbook laborers, 49, 123
  first stage for, 127–31
Thacker, Stephen B., 190, 195, 202

Thalidomide, 38
Toxemia, nutrition and, 29–30
Transition. *See* pp. 115–19 (Third Emotional Signpost)
Twins, 45, 163

Ultrasound. *See* Fetal monitoring
Umbilical cord, 45–47, *46*, 182
  in birthings on way to the hospital, 184, 185
  clamping and cutting of, 46–47, 223
  prolapse of, 207
Uterine inertia, 204, 205, 211
Uterus, 41–47, *42, 44, 46, 47, 51*
  contractions of, 10–11, 50–54, 56–57, 78, *100–101*
    backache during, 86–89, 87
    after birth, 56–57, 224–25
    breathing and, 91–95, *92, 95*
    drug for, 168
    emotional signposts for, 110–22, *111, 113, 116, 118*
    in "false labor," 76
    length of, 113
    mental imagery for, 100–102
    relaxation for, 11, 77–85, *79, 80*
    round ligament ache during, 89–90, 89
    telephoning between, *151*
    timing of, 96
    on way to bathroom or car, 105, 129–30, *130*
  See also Labor
  infections of
    after caesarean surgery, 199

after induction of labor, 215
after water bag breaks, 220
ligaments of, *51*, 86, 89
PC muscle and, 67–68, 67
  episiotomy damage, 192
rupture of, 215

Vacuum extraction, 9, 168, 218, *218*
  doctors' preference for, 21
Vagina, 41–44, *42, 43*
  infection from exam of, 220
  PC muscle and, 67–69, *67, 68*
  wetness of, 45
Varicose veins, exercise vs., 65, *65*
VBAC (vaginal birth after caesarean), 199
Vitamins, 37
Vomiting during labor, 116

Wainer-Cohen, Nancy, 207, 219, 232
Water bag. *See* Bag of waters
Weekly practice plans, 106–107
Weight gain by mother, 30–31
  toxemia and, 29–30
Whole wheat, 33
Williams Obstetrics, 8

X-rays, 39–40
Xylocaine, 168

Yoga, 67
Yogurt, 33
Young, Diony, 204

THE BRADLEY METHOD® FEEDBACK FORM

Please help us serve the unborn by communicating and sharing with the American Academy of Husband-Coached Childbirth.®

Name_____

Address_____

City, State, Zip_____

Baby's name_____

☐ I am looking for a Bradley® teacher. Please send me a FREE National Directory of all affiliated teachers.

☐ I had such a great birth that we want to share what we have done. Please send FREE information about becoming a Bradley® teacher.

☐ I want to share the following information, so you can update the statistics in your computer.

FOLLOW-UP REPORT

BIRTH: ☐ I pushed the baby out.
☐ They pulled the baby out (forceps).
☐ Caesarean surgery
☐ Vaginal birth after previous caesarean (VBAC)

DRUGS: ☐ None
☐ Local anesthetic for episiotomy only
☐ Analgesic (pain reliever): Demerol, Nistetil, Vistaril, Valium, Phenergan, etc.)
☐ Anesthesia (pudendal block, epidural/spinal/ saddleblock, gas)

ATTENDANT: ☐ MD ☐ DO ☐ DC ☐ CNM ☐ Midwife ☐ None

BABY/MOM: ☐ Boy ☐ Girl ☐ First baby ☐ Second baby
☐ Third or more ☐ Twins
Baby's weight _____lbs_____ozs
Mom's weight gain _____lbs
Mom's daily average protein intake
_____grams

CLASSES: ☐ Bradley® ☐ Lamaze ☐ Other _____
Number of classes: ☐ Four ☐ Six ☐ Eight
☐ Ten ☐ Twelve ☐ More

ULTRASOUND: ☐ Scan ☐ Doptone used in office or in labor
☐ External fetal monitor
Total radiation time: _____hours.

	DOCTOR/ MIDWIFE	HOSPITAL/ BIRTH CENTER	TEACHER
NAME	_____	_____	_____
ADDRESS	_____	_____	_____
CITY/ST/ZIP	_____	_____	_____

Send to: American Academy of Husband-Coached Childbirth®
THE BRADLEY METHOD®
Box 5224-R, Sherman Oaks, CA 91413-5224
(800) 423-2397 or (818) 788-6662 (California)

CUT ALONG DOTTED LINE